MW00559003

SPLENDIDLY VICTORIAN

Professor Walter L. Arnstein

Splendidly Victorian

Essays in Nineteenth- and Twentieth-Century
British History in Honour of Walter L. Arnstein

Michael H. Shirley
Todd E. A. Larson
Editors

Ashgate

Aldershot • Burlington USA • Singapore • Sydney

Published by
Ashgate Publishing Limited
Gower House
Croft Road
Aldershot
Hants GU11 3HR
UK

Ashgate Publishing Company
131 Main Street
Burlington, VT 05401–5600 USA

Ashgate website: http://www.ashgate.com

British Library Cataloguing-in-Publication Data

Splendidly Victorian: Essays in Nineteenth- and Twentieth-Century British History in Honour of Walter L. Arnstein.
        1. Great Britain—History—Victoria, 1837–1901 2. Great Britain—History—20th Century 3. Great Britain—Social Conditions—20th Century
        I. Shirley, Michael H. II. Larson, Todd E.A.
        941'.081

US Library of Congress Cataloging in Publication Data

The Library of Congress Control Number was preassigned as: 00–108827

ISBN 0 7546 0289 3

This book is printed on acid-free paper.
Typeset in *Times New Roman* by Password, UK.
Printed and bound by Athenaeum Press, Ltd.,
Gateshead, Tyne & Wear.

Contents

List of Illustrations and Tables

Notes on Contributors

John Beeler is Associate Professor of History at the University of Alabama. His Ph.D. dissertation, on British naval policy, was directed by WalterArnstein. After completing the degree he spent a postdoctoral year at Yale, and taught at Eastern Illinois University before joining the University of Alabama faculty in 1993. His book, *British Naval Policy in the Gladstone–Disraeli Era, 1866–1880* (Stanford University Press, 1997), won the American Historical Association's Paul Birdsall Prize for 1997 and 1998 for the best book in European military and strategic history for the period since 1870.

Lucinda McCray Beier received her bachelors degree in history and English from Indiana University, her masters degree in history from the University of Illinois, and her Ph.D. in the history of medicine from Lancaster University in Great Britain. She is the author of *Sufferers and Healers: The Experience of Illness in Seventeenth-Century England* (Routledge and Kegan Paul, 1987), and *A Matterof Life and Death:Health, Illness and Medicine in McLean County, 1830–1995* (McLean County Historical Society, 1996). Beier has faculty appointments in the departments of History and Political Science at Illinois State University in Normal, Illinois. In addition, she directs ISU's College of Arts and Sciences Research Office. Her current research focus is the comparative history of health policy development.

Helen S. Hundley is a Russian Historian at Wichita State University. She is the author of 'The Buddhist Agent: Tibet's Part in the Great Game,' in *History Today* 43 (Oct. 1993): pp. 45–50, and a number of articles concerning Buddhism in the Russian Empire in the *Modern Encyclopedia of Religions in Russia and the Soviet Union.*

Tamara Hunt is Associate Professor of History at Loyola Marymount University. Her book, *Defining John Bull: Political Caricature and National Identity in Late Georgian England,* will shortly be published by Ashgate.

Marsh Wilkinson Jones is a lecturer in History at Parkland College in Champaign, Illinois. He was awarded a Ph.D. in history from the University of Illinois at Urbana-Champaign in 1995. His dissertation, *Pulpit, Periodical, and Pen: Joseph Benson and Methodist Influence in the Victorian Prelude,* was completed under the direction of Walter L. Arnstein.

Todd E.A. Larson received his B.A. from the University of Minnesota and his M.A. in History from the University of Cincinnati and is currently completing work on his doctoral dissertation at the University of Illinois at Urbana-Champaign under the direction of Walter L. Arnstein. He has written extensively on the subject of computers and history, and is the co-author of *The History Highway: A Guide to Internet Resources* (Armonk, NY: M.E. Sharpe, 1997).

Scott Myerly is an independent scholar, and is the author of *British Military Spectacle from theNapoleonic Wars through the Crimea* (Cambridge, MA: Harvard University Press, 1996).

James Schmiechen is Professor of History at Central Michigan University. He is the author of *Sweated Industries and Sweated Labor: The London Clothing Trades, 1860–1914* (Urbana, IL: University of Illinois Press, 1984). His latest work, *The British Market Hall* (co-authored With Kenneth Carls), was published in 1999 by Yale University Press.

Paul W. Schroeder is Professor of History Emeritus at the University of Illinois at Urbana Champaign. A specialist in the history of European international relations, he is the author of *The Transformation of European Politics, 1763–1848*, Oxford History of Modern Europe series, (Oxford: Oxford University Press, 1994), and numerous other books and articles.

Stephen Shafer, who earned five degrees from the University of Illinois at Urbana-Champaign, is now Assistant Dean of that university's College of Liberal Arts and Sciences, where he also serves as the university's Pre-Law Advisor and has an appointment as Adjunct Assistant Professor of Cinema Studies. For the past twenty-five years he has developed and taught courses on Film and History, and his 1997 book, *British Popular Films, 1929–1939: the Cinema of Reassurance*, was published in New York and London by Routledge. He is a past president of the Midwest Association of Pre-Law Advisors and currently is editor of the organization's newsletter.

Michael H. Shirley who holds graduate degrees in law, education, and history, is Assistant Professor of History at Eastern Illinois University in Charleston, Illinois. His doctoral dissertation, *On Wings of Everlasting Power: G.W.M. Reynolds and 'Reynolds's Newspaper' 1848–1876*, was researched and written under the direction of Walter L. Arnstein.

Richard Frances Spall, Jr who earned his Ph.D. in History at the University of Illinois in 1985, is Cornelia Coles Fairbank Professor of History at Ohio Wesleyan University. His publications include articles in the *International History Review*, *The Journal of Church and State*, *Victorian Britain: An Encyclopedia* and *Historic Leaders of the World*. Since 1993 he has served as Book Review Editor of *The Historian*.

All the contributors to this volume studied British history at the University of Illinois with Professor Walter L. Arnstein. Other than Lucinda McCray Beier, all completed (or are completing) Ph.D. degrees in History at that institution. Professor Arnstein served as thesis advisor for all of the rest except for Helen Hundley, whose major field was Russian and East European History.

Acknowledgements

We wish to thank Walter and Charlotte Arnstein for their support, the people at Ashgate for their encouragement, and the contributors for their splendid work. We especially want to thank Charlotte Arnstein for her stellar proofreading and Kirsten Weissenberg for her unfailingly good humoured assistance.Finally, in a spirit of delighted uxoriousness, we thank Debra and Heidi for putting up with us.

CHAPTER 1

Walter L. Arnstein, Teacher and Mentor

Michael H. Shirley and Todd E. A. Larson

Festschrifts are, of course, written to honor great scholars, and this one is no exception: Walter L. Arnstein's scholarly interests are numerous and diverse, and his publications continue to be influential. Precious few Festschrifts, however, honor three-time Jeopardy© champions, which he was back in 1974.[1] We mention this fact, not because it is evidence of his vast store of knowledge (which it is), nor because it indicates that he has a whimsical side (which he does). We mention it because what he said on that show says something fundamental about him. When asked to introduce himself, he responded 'I am a history teacher from Illinois.' Over a span of more than forty years, both in the classroom and through his publications, he has arguably introduced more students to British history than has any other American historian. In everything he does – in his scholarship, his classroom work, his advising, his life – he is a *teacher*.

The obvious hallmarks of great teaching are all certainly present in Walter Arnstein. His lectures are clear, organized, energetic, and laced with humor.[2] His standards can be met, but only through diligent effort. His undergraduate lecture courses have always been among the most popular at the University of Illinois, his name has appeared on the list of outstanding teachers almost every year since 1968, and in 1987 he was awarded the University-wide prize for Excellence in Undergraduate Instruction. Numerous graduate students have found him a sympathetic and conscientious advisor, and twenty-one of them have thus far successfully defended doctoral dissertations which were written under his direction.

His ability to teach writing is remarkable, both through example (his own writing is notable for its clarity and elegance) and through his evaluation of students' papers. All of his graduate and advanced undergraduate students have had the experience of turning in a 'polished' paper, only to have it returned with extensive marginal notations and several pages of single-spaced typed comments raising points missed, arguments in need of clarification, and suggestions for rephrasing. This attention to detail has a double effect: students learn to seek perfection in their own writing, and graduate students seek to emulate him in their own teaching.[3]

It is not just these "standard" characteristics which mark him as a great teacher. One of the most important legacies of Professor Arnstein's tenure at the University of Illinois has been the British History Association, known as the BHA, the founding of which he inspired in 1971 and which until 2000 persisted. Its intent was to bring scholars in the broad field of British studies to the University to present their research in a relatively informal setting. While many universities and colleges sponsor academic talks, the BHA was unique in that it was a student-run organization and provided an informal and relaxed atmosphere in which the speaker and an audience made up of professors, graduate students, undergraduate students, and members of the general public could interact collegially. Scholars such as Richard Davis, J.C.D. Clark, Marjorie Morgan, Lacey Baldwin Smith, Nicholas Temperley, Jeremy Black, Harold Perkin, Emmet Larkin, James Sack, Newton Key, and Rajmohan Gandhi, to name just a few, came to Champaign, Illinois, to enjoy a meal (dining is inevitably part of the BHA experience[4]), to present a paper, and to converse with students and colleagues.

Through all of the years of the BHA, Walter Arnstein served as its guiding hand. He provided advice, contacts, institutional memory, continuity, and financial support. The BHA met in private homes, and Professor Arnstein has hosted its meetings dozens of times. He has not been so generous merely because he enjoys fine dining, but also because he long ago perceived a gap in graduate training for which no obvious remedy existed, a remedy that the BHA provided. The BHA gave graduate students the opportunity to learn academic leadership skills, to see the business of academia as being an inevitable and invaluable part of scholarship, and to meet great scholars in an informal setting. Walter Arnstein's students understand and value academic conferences, not just because they present papers at them, but because they organized small ones several times a year.[5]

In none of his teaching is he dogmatic. As Professor Paul Schroeder notes in his appreciation following this essay, Walter Arnstein is not enamored of theory, but neither is he averse to his students' use of it if they can convince him that it is indeed useful. Although he may find an argument unconvincing, he is always willing to listen politely and to help his students clarify their positions. He is invariably courteous in doing so, and the advice he gave in a 1995 interview with *The Historian* is advice he gives all his students, if only through example:

> I was taught a pioneering course in historiography by Professor Jacques Barzun at Columbia University. The advice he offered in the 1950s strikes me as equally valuable to historians in the 1990s: be accurate; be orderly; be honest; and be self aware. To that I might add: be

imaginative in the questions you ask, but remain judicious in the conclusions that you reach.[6]

Ultimately, his students learn the most from his example, and, for what are probably more years than he cares to remember, Walter Arnstein has demonstrated that brilliant scholarship and splendid teaching can be accompanied by kindness and decency. He is the very model of a gentleman, and, with his unflagging spirit of scholarship and service, he continues to teach us what we can become as scholars, teachers, and human beings.[7]

NOTES

1 Jeopardy©, for those unfamiliar with it, is a televised game show which has been broadcast in the United States for many years. Contestants are required to come up with questions to match answers within several varied categories. Unlike most game shows in the United States, it requires a detailed and occasionally esoteric fund of information which must be disgorged under the pressure of head-to-head competition.

2 At the beginning of one lecture in 1989, he hung a map of the British Empire on the wall and announced 'Today we shall be discussing the British Empire and noting the manner in which it achieved its greatest size in terms of territory in the years immediately following the First World War.' Whereupon the map, wooden frame and all, fell with a crash to the floor. He raised an eyebrow and remarked, 'Well, it did fall, but not quite that precipitously.'

3 As Professor Paul Schroeder notes in his appreciation following this introduction, Professor Arnstein's examination questions are models of challenging clarity.

4 Meals are normally prepared by students, but one of the contributors to this volume, Professor John Beeler, a long-time member of the BHA, achieved a unique hat-trick at one meeting: a former professional chef, he prepared the meal, served it, and then gave the talk.

5 His more advanced graduate students certainly present papers at major conferences, but he encourages others as well. Professor Arnstein has was for many years the faculty advisor to the University of Illinois' chapter of Phi Alpha Theta, the history honor society, and pushed his students – both beginning graduates and undergraduates – to present their work at Phi Alpha Theta conferences.

6 Roger Adelson, 'Interview with Walter L. Arnstein,' *The Historian* 57 (Spring 1995); p. 488.

7 His service to the University of Illinois and to the profession at large has been significant. At the University of Illinois he was twice director of graduate studies for the Department of History and served as department chair from 1974 to 1978, and again in 1989. He has served on the editorial boards of *The American Historical Review, Albion,* and *The Historian*, on the advisory board of *Victorian Studies,* and as president of the Midwest Victorian Studies Association, the Midwest Conference on British Studies, and the North American Conference on British Studies.

CHAPTER 2

Walter L. Arnstein: A Collegial and Personal Appreciation

Paul W. Schroeder

This opportunity to contribute to a much-deserved *Festschrift* for Walter Arnstein is one I welcome for several reasons. First, it is a chance to discharge the debts of a long friendship. We have been colleagues in the same history department at the University of Illinois for thirty years, and friends for just as long – which means that I can speak personally without awkwardness, frankly without offense, and warmly without seeming to flatter. Second, I feel able to comment on his contributions to the historical craft as scholar, writer, teacher, and in other capacities (administrator, officer in various societies, guest lecturer and public speaker, etc.), not because I am especially expert in any of these areas or knowledgeable about his activities, but because Walter's particular contributions and his blend of qualities have been so obvious and consistent in all these fields (on that, more later). Finally and most important, in evaluating and praising his career and accomplishments, I can honestly, without artful dodging, careful omission, or stretching the truth, say something about the historian's craft as I believe it should be practiced. This is not because Walter and I do the same kind of history, except in the very broad sense of being concerned with the history of politics in the modern era, or that we have similar styles (we do not) or that we regularly agree in our views. Since he would be surprised and possibly a bit disappointed if I did not do so, I will even include one or two such small disagreements in this essay. It is rather that in looking at the whole picture and on balance (one of his most characteristic phrases), I conclude that he represents in his career the kind of historical work one not only can value and affirm, but must also hope will continue to be done.

Of the three areas on which we normally judge a historian's career (scholarship, teaching, and service), I will say by far the most about the first. This represents no distortion of his work, however, for to a remarkable degree, as noted earlier, Walter Arnstein is the same person in all three. We all know scholars who are in various respects Jekyll and Hyde—cautious and moderate in their scholarship, radical in their political and social views, or extremely conscientious in research while sloppy in their teaching, or even, occasionally, scrupulously honest on historical fact, but you would not want to buy a used car from them. With Walter Arnstein, what you see in one field is what you get in all three: the characteristics of his scholarship are equally those of his teaching and service.

The first thing that must strike anyone on reading Walter Arnstein's work is the remarkable thoroughness of the research and comprehensiveness of the treatment of any subject he takes up. This is what impressed me once again in re-reading his two major monographic works, *The Bradlaugh Case*[1] and *Protestant versus Catholic in Mid-Victorian England*,[2] for this assignment, and it has impressed outside reviewers and other historians as well. It is a mistake or at least an exaggeration ever to say of a book that the research is exhaustive or the treatment of the subject complete; there are always more possible sources that could be consulted, additional angles from which it could be viewed. Yet it is hard to imagine what additional research or further questions could have been taken up for these books. Something I always do in reading scholarly works of history (almost a game or challenge) is to scan the bibliography to see whether I can find things the author should have read and did not. I seldom fail, but on *The Bradlaugh Case* I struck out, and on *Protestant versus Catholic* scored only one scratch single—one book (in German) that I thought should have been consulted and one question or aspect of the subject that I thought could have been more thoroughly explored.[3] This thoroughness and comprehensiveness is not just a matter of fact-grubbing, getting the data all in and straight. That is important, but we all know books that numb by simply throwing all the 'facts' at the reader. To be genuinely thorough in research and comprehensive in treatment requires, beyond patience and hard, determined work, a high level of intelligence, insight, imagination, and analytical and organizational skill. One cannot simply let the 'facts' tell the story (though real skill at narrative often gives the impression that the author is doing this). One has at once to seek out all the evidence available, to interpret it with care and insight, and to drag out of it the story that the historian sees is there. This is what Walter Arnstein does admirably.

This means in turn that he has a gift for clear, elegant style and a coherent, interesting narrative. It is hard to find a muddy thought or an awkward sentence in Walter Arnstein's work. It is not at all hard to find neat phrases, cogent summaries, lucid expositions of complicated material, penetrating insights, even dashes of understated wit. For an example of such insights: 'A significant aspect of any historical incident is the tendency for both the newspaper-reading audience and the very actors themselves to forget the details of Act One by the time Act Two is well under way.'[4] (I could not help thinking of this in regard to the Clinton impeachment trial in its transition from House to Senate.) For an example of subtle wit: 'As Bradlaugh advanced to the Table, Northcote, who had been leaning forward with his hands on his knees like a dog held in leash, rose to interrupt.'[5] More important still, one cannot read what Walter Arnstein writes without seeing how his subject (historical event, development, argument, discussion, whatever) goes somewhere, has a beginning, development, and end that hang together. This applies to his textbooks, his numerous articles, and even his book reviews as well as his monographic books. One always is told clearly what happened, when, where, how, and (where the evidence permits) why. This flair for coherent, interesting narrative development, I am certain, helps account for the great success of his textbooks and undergraduate and public lectures. It even shows up in a most unlikely place: his examinations. For years I served as second reader on qualifying doctoral examinations in his field of Modern Britain, in which we had a most satisfactory division of roles: he cheerfully drew up the exams and I cheerfully accepted them. Every university professor knows what a deadly dull task composing such exams can be, and how often the questions are mind-numbing in their unimaginative vagueness ('Discuss the rise of labor movements in nineteenth century Europe'). Walter Arnstein always wrote new, different exams, and they were always interesting. We regularly hold that examination questions are supposed to make students think (which in some instances, I fear, means making them think, 'What on earth does this question mean?'). His questions really did make students think about the subject of the question, and drew out what they did and did not know about it.

Along with these gifts of a lucid style and interesting exposition go two other combinations of qualities, each one involving an uncommon juxtaposition of opposites: first, an unusual capacity for scholarly detachment and at the same time for empathy with the historical actors with whom one deals; and second, the ability to reach firm, clear judgments and conclusions while at the same time maintaining a sense of balance, restraint, and moderation, giving all sides their due and weighing all the facts impartially. Here, I need to say, is where I see the greatest difference between Walter Arnstein's style in history and my own. Not for him the deliberately provocative assertion, the paradox, the bold counterfactual, the seemingly outrageous thesis, the sly gibe or the blunt attack. He is clearly reluctant to draw parallels between his story and other eras, or to use it to say something about current problems. He shows an even greater reluctance to impose his opinions on the reader or to make history teach lessons. He shows a far greater disposition to say instead, in dealing with conventional verdicts, 'Well, not exactly.' A favorite and characteristic phrase in his conversation and an attitude easily detected in his work is 'On balance.' This is not at all the product of intellectual timidity or that common disease among historians, acute paralytic cautionitis. When he comes to conclusions, they are clear and unequivocal (see, for example, the final pages of *The Bradlaugh Case*). When he has theses to propose and revisionist interpretations to offer, they are equally so (see, for example, the introductory chapter of *Protestant versus Catholic*). These characteristics of balance and moderation arise instead, I am sure, from a good historian's recognition of the intractable complexity of his material, and still more from his willingness and ability to empathize (not sympathize) with the situations, feelings, thoughts and motives of historical actors. It goes even beyond that, to a recognition with Leopold von Ranke that 'Every age is immediate before God' – that is, every era deserves to be understood and judged on its own terms, and not on ours or by the values of a particular historian.

It is precisely because of these latter qualities, I would guess, that Walter Arnstein has had a major impact on Modern British History in general and Victorian Studies in particular. He has not attempted flatly to deny or in sweeping fashion to overthrow the reigning interpretations; he has instead quietly and successfully demonstrated that they are at best incomplete and at worst seriously distorting; that there is another side which cannot be ignored, other evidence which must be taken into account and which makes the whole picture substantially different. He does not deny, as I understand it, the long-term trends of secularization which many have discussed, but he does insist, and in my view demonstrates convincingly, that religion was far more important and had far more to do with many vital issues in nineteenth-century Britain than many have supposed. He does not deny the importance of class (though I am sure he does reject the Marxist interpretation of it), but he does argue, again convincingly, that much else besides class shaped the history of that era. He does not sweep aside notions of the decline of the aristocracy or the invention of tradition, but he does confront them with evidence of a persistence and even revival of aristocracy and tradition. He does not make Queen Victoria one of the greatest active rulers or intellects of all time, but he does show that she was both more active and more serious in her role as Queen than many have supposed, and so on. Nor should one overlook the great contribution he has made and impact he has had through his numerous book reviews in all the major journals – a kind of historical work too often underrated. Here too these qualities of balance and firm, sensible judgment are constantly in evidence. Judging from the many reviews of his I have read, I am sure that quite a few of the authors involved were not happy with his judgments (though I would guess the majority were). I cannot believe, however, that any of the authors could legitimately feel that his/her work had not been carefully read, its contents and arguments fairly presented to the reader, and the reasons for the judgment, good or bad, not stated clearly or not shown to be germane.

This account of Walter Arnstein's intellectual achievements and qualities as a historian does not, of course, fully account for the many honors he has received and offices he has held locally, nationally, and internationally as a scholar and teacher. It leaves out many personal qualities that, though imponderables, are equally vital: his genial personality, his elegant, if at times a bit Gladstonian, turns of phrase, his sense of humor, his clever wit (despite an occasional excruciating pun),[6] his great and genuine interest in his students and willingness to devote much time to promoting their projects and undertakings (this *Festschrift* is above all a tribute to this), and his unmistakable love of history and joy in teaching it. He also possesses (again I sense the contrast with myself) some of the talents of a good administrator—an eye for detail, a willingness to take pains, an ability to persuade people to do things they would prefer not to do for the sake of the general good, a willingness patiently to endure committees and meetings and the whims and idiosyncracies of colleagues, and the like.

Is there something old-fashioned in all this? Undoubtedly so, both in the kind of history Walter Arnstein does and in the ways he goes about it, in research and writing, in teaching, and in service. There is even something old-fashioned in the historical *credo* he gives in the interview published in Roger Adelson, ed., *Speaking of History: Conversations with Historians*, where, speaking of his concern at the impact of post-modernism and of theories from literary criticism and social science on the current practice of history, he says:

> At one time historians may have had too much of a sense of certainty, but nowadays we have too much of a sense of relativity. All historians are necessarily circumscribed in their work by the limits of the available evidence, by the limits of their own understanding, and by the need to take into account their own preconceptions. But I find myself deeply troubled by scholars who seem to have reached the conclusion that writing history is identical to writing a work of fiction, as if there were no fundamental difference between a historical monograph and a novel.[7]

This is doubtless old-fashioned language, and in one small particular I somewhat disagree with it. That is, I do not see quite the danger in theories imported from social science into history that Walter Arnstein seems to. But if it is also old-fashioned to concentrate, as he further urges historians to do, on the relative, partial truths we can attain to, the 'innumerable "facts" … we can establish with a high degree of reliability', and the many generalizations on which we can reach a considerable level of intersubjective consensus and verification, thereby keeping history alive as a method of genuine scholarly discovery, *sui generis* and indispensable to the examined life which is the only kind worth living—if this is old-fashioned, then I will wear the term along with Walter Arnstein as a badge of honor, and trust that

this old-fashioned kind of history will endure when a good many current
fashions have been forgotten.

NOTES

1 Walter L. Arnstein, *The Bradlaugh Case: Atheism, Sex, and Politics among
    the Late Victorians* (Oxford: Oxford University Press, 1965; reprint,
    Columbia: University of Missouri Press, 1983).
2 Idem, *Protestant versus Catholic in Mid-Victorian England: Mr. Newdegate
    and the Nuns* (Columbia: University of Missouri Press, 1982).
3 Just for the sake of pedantic completeness, the book is Matthias Buschkühl,
    Great Britain and the Holy See, 1746-1870 (Dublin, 1982) – not a particularly
    good book, but one which makes some points about the impact of religion
    and particularly of anti-Catholic sentiment in Britain on British foreign policy
    which would have contributed to Arnstein's thesis. This, it will not surprise
    him to hear, is also the one theme I thought was somewhat neglected .
4 *Bradlaugh Case*, p. 102.
5 Ibid., p. 109.
6 Editors' note: his puns are, indeed, often excruciating.
7 Roger Adelson, ed., *Speaking of History: Conversations with Historians* (East
    Lansing, MI, 1997), p. 19.

CHAPTER 3

'The Prince of Whales': Caricature, Charivari, and the Politics of Morality[1]

Tamara L. Hunt

In 1812, John and Leigh Hunt, proprietors of the *Examiner* newspaper, were convicted of seditious libel for publishing an article on the Prince Regent that read in part: 'This *delightful, blissful, wise, pleasurable* [sic], *honorable, virtuous, true*, and *immortal* Prince [quoting the *Morning Post*], was a violator of his word, a libertine over head and ears in disgrace, a despiser of domestic ties, the companion of gamblers and demireps, a man who had just closed half a century without one single claim on the gratitude of his country, or the respect of posterity!'[2] This prosecution was undertaken because it met the definition of seditious libel: 'to bring into hatred or contempt or to excite disaffection against ... the person of His Majesty, his heirs and successors.'[3] However, the government was not only interested in enforcing the law; it also believed that ridiculing the royal family could have grave consequences. As John Croker, a secretary of the admiralty, noted in 1817, 'the public is in, I think, a sulky humor, waiting for any fair or unfair excuse to fly into a passion ... . If there should arise any division in the Royal Family, it will be that match to fire the gunpowder.'[4] Yet even though the government believed that public perceptions about the royal family could set off a revolution, no attempt was made to stop the production of one of the most virulent, widespread, and outspoken forms of attack on George III's family: caricature.

There is evidence that the government did not prosecute caricatures because the resulting trial would require the prosecutor to give a detailed explanation of every allusion in the print. The Solicitors General gave this as their reason for advising against prosecuting the artist and publisher of *Princely Predilections or Ancient Music and Modern Discord*, apparently the only print seriously considered for prosecution during the Regency.[5] They noted that this 'most indecent and impudent' satire on the royal family 'would require so much of difficult explanation in stating it as a Libel upon the Record' as to make it unsuitable for prosecution.[6] Their recommendation was undoubtedly affected by the fact that once the charges were read aloud in court, they could be printed in newspapers, thereby further publicizing objectionable prints.

The government also knew that juries were unlikely to convict if the charges were believed to be true.[7] This made it especially difficult to stop attacks on the royal family, for during the reign of George III, the public was particularly well-informed about royal immorality. In addition to official government action taken as the result of the sexual escapades of various members of the royal family,[8] some royals published their private correspondence as a means of attack – or of justifying their actions – in purely private quarrels.[9] Gossip was further fueled by 'private' or 'secret' court histories which circulated freely among the aristocracy and led to veiled or open allusions in newspapers and caricatures.[10] Lord Glenbervie's attitude towards such reports may be representative; after confiding several of these highly scandalous rumors to his diary, he concluded 'Is all this really true? It is so like many stories one has heard! But that such things have happened is almost certain, and they probably have happened and will happen not once or twice, but over and over again.'[11]

While the children of George III were hardly the first members of the ruling family to be notorious for their behavior, their foibles were far more well-known than those of any previous generation. Significantly, in the course of George III's reign, caricaturists shifted their focus from royal oppression and political misconduct to the immorality of the ruling family.[12] Yet in the era of the French revolution, even prints that satirized the private behavior of royalty were intrinsically political.[13] While caricaturists generally did not credit the royal family with political motivations or accuse them of interfering in the government or threatening the constitution, their satires were political in that their complaints about the expense and immorality of the royal family often included the suggestion that such behavior threatened the security of the throne by undermining respect for the monarchy.

In some respects, it is not surprising that caricatures commented at length on the private lives of royalty. In late Georgian England, caricatures had come to form a fundamental part of the often highly ritualized political dialogue,[14] and graphic satires took on some of the symbols and concerns reflected in these rituals, especially that of rough music or charivari. Mentions of charivari occur as early as the fifteenth century, and instances continued well into in the nineteenth, with its elements often being incorporated into other forms of protest.[15] Charivaris often targeted people in positions of influence or authority, suggesting a connection to continental carnival, or the 'world turned upside down,' where behavior normally prohibited became the order of the day.[16] Mockery was not restricted to local men, however, and well-known figures who were seen as deserving special denigration could be targeted; Tom Paine, Napoleon Bonaparte and even the Pope were popular substitutions for 'the Guy' on November 5.[17]

It has been suggested that this ritualized mockery of authority is a form of communication by which means those normally excluded from political power are able to express their opinions with relatively little fear of reprisal.[18] Other scholars have posited that such mockery provides an outlet for feelings and beliefs normally repressed by the authorities, and thus it tends to partially defuse potential conflicts.[19] Still others have suggested that public mockery is ambiguous, alternating between disapproval of and support for the status quo.[20] The behavior of the royal family would have merited rough music had they been private citizens, yet their very public position made their lives and even private decisions a matter for political debate. Thus, many caricatures on the royal family contain elements of charivari, allowing those who did not have political power to join in the general ridicule of their rulers for inappropriate behavior.

Unsuitable marriages in private life were often the focus of charivari, and a spate of royal marriages during the Regency between aging grooms and young brides (some of dubious morality) or wealthy princesses and poor foreigners made a likely target. The first occurred in 1815, when the Duke of Cumberland married his cousin, the twice-widowed Princess of Solms-Braunfels. Notoriety surrounded the marriage; Queen Charlotte published in newspapers her reasons for refusing to receive her new daughter-in-law (who was also her niece), citing the latter's reputation for immorality,[21] and Parliament turned down the Duke's application for an additional £6000 annual grant.[22] Although some believed that it was solely the Duchess's past indiscretions that raised opposition to the grant,[23] MPs apparently did not forget that the Duke's unsavory reputation included rumors of incest and murder. During the debate one MP stated that the marriage 'was an improper one, however much the parties might be suited to each other from their habits and morals.'[24] Rumors about the couple were summed up in the caricature *Financial Survey of Cumberland or the Beggar's Petition.*[25] The new Duchess looks longingly at three grotesque Grenadiers, saying, 'Ah! who could resist such Lovers as these. Happy is the woman whose husband is a Grenadier.' To emphasize further the Duchess's questionable past, Cumberland wears cuckold's horns. Lord Cochrane, whose vote tipped the scales to defeat Cumberland's grant, fires a cannon at the Duke, expelling him from Parliament. The large black area on the right of this self-censored print covers the figure of Cumberland's late valet, who allegedly cut his own throat after unsuccessfully trying to murder the Duke in 1810. He holds a bloody razor, crying 'Is this a razor that I see before me? Thou canst not say I did it,' echoing the popular rumor that the Duke had murdered him.[26]

Political and economic troubles quickly turned the public's attention away from the Duke and Duchess, but in 1816 Princess Charlotte of Wales's

Plate 1: 'A Financial Survey of Cumberland'

marriage to Prince Leopold of Saxe-Coburg inspired numerous satires. As the only legitimate child of the Regent, Charlotte was heiress presumptive to the throne, and she was arguably the most popular member of the royal family. The public's attention (and affection) had been caught in 1815 when she broke off her engagement to the Prince of Orange because she refused to live outside of England. In the eyes of many, this showed proper respect for the country and her position, and as Robert Patten points out, even the caricatures that complained about her wedding's cost and the prospect of numerous, expensive progeny were relatively mild, since 'hopes for a peaceful and perhaps redemptive succession rested on the offspring of this union.'[27]

These attitudes are reflected in the caricature *Buying a German Sausage or a Foreign Dainty for the Wedding Feast*.[28] Leopold, a butcher's apron over his hussar's uniform, offers a 'German Sausage' to Princess Charlotte. John Bull, a grotesque figure, stands behind the Princess, holding out two large moneybags, labeled '£60,000 per annum' and '£60,000 outfit.' John says, 'Here's the Money! The family always expect me to make good all their Bargains at home & abroad! I hope young man (as you have charg'd such a swinging price for it) that it is a good article quite clean and wholesome & will not do the Lady any harm!!'[29] Charlotte's reply reflects the popular belief that she wished to marry an Englishman: 'If I was left to my own free will in these things, I would rather choose a Rump Stake [*sic*] from an English Buttock than all the German sausages in the world!!'

The 'German Sausage' also figures prominently in other prints, along with the suggestion that a reversal of gender roles might occur when a relatively penniless young man married a far wealthier woman and instantly gained status and position.[30] Had such a marriage taken place between private individuals whose disparity of rank and fortune were similar, the couple could have faced an evening of rough music.[31] But would this bride who was destined to be the Queen of England be submissive to her far less important husband? This was reflected in the satire *Hercules and Omphale, or Modern Mythology*.[32] Charlotte holds a large sausage topped by a small crown, and she wears Leopold's chapeau-bras and breeches, while he wears a woman's cap and skirt and holds a distaff. He pleads with his wife to return his breeches, but Charlotte replies, 'Can't spare them yet love! I must use myself [*sic*] to them that they may sit easy when I am obliged to wear them for good my dear! Queen Ann [*sic*] did so before me.'

Yet while Charlotte's words point out the political significance of 'wearing the breeches,' the print's caption notes that '[when] Beauty so bewitches, With Married pairs, tis ten to one the Wife will wear the Breeches.' This links the print to traditional charivari, for in private life, a woman who ruled her husband—and thereby inverted the 'natural' order—was a likely target for a mocking ritual.[33] Yet in this case the private and the public

Plate 2: 'Hercules and Omphale'

Plate 3: 'Balancig Accounts'

clashed; a native-born sovereign was preferable to a foreign prince, even if a queen ruled her husband. This sentiment was clearly expressed in *Balancig [sic] Accounts—i.e. Proving the Weight of a Crown.*[34] John Bull supports a see-saw on his back, and Charlotte, resting on a pillow inscribed 'Amor Patriae,' far outweighs her husband, who carries a German Sausage.[35] Near Charlotte lies a pile of broadside ballads, one of which is 'The Days of Queen Bess.' In the meantime, John assures her that he intends to see that the balance will stay in her favor. Thus, in a curious way, xenophobia appeared to overcome fears about the 'unnatural' domestic arrangements of Charlotte and Leopold, yet caricaturists reminded the Princess—and the public—that her position was indeed unique because of its special importance to the country.

The public's preference for British grooms for their princesses was also reflected in the satires that appeared later that summer when Princess Mary wed her cousin and long-time suitor, the Duke of Gloucester.[36] Mary was popular, and her choice of a native-born husband met with public approval, as is reflected in prints such as *Farmer George's Daughter Polly Longing for a Slice of Single Gloucester!*[37] Mary is a dairy maid who is courted by the Duke, dressed in military uniform and wearing a long apron. They look at each other with longing, and, using *double-entendres* cloaked in language connected with the dairy, each makes a sexually suggestive speech. Meanwhile, a small figure representing the Prince Regent's private secretary holds out a field marshall's baton, saying 'Please sir my Master has sent you this <u>Churning Stick</u> as you are so kind as to <u>work in</u> his Sisters <u>Buttery</u>.' Thus, this print suggests that while the Duke was in love with Mary, he also was something of a fortune hunter – receiving a military promotion on his marriage. The print *Gloucestershire Glory*[38] makes this point more clearly. Mary carries her new husband on her back through the doorway of the Horse Guards, while the lines beneath the title read: 'Dear double inducement / of <u>baton</u> and <u>Bed</u> / For such sweet amusement / Oh! – who would not wed!!' Criticism was far less muted in 1818 when Princess Elizabeth married the Prince of Hesse-Homburg,[39] and caricaturists had several reasons to invoke charivari's imagery. The public did not consider the Prince to be an eligible spouse; at the age of forty-nine, he was immensely fat, smelled of garlic and tobacco, and rarely washed.[40] In addition, he was a foreigner and seemed to offer little in terms of personal worth or advantages through diplomatic alliances. As was the case of Prince Leopold in 1816, Hesse-Homburg was charged with being a fortune-hunter. This was the theme of *More Humbugs,– or–Another Attack on John Bull's Purse*[41] which shows the bridal couple walking arm-in-arm behind a glum John Bull. The Prince declares: 'Now Mr. Bull! I try my best, I erect my Crest And at your expence I shall be Blest. I be com [sic] for your <u>goods</u> – ' to which John replies: 'Aye and my Chattels too, I suspect!!!'

Plate 4: 'Farmer George's Daughter Polly'

This print merits closer scrutiny, for Elizabeth's words reflect another reason for charivari. She declares, 'Yes Johnny you know me before to Day, be assured I am no chicken And you shall see that merry Bess, In concert join'd with Humbug Hesse With Heirs old England soon shall Bless, But you must find the Money.' It was unlikely that she would become a mother at forty-eight, but her assertion that 'you know me before to Day.... I am no chicken' is a veiled reference to the persistent rumors that nearly thirty years earlier Elizabeth had secretly married a courtier and had children by him.[42] 'Betts Chickens' was a phrase used to signify Elizabeth's supposed children in *Found it Out; or, A German P—Humbuged* [sic].[43] On the morning after the marriage, Elizabeth and Queen Charlotte try to assure the doubting Prince of his bride's virginity, while a servant smuggles away two infants in a basket inscribed 'Betts Chickens.' Other prints also suggested that Elizabeth deceived her new husband about her virginity. The simplest of these merely made use of the traditional cuckold's horns, such as *The New German Waltz* which shows the newlyweds dancing.[44] As the Prince lifts the Princess into the air, she makes the sign of horns behind his head, implying that he is a cuckold.

While Mary and Elizabeth married for personal reasons, Princess Charlotte's death while giving birth to a still-born son in November 1817 suddenly gave the unmarried royal dukes a political reason to seek brides. Charlotte's death left the Regent without a legitimate heir, and both he and his childless next eldest brother, the Duke of York were estranged from their aging wives and unlikely to produce offspring. Thus, their younger brothers had an opportunity to become the father of the new heir presumptive. Although the Duke of Cumberland had married in 1815, he had as yet no surviving heir, and since the Dukes of Clarence and Kent preceded him in the succession, they scrambled into matrimony, along with their younger brother the Duke of Cambridge. The situation was ripe for ridicule: all the grooms were well beyond the traditional age of first marriages when they hurriedly selected brides, and the two eldest had been involved in long-standing relationships with mistresses.[45] Further, for more than seven years – after leaving the actress who had supported him and borne his ten illegitimate children – Clarence ardently (and unsuccessfully) pursued a bride among women less than half his age whose major attraction seems to have been their wealth.[46] Although Kent was active in charitable work, supported moderate political reform, and had been faithful to his mistress for nearly thirty years, his severity as an officer had provoked two mutinies, and he had been forced to assign three-quarters of his income to his trustees in an effort to pay off his enormous debts.[47] Only Cambridge was known for his polite manners and filial behavior and he apparently never had an illicit romance; as the youngest (at age forty-three) and most virtuous of the bridegrooms, he seemed most likely to marry respectably

Plate 5: 'Found it Out; or, a German P— Humbuged'

Plate 6: 'The New German Waltz'

and produce an heir to the throne.[48] Nevertheless, caricaturists condemned this unseemly scramble for wives, as well as the fact that the British government was expected to find funds to cover the costs of their weddings and new establishments, despite the country's economic distress.[49]

These features came together in several caricatures castigating the expense occasioned by this spate of royal marriages. In two different prints, *The Matrimonial Mania–or–Poor Jonny [sic] Ridden to Death*[50] and *John Bull Supporting the Nuptial Bed!!!*,[51] John Bull is shown literally bearing on his back the expense of the royal weddings, while the dialogue in each print allude to the salacious stories surrounding many of the participants. Several other satires produced at this time broadly criticized the royal family's lack of morals using the motif of balls or dances, such as in the broadside *The R—l Masquerade,*[52] which comments on recent repressive political decisions and ongoing economic distress, as well as on the foibles of the royal family; for instance, in reference to Clarence's unsuccessful attempts to secure a bride, he is shown singing 'Young froggee [sic] would a wooing go ... .' *The Hombourg Waltz, with Characteristic Sketches of Family Dancing!*[53] focuses solely on the marriages and sexual improprieties of the royal family, using 'dancing' as a metaphor for sexual intercourse. While it refers to the rumors surrounding the four royal marriages of 1818, it also makes mention of earlier royal scandals, such as the Prince Regent's disastrous marriage and his continuing illicit affairs: in the print, the Regent declares that, having selected a partner early in the evening, 'it has spoild my Waltzing' to which his mistress replies, 'Not altogather [sic] your Dancing tho' I Fancy.'

Such caricatures make it clear that the children of George III were hardly respectable, and their behavior had been the subject of gossip and published innuendo for years. Much of this focused on George III's two eldest sons, the Prince of Wales and the Duke of York. Although each married relatively early in life, neither emulated their father's well-known domesticity, good manners or frugality. The public knew that they were estranged from their wives, openly kept mistresses, and ran up enormous debts. But this behavior was more than a private concern for the royal family; during this revolutionary period any royal immorality became a significant political problem. The monarchy had to present itself as a desirable counterpoint to republican government as espoused by France, and for that reason, the royal family had to maintain its regal station and the public's respect. Yet this was increasingly difficult as the follies of the Duke and the Prince became glaringly public.

This connection between royal morality and the good of the state was stated quite openly in the caricature *John Bull Advising with his Superiors*, published in 1808.[54] In this remarkable satire, John Bull is a country bumpkin who not only gives advice, but directly confronts the Prince of Wales and the Duke of York about their immoral private lives compromising the country:

Sarvant Measters. I be come to ax a bit of thy advice because our great Parliament man a been telling us that the great folk in France be committing all sorts of Abominations & that they be likely to loose their places for it, & moreover he tells us that the great rulers before them did the same, & therefore God punished them for it. I has heard some strange things o' late of our great Folk in that way (Crim Con) I thinks they calls it, & so forth. Now I & my Family a been thinking that the stream should run pure from the fountain head or else it is apt to get thicker & thicker and I reads that no Adulterers nor whoremonger nor Fornicator nor those tha marry Roman Catholics nor keep Catholic Whores shall inherit the Kingdom of Heaven, now does the think such like should ever be promoted on Earth either? he!!! why thee doesn't answer. the seems astounded, why doesn't the knaw this?!!! Well if the won't answer I must go & ax our Parliament man, so good bye Measters I hope no offence — Good Old King Georg for Ever I does love good old Georg by goles! because he is not of that there sort! God send he may live for ever I says - that won't affront thee I hope!!!

Masked behind a simple countryman's language is a very significant condemnation. John denounces the royal brothers' licentious behavior (their mistresses' portraits hang on the wall behind them), and stresses that personal virtue is an indispensable prerequisite for a monarch. His praise of George III further emphasizes the link between good character and the right to rule.

The public had further reason to criticize the Duke's conduct in 1809, as Parliament began an official inquiry into allegations that officers had bribed the Duke's mistress, Mary Anne Clarke, to use her influence with the Commander-in-Chief to obtain promotions for them. In the course of the investigation, many details about the Duke's private life with his mistress emerged, and his puerile letters to her, overflowing with excessive sentiment, were published as part of the evidence in the case. Dozens of caricatures were published on this topic between January and April, and virtually all suggested that the allegations were true, often incorporating material drawn directly from Parliamentary testimony. For example, *The Modern Circe or a Sequel to the Petticoat*[55] shows Mrs. Clarke using the Duke's military cloak to shelter a crowd of tiny petitioners, while from her waist hangs a notice 'Who'll buy good luck Who'll buy Who'll buy Promotion tickets here am I.' A more explicit allegation is depicted in *The Bishop and His Clarke. Or a Peep into Paradise.*[56] The Duke, who had also been the secular bishop of Osnabrück for many years, is shown in bed with Mrs Clarke, his mitre sitting on a commode. In language similar to that found in his letters, the Duke says, 'Ask any thing in reason and you shall have it my dearest dearest dearest Love.' She replies, 'Only remember the promotions I mentioned I have pinn'd up the list at the head of the Bed'; her words echo her testimony before Parliament in which she claimed that such a transaction, complete with a written list pinned to the bedpost, actually took place.[57]

Yet while most prints focused on the salacious details which were revealed daily before Parliament, there was a deeper public concern over this affair which was reflected in prints such as *Sampson Asleep on the Lap of Dalilah*.[58] In this satire, the Duke of York dozes while Mrs. Clarke cuts off his pigtail; she shows it to two men standing to one side and says 'Gentlemen you may now take him with safety, his strength is gone, I have cut off his regulation tail, and there is no danger.' Her companions, Colonel Wardle, the Duke's chief accuser, and Viscount Folkestone, an ally of radical Sir Francis Burdett and a supporter of the investigation of the Duke,[59] reflect the fact that the Duke's affair became a source of political controversy; the opposition supported the inquiry, while the government opposed it. But the sordid affair – and the public's reaction to it – also had implications for the nation at large. Early in the proceedings, one MP declared that '… this was the foulest conspiracy that ever was set on foot against the Son of the Crown, and indirectly against the Crown itself.'[60] Another long-time member of Parliament wrote to a friend that 'I see no means myself, in the present state of the world, of preserving our liberty but by the act of settlement and the House of Brunswick; but we are dependent, even for that, upon the family itself; and it is in their power, no doubt, by outraging every sentiment of public opinion, and every decorum of English manners, to render it impossible to maintain them.'[61]

Although Parliament voted to acquit him, the Duke felt obliged to resign because of the large number who had voted to convict, and interest in the affair subsided. However, the ongoing romantic entanglements of the Prince of Wales – who became Prince Regent in 1811 after George III subsided into madness – were more than sufficient to catch the public's attention. Since his first serious affair in 1780 at age seventeen with actress Mary Robinson, the Prince's romantic liaisons had been standard fodder for caricaturists. Unfortunately, so was his marriage in 1795 to his cousin, Caroline of Brunswick; little more than a year after the wedding (and less than six months after the birth of their only child), the Prince separated from his wife after she demanded that he dismiss his current mistress, Lady Jersey, from her position as one of the Princess's chief attendants.[62]

The Prince was roundly condemned in caricature and in the press for the separation; he seemed to have wantonly rejected a proper domesticity with his wife in order to indulge in an illicit liaison with a married woman. This formed the basis for a number of satires using symbols of charivari, including *Future Prospects or Symptoms of Love in High Life* which appeared at the time of the separation.[63] The Prince kicks over the tea table in a rage, saying 'Marriage has no restraint on me! No Legal tie can bind the will. 'Tis free

Plate 7: 'Future Prospect or Symptoms of Live in High Life'

and shall be so – '. Through an open doorway a semi-nude woman is visible, sprawling on a couch, and her horned (i.e. cuckolded) husband smiles and says 'My Wife is waiting for you in the next room.' The 'Map of Jersey' protruding from his pocket shows that this couple is Lord and Lady Jersey. Meanwhile, the Princess, a sad and demure mother, cradles her baby daughter in her arms and declares that she will obey. The artist clearly contrasts this improper behavior to that of George III through a painting of 'Farmer George' and his wife riding together that hangs on the back wall of the room.

Lord Jersey was only one of a number of husbands to be portrayed with the cuckold's horns, yet these complaisant spouses also received honors, sinecures or gifts from the Prince. Such a situation is reflected in a print from 1816, *The Court at Brighton a la Chinese!!*[64] The Regent is dressed in oriental clothing and surrounded by lavish eastern trappings, an allusion to his predilection for oriental design. His current mistress, Lady Hertford, lounges next to him, her elbow carelessly propped up on his shoulder. Her husband, standing by her side, abounds in symbols of cuckoldry. Not only does his wife hold two fingers symbolizing horns behind his head, but his oriental-style dress is covered with an antler design, and his Lord Chamberlain's staff (he received the office through his wife's connection with the Prince) is topped by a tiny stag's head with antlers adorned by tiny bells, a symbol of folly.

Even a mere rumor that the Regent had entered into a new liaison inspired caricaturists, and his well-known amorous disposition gave them plenty of material. For example, in 1819, several caricatures suggested that the Duchess of Richmond had become the Regent's new paramour, even though there seemed to be virtually no basis for this rumor.[65] In *The P****e's Privy Pimp!!!*[66] the Prince's secretary, Sir Benjamin Bloomfield, negotiates with the Duchess on behalf of his master, assuring her that the Duke will never know of her indiscretion, since '*the P— will cover all that with a good Place.*' Discreetly-placed cuckold's horns reflect the illicit nature of this affair: the conspirators stand on a carpet decorated with antlers and stags' heads, while a picture hanging on the wall entitled *Horned Cattle of Canada* shows the Duke (and his two servants) wearing antlers.

This disparaging view of the Regent received additional impetus in the waning days of the Regency through his own undignified public actions. For example, on a whim in 1819, he held an informal supper in the Brighton Pavilion's elaborate kitchen. Many considered this to have been inappropriate behavior for one in his position; when caricaturists combined this with his already immoral reputation, the result was a spate of caricatures such as *He Stoops to Conquer or Royal George Sunk!!!*[67] in which the Regent makes amorous advances to a bashful cook. His speech, and the cook's reply, imply a belief that her sexual favors would be rewarded by a

Plate 8: 'The Court at Brighton a la Chinese!!'

Plate 9: 'He Stoops to Conquer or Royal George _Sunk!!!_'

title. This print was so popular that the publisher felt obliged to publish the
following notice:

> It has been falsely reported that the highly humourous caricature
> of *He Stoops to Conquer or R–l George Sunk* has been worn
> out, I take this opportunity of informing the Public that the Plate
> [is] perfect, and may be had where this is bought.[68]

*Royal Kitchen Stuff! – or, a Great Man <u>come down</u> to Visit his most <u>Obedt</u>
humble Servants!!! (vide, the amusements of Brighton)*[69] more pointedly
criticizes the Regent's demeaning himself by associating with servants. Once
again, he amorously accosts a stout cook; this one, however, declares 'La
Sir! what will the people say when they hear of your meddling so often with
things beneath you! Depend on it, you'll be haul'd over the coals & finely
<u>Roasted</u> for this!'

The Regent certainly was 'hauled over the coals' for his kitchen supper,
since at least five different caricatures on this subject appeared in late March,
1819. Caricaturists next depicted him and his mistresses even more
ridiculously on an early form of bicycle called a velocipede, popularly known
as hobby-horses or 'hobbies,' which had recently become the rage in society.
Royal Hobby's[70] linked the kitchen supper with the hobby craze, but in this
print, the Regent's 'hobby' is his cook, and he gleefully holds aloft a bottle
of gin and a goblet, exclaiming 'Ha! Ha! D—me! This is glorious! This is
<u>Princely</u>!! – better fun than the Hertford Hobby <u>– Kitchen</u> stuff and <u>Dish
clouts</u> for ever I say D—me!! – If the rascals caricature me <u>I'll buy 'em All
up</u> d—me.' The cook looks up in dismay, and her words are a play on the
public disapproval at such unprincely behavior: 'Oh! master do let me alone
& see! You've thrown the Cod's head[71] & shoulders all in the dirt!' On the
right side of the print, the Duke of York and his current mistress, Mrs.
Carey, ride on a velocipede loaded down with money bags, a reference to
the £10,000 per year he had recently begun receiving as the newly-appointed
Keeper of the King's Person. He received this sum merely for riding to
Windsor several times per month to consult with George III's doctors. The
Duke tips his hat to John Bull, who fumes, '<u>£10,000 a year</u> for a son to do
his <u>duty</u> to his Father !!!!!! Whilst my children are starving!!!'

The motif of riding a hobby can be seen as a form of charivari, for some
traditional charivari processions paraded the victim or effigy on a horse or
a pole, preferably facing backwards.[72] *Royal Hobby's* makes it clear that
the private lives of George III's two eldest sons did not meet the public's
standard of acceptable behavior. Yet this print pointedly criticizes their
behavior for its official implications as well – the Regent's words emphasize
his unregal behavior, while John Bull's condemnation of the Duke of York
highlights the public's disgust at the royal family's apparent lack of concern
about the extreme economic hardship faced by many ordinary Britons.

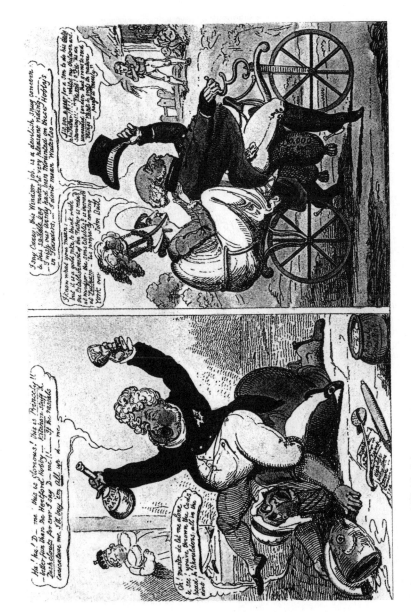

Plate 10: 'Royal Hobby's'

Plate 11: 'Royal Hobby's, or The Hertfordshire Cock-Horse!'

Similar complaints about the Regent and the Duke appeared in another hobby print, *Royal Hobby's, or The Hertfordshire Cock-Horse!*[73] The Regent lies prone, his body forming part of a hobby. Lady Hertford rides on his back and steers him 'To the Horns Inn, Hertford.' She clearly dominates the Regent, for not only does she ride on his back and hold the reins which guide him, she also wears a crown and flourishes a whip that has a scepter for a handle. This provided a dual incentive for charivari: not only was the Regent guilty of sexual misconduct, but he was henpecked into the bargain.[74] Meanwhile, the Duke of York rides towards Windsor on a hobby which is 'one of £10,000.'

The implication that the Regent was managed by his mistresses was as much a source of serious concern as a butt of humor. As in the case of Charlotte and Leopold, a man being dominated by his wife or mistress was possible grounds for a charivari, since this situation overturned the 'natural' order in a family. Moreover, the influence of the Prince's mistresses had significant political implications. These ladies openly sided with—and indeed were related to—leading politicians. Thus, 'petticoat government' appeared to jeopardize the supposedly impartial nature of sovereign power. Not only could these women lead the Regent into debauchery and extravagance, but they might also improperly or even dangerously influence his policies.[75]

Such consequences were the theme of *The Prince of Whales or the Fisherman at Anchor*,[76] where one artist utilized the pun on the Regent's title and his excessive girth. Here he is a whale with a human head, swimming in the 'Sea of Politics.' He is controlled by Prime Minister Perceval who guides him using a chain and anchor, and from the Prince's nostril spews the 'Dew of Favor' which showers Perceval and his companions. The Regent is urged along this course by a buxom mermaid who swims beside him, playing a lyre while her husband struggles with his newly sprung cuckold's horns, scowling in anger.

Other satires suggested that the Prince had abandoned the Whigs, his long-time political allies, at the direction of his mistress, Lady Hertford. In one such caricature, *Delilah Depriveing [sic] Sampson of those Locks in Which Consisted His Strength*,[77] Lady Hertford plays the part of Delilah to the Regent's sleeping Sampson. She discards locks of hair snipped from his head which are inscribed with the names of leading Whig politicians, suggesting that she directed the Regent's political allegiances. *An Accouchment or Lady .... Delivering the Present Administration*[78] goes even further, alleging that Lady Hertford chose the Regent's Ministers. Five tiny men appear from under her skirts as she lies on a couch as if giving birth, and the Regent encourages her to 'bring forth some more.' Unlike the *Delilah* print which implied that the Regent was unaware of her machinations, this satire shows him as a willing participant, eager to be

Plate 12: 'Delilah Depriveing Sampson of those Locks'

dominated by his mistress.

Yet the most spectacular examples of caricature as charivari on royalty were produced in 1820-21 after the Regent had become George IV and attempted to divorce his wife on charges of adultery.[79] The spectacle of an aging, obese libertine insisting that he was a cuckolded victim solely for the purpose of divorcing the wife he had mistreated from the day they met was clearly ridiculous, and it inspired hundreds of graphic satires, many of which utilized the symbols of charivari. In some prints, the King wears cuckold's horns; while this implies that the Queen was guilty of adultery, she is not the satire's target. Rather, such prints ridicule the King's claim that he was the injured party. For example, in *A Struggle for the Horns!*[80] John Bull attempts to wrest a pair of cuckold's horns from the King's grasp, declaring, 'I'll be D—n'd if you do wear them yet, however much you may deserve them so it is useless contending G—e.' In *Baise-Mon-Q*,[81] the King and his mistress sit on a sofa, kissing, yet above the King's head is a picture that refers to the king's claim to be an injured husband; a fat mandarin wears a hat topped with antlers, while the half of a crown on his stomach indicates that he symbolizes George IV.

The Queen's cause was phenomenally popular, and some caricatures suggest that the public's anxiety about the stability of the throne in the face of royal misconduct was even greater than it had been during the French wars or at the time of Mary Anne Clarke scandal. The American Minister in London marveled at

> the boundless rage of the Press, and liberty of speech. Every day produced its thousand fiery libels against the King and his adherents; and caricatures, under the worst forms, were hawked about all the streets ... . This tempest of abuse incessantly directed against the King and all who stood by him, was borne, during several months, without the slightest attempt to punish or check it.[82]

But many also agreed with Sir Robert Peel, who in August, 1820 bemoaned the Ministry's apparent blindness to the seriousness of the situation:

> I do think the Queen's affair very formidable. It is a famous ingredient in the cauldron which has been bubbling a long time, and upon which, as it always seemed to me, the Government never could discern the least simmering. They applied a blow-pipe, however, when they ... established a precedent of dethronement for imputed personal misconduct. Surely this was not the time for robbing Royalty of the exterior marks of respect... .[83]

Peel was not alone in recognizing the implications of dethroning the queen for personal misconduct. Early in July, Earl Fitzwilliam wrote to Earl Grey:

We are to dethrone a queen and dissolve her marriage with the
king, for the crime of disgusting intimacy with a menial servant,
for bestowing on him marks of favour, etc., etc. But if these be
crimes in a queen, that call down upon her the vengeance of the
nation, what is the nation to do in the case of king, guilty of
similar crimes – is [Prime Minister] Liverpool bold enough to
tell us, that he will dethrone from his hereditary throne a king,
*not charged with attempts to overthrow the liberties of the
country*, but guilty of the crimes alleged against the queen?[84]

The suggestion that the King's unchecked licentiousness was a threat to the
stability of the country can be found in a number of prints. For example, in
Royal Gambols!! or the Old Oak in Danger[85] George IV and two of his
mistresses swing on the 'Old Oak' of England; the King exclaims. 'Here I
go–Up–up–up, But fear I'll fall down, down, downy.' The base of the oak
is composed of the heads of the Ministers (one of whom wears cuckold's
horns), and it is being attacked by demons armed with an axe, a shovel, and
a saw. John Bull, a stout countryman, looks on the scene with an expression
of great concern; he exclaims, 'Oh dear! my poor Old Oak–how it shakes–
I fear they will break it down with their d—nd tricks.'

Because of the sexual nature of the conflict between the King and Queen,
it is perhaps not surprising that charivaris occurred in a number of places
throughout the country. One observer in York described the citizens as being
'in much tumult and disorder, being engaged in burning an effigy of the
reigning king (George IV.), whose cruelty and baseness towards his wife
had drawn upon him the odium and contempt, not only of his own subjects,
but of every feeling and enlightened man in the world ... .'[86] Magistrates
and clergymen who appeared to favor the action against the Queen faced
mocking parades and rough music in several districts; in Lincoln a pro-
Queen crowd paraded an effigy of the local magistrate through the streets
then burned it, while in Cambridgeshire, a clergyman who refused to ring
his church bells to celebrate the dropping of the charges against the Queen
was 'serenaded' by a crowd of her supporters until 4 a.m.[87] The chief
witnesses against the Queen also became victims of charivari in a number
of places. On Guy Fawkes day, the effigy of a former servant who testified
against her took the place of the Guy in a number of cities, while in Warwick,
effigies of two witnesses were hung from the gallows, paraded through the
streets to rough music, then burnt.[88]

In this instance, the public won, and George IV remained married.
However, because many believed Caroline had committed adultery, she
became a focus of a caricature charivari after the charges against her were
dropped. *Grand Entrance to Bamboozl'em*[89] is a comprehensive satire
incorporating allusions to the charges against the Queen and condemnation
of her radical supporters. Of particular note is a line of butchers who are

Plate 13: 'Royal Gambols!! Or the Old Oak in Danger'

making rough music as the Queen passes in procession, suggesting public condemnation of her behavior.

These satires on George IV and his wife are the most telling examples of the way in which traditional charivari became incorporated into political debate. But more importantly, they show a demand by the public that the monarch and the royal family conform to its standards of morality. Although members of government worried that satiric attacks on the royal family reflected a revolutionary republicanism similar to that which had overthrown the Bourbons in France, they linked such parody to the wrong tradition. Instead, caricatures were closer to charivari or rough music in which groups could unofficially enforce community standards of behavior. Thus, caricature charivaris against the royal family reflected public support for an idealized conception of royalty rather than a republican attack on one of Britain's oldest institutions. Ultimately, it could be argued that caricatures were one way of defusing a potentially dangerous situation by allowing the public to castigate its leaders for unacceptable behavior, urge reform of such conduct, and reinforce community beliefs and social structures. It also reflected the growing demand by the largely unenfranchised public that the government and monarchy listen to public opinion and shape their actions accordingly, making this a significant step in the evolution towards democracy in Britain, while maintaining the central ceremonial role of the monarchy.

NOTES

1   This paper is based on a chapter in my forthcoming book, *Defining John Bull: Political Caricature and National Identity in Late Georgian England* (Ashgate, 1999). I want to thank Walter Arnstein, Scott Hughes Myerly and Alexis Dolan for their comments and suggestions.

2   The *Examiner*, 12 March 1812. A hand-picked jury found them guilty and sentenced each of them to two years in prison and £500 in fines. Significantly, the government offered to drop the prosecution if the Hunts would promise never again to attack the Regent in print: they refused. Other prosecutions of journalists and authors were discussed throughout the Regency by the law officers of the crown: for examples, see PRO TS 11/155/485; PRO HO 41/4/117; and PRO HO 119/6/13.

3   Cited in William Wickwar, *The Struggle for the Freedom of the Press, 1819–1832* (London: G. Allen and Unwin, 1928), p. 27. One contemporary legal scholar also argued that special emphasis ought to be placed on libels against the king and his ministers, as being 'proportionately more criminal as it presumes to reach persons to whom special veneration is due.' F.L. Holt, *The Law of Libel*, 2nd edn. (London: J. Butterworth, 1816), p. 118.

4   John Croker, *The Correspondence and Diaries of the Rt. Hon. John Wilson Croker*, ed. Louis J. Jennings, 3 vols (London: J. Murray, 1844), 1: p. 110.

5   BMC 11864, published in the *Scourge* 3 (1 April 1812), p. 259. I have been unable to find any other references in the Treasury Solicitor's papers of prosecutions of caricatures until the Queen Caroline agitation.

6   PRO TS 11/580/1913.
7   Ironically, a libel defendant could not argue that the libel was true; indeed, some legal scholars believed the truth of an allegation against the government increased its gravity. Holt, *Law of Libel*, 118. The government also recognized that a prosecution could actually benefit the publisher by increasing demand for the caricature, a fact which was noted in the 1820 print *His most gracious Majesty Hum IVth & his Ministers going to play the Devil with the Satirists*, PRO TS 11/115/326, No. 56. George IV prepares to take steps against satirists, but the ghost of George III warns 'O my dear Son! my dear Son! if you prosecute them you will make their fortunes – but if you will only conduct yourself like a man and a gentleman you will destroy their profession. Farewell!!'
8   The Prince of Wales's illegal marriage to Maria Fitzherbert was introduced into Parliamentary debate in 1787; in 1794, George III petitioned the ecclesiastical courts to annul the clandestine marriage of his fifth son, Prince Augustus; the Princess of Wales's behavior was investigated in 1806 following charges that she had borne an illegitimate child, and the proceedings were published in full in 1813; and the Duke of York resigned as commander-in-chief in 1809 after it was revealed that his mistress had sold her influence with the Duke to men who wanted military commissions.
9   For example, Lord Glenbervie noted in 1804 that 'Many people about the Court ascribe the King's present attack (of illness) to the publication' of correspondence between the Duke of York and the Prince of Wales over the latter's request for an active military appointment. Sylvester Douglas, Lord Glenbervie, *The Diaries of Sylvester Douglas*, ed. Francis Bickley, 2 vols. (New York: Houghton Mifflin Co., 1928), 1: pp. 364–5. In 1812, a letter from the Princess of Wales to her estranged husband stating her grievances was published in the *Morning Chronicle*, and printshops also sold copies for sixpence. Thea Holme, *Caroline* (New York: Atheneum, 1980), pp. 110–11.
10 Roger Fulford, *The Royal Dukes*, rev. edn. (London: Collins, 1973), p. 46.
11 Glenbervie, *Diaries*, 2: p. 96.
12 For a fuller exploration of this, see Hunt, *Defining John Bull*.
13 Lynn Hunt's study, *The Family Romance of the French Revolution* (Berkeley: University of California Press, 1992), makes this point for the pre-Revolutionary French monarchy.
14 A number of recent works have suggested how widespread was political ritual throughout this period. See E.P. Thompson, *Customs in Common: Studies in Traditional Popular Culture* (New York: The New Press, 1993); Frank O'Gorman, 'Campaign Rituals and Ceremonies: The Social Meaning of Elections, 1780–1860,' *Past and Present* 135 (1992), pp. 72–101; Jack Goody, 'Knots in May: Continuities, Contradictions and Change in European Rituals,' *Journal of Mediterranean Studies* 3 (1993), pp. 30–45; Marc Baer, *Theatre and Disorder in Late Georgian London* (Oxford: The Clarendon Press, 1991); and James A. Epstein, *Radical Expression: Political Language, Ritual and Symbol in England, 1790–1850* (Oxford: Oxford University Press, 1994), especially Chapter 3, 'Understanding the Cap of Liberty: Symbolic Practice and Social Conflict in Early Nineteenth-Century England,' and Chapter 5, 'Rituals of Solidarity: Radical Dining, Toasting, and Symbolic Expression.'
15 Richard Hendrix, 'Popular Culture and the *Black Dwarf*,' *Journal of British Studies* 16 (Fall 1976), pp. 118–19; Thompson, *Customs in Common*, pp. 469, 477. Charles Tilly mentions an itinerant Evangelical preacher who was subjected to rough music in the 1790s. *Popular Contention in Great Britain*,

1758–1834 (Cambridge, MA: Harvard University Press, 1995), p. 217. Bob Bushaway discusses the traditional and ritual significance of various episodes of the Captain Swing riots of 1830 in his *By Rite: Custom, Ceremony and Community in England 1700–1880* (London: Junction Books, 1982), pp. 190–202. Cross-dressing, a familiar part of charivari and carnivalesque protest, played a significant role in even later political disturbances, particularly the Welsh 'Rebecca riots' in 1843; for a detailed account, see David Williams, *The Rebecca Riots: a Study in Agrarian Discontent* (Cardiff: University of Wales Press, 1953).

16   Not all local officials took such satire with equanimity; magistrate Zachariah Button of Essex went to court in 1791 in an effort to prosecute the artist and publisher of a print that depicted him in the pillory. PRO KB1/27, part 1, Michaelmas, 32 Geo. III, no. 2.

17   See Robert W. Malcomson, *Popular Recreations in English Society, 1700–1850* (New York: Cambridge University Press, 1979), p. 64; Robert D. Storch, '"Please to Remember the Fifth of November": Conflict, Solidarity and Public Order in Southern England, 1815–1900' in *Popular Culture and Custom in Nineteenth-Century England*, ed. Robert D. Storch (London: Croom Helm, 1982), p. 73.

18   Michael D. Bristol, *Carnival and Theater: Plebeian Culture and the Structure of Authority in Renaissance England* (New York: Routledge, 1989), p. 57.

19   Lewis Coser, *The Functions of Social Conflict* (London: Routledge & Keegan Paul, 1956), p. 41.

20   Thompson, *Customs in Common*, p. 482.

21   The new duchess had been married twice, first to Prince Frederick of Prussia, and second to Prince Frederick of Solms-Braunfels, but this second marriage had taken place while she was engaged to the Duke of Cambridge, Cumberland's younger brother, because she found herself pregnant by the Prince of Solms-Braunfels.

22   This was the first instance in modern British history that Parliament refused to vote money to a member of the British royal family. Fulford, *Royal Dukes*, p. 221.

23   Artist Joseph Farington stated that 'The immoral character of the Duchess of Salm [*sic*] ... caused this opposition [in Parliament].' *The Diary of Joseph Farington*, ed. Kathryn Cave, 16 vols (New Haven: Yale University Press, 1983), 13: p. 4661.

24   Quoted in Fulford, *Royal Dukes*, pp. 220–21.

25   BMC 12591, published by W.N. Jones, 1 August 1815, George Cruikshank, artist.

26   This appears to be the only Regency caricature to have been partially censored by the publisher and the artist to avoid a prosecution for libel, and only a few unaltered copies exist. Cumberland prosecuted anyone who accused him of the murder in print, such as journalist Henry White, who was sentenced in 1815 to 15 months' imprisonment and fined £200 after publishing the rumor. George S. Layard, *Suppressed Plates, Wood Engravings, etc.* (London, 1907), p. 60.

27   Robert L. Patten, *George Cruikshank's Life Times, and Art*, vol. 1, *1792–1835* (New Brunswick, NJ: Rutgers University Press, 1992), pp. 105–6.

28   HEH 216/97, March 1816.

29   This 'hope' undoubtedly sprang from a rumor that Prince Leopold had contracted venereal disease at Dover. Joseph Farington hinted at this in his diary entry for 25 March 1816: '[Capt. Farington] mentioned a report of the

nature of the indisposition of the Prince Leopold of Sax Cobourg [*sic*] which is said to have originated at Dover, – also that the Princess Charlotte had resolved not to marry Him. Such are the floating rumours of the day.' *Diary*, 14: p. 4801. This allegation is made much more pointedly in *A Brighton Hot Bath, or Preparations for the Wedding!!* BMC 12765, published by J. Sidebotham, *c*. April 1816, George Cruikshank, artist, which shows the Prince being dosed with various remedies for venereal disease in preparation for the wedding.

30   Joseph Farington had several different people tell him that when Leopold first came to England in 1814, he had 'lodged at a Grocers in Marybone [*sic*] St. and his apartments were up *two pair of stairs* ... [He] sd. He was so lodged because he was afraid His money wd. not hold out.' *Diary*, 14: p. 4831.

31   Thompson, *Customs in Common*, p. 493.

32   BMC 12780, published by T. Tegg, June 1816.

33   Thompson, *Customs in Common*, 469; Martin Ingram, 'Ridings, Rough Music, and "Reform of Popular Culture" in Early Modern England,' *Past and Present* 105 (1984), pp. 96–7.

34   BMC 12785, published by T. Tegg, June 1816, Williams, artist.

35   Significantly, the Prince Regent tries to help Leopold by placing liquor bottles on his end of the see-saw. While it is possible that the artist meant to suggest that the Regent wanted Leopold to rule his daughter, it is more likely that this is intended to contrast the anticipated reign of Charlotte with that of her dissolute father, who was both prone to drunkenness and submissive to his mistresses. His life is discussed more fully below.

36   Gloucester had been Mary's suitor for nearly twenty years, but her parents' opposition to marriage for any of their daughters delayed the wedding for decades. *Letters of George IV,* ed. Arthur Aspinall, 3 vols (Cambridge: Cambridge University Press, 1938), 2: p. 166. Princess Elizabeth suffered a similar fate; see note 39 below.

37   BMC 12783, published by T. Tegg, 21 June 1816, George Cruikshank, artist.

38   BMC 12789, published in the *Busy Body* 1 (1 July 1816), p. 196.

39   Farington reported that the Prince had first proposed in 1806 but George III had 'put the letter into the fire.' *Diary*, 15: p. 5169.

40   Christopher Hibbert, *George IV Regent and King* (New York: Harper and Row, 1973), pp. 118–119.

41   BMC 12986, published by S.W. Fores, April 1818, Williams, artist. 'Humbug' was the nickname given to the Prince in the press.

42   George, *Catalogue,* 9: p. 798. Some claimed that Elizabeth had committed incest with her brother, the Duke of Cumberland, and that any children she may have borne were the result of that liaison. See John Sartain, *The Reminiscences of a Very Old Man, 1808–1897* (1899; reprint, New York: B. Blom, 1969), p. 76. Others attributed the illegitimate child by Cumberland to another sister, Princess Sophia; see Glenbervie, *Diaries*, 1: pp. 363–364.

43   BMC 12991, published by J.L. Marks, *c*. April 1818.

44   BMC 12993, published by S.W. Fores, *c*. April 1818, Capt. Hehl (?), artist.

45   Clarence came in for a great deal of condemnation during the Regency, for while he had been supported by the popular actress Dorothy Jordan for many years and had ten children with her, he abruptly broke with her in 1811 to seek a legitimate marriage at the age of forty-six. The reasons for their separation were never publicly known, although the press castigated Clarence for having cast off Mrs Jordan, who died in seeming poverty in France in

1816. There is no doubt, however, that Clarence began courting the heiress Catherine Tylney-Long in the summer of 1811, even before he broke with Mrs. Jordan. Philip Ziegler, *King William IV* (Bungay, Suffolk: Fontana Books, 1973), pp. 104–5. However, he did make provisions for her, and it seems unlikely that she was as destitute as was alleged; Jonah Barrington, a close friend of the Duke and Mrs Jordan, claims that in addition to the sums settled on her at the separation, she made 'a clear profit of near £7,000' from her work on the stage the year before she left England. Jonah Barrington, *Recollections of Jonah Barrington* (Dublin: Phoenix Publishing Company, n.d.), pp. 363, 362.

46   His pursuit of a young bride occasioned much ridicule, for he behaved with 'all the anxiety of an enamoured Youth,' yet despite his ardor, he easily transferred his affection from one wealthy woman to another. Farington, *Diary*, 15: p. 5204.

47   Fulford, *Royal Dukes*, pp. 178–179, 191.

48   Fulford, *Royal Dukes*, p. 281.

49   It was argued in Parliament that these grants were necessary to secure the succession. George, *Catalogue*, 9: p. 798.

50   BMC 12987, published by S.W. Fores, April 1818.

51   BMC 12989, published by J.L. Marks, April 1818.

52   BMC 12994, published by John Fairburn, *c.* April 1818.

53   BMC 12996, published by G. Humphrey, 4 May 1818, George Cruikshank, artist.

54   BMC 10978, published by S.W. Fores, 3 April 1808, Isaac Cruikshank artist.

55   BMC 11252, published by S.W. Fores, 14 March 1809, I. Cruikshank, artist.

56   BMC 11227, published by T. Tegg, 26 February 1809, Thomas Rowlandson, artist.

57   *Parliamentary Debates*, 12:988.

58   BMC 11262, published by T. Tegg, 19 March 1809, Thomas Rowlandson, artist.

59   Dorothy George makes these two tentative identifications. *Catalogue*, 8: p. 768.

60   Quoted in George, *Catalogue*, 8: p. 755.

61   Francis Horner to J. A. Murray, 16 February 1809, *Memoirs and Correspondence of Francis Horner, M.P.*, ed. Leonard Horner, 2 vols. (Boston: Little Brown and Company, 1853), 1: p. 483.

62   Flora Fraser, *The Unruly Queen: The Life of Queen Caroline* (London: Macmillan, 1996), pp. 88–91.

63   BMC 8810, published by S.W. Fores, 31 May 1796.

64   BMC 12749, published by J. Sidebotham, March 1816.

65   As Dorothy George points out, the Duke of Richmond's appointment as Governor of British North America and his subsequent departure for Canada were coupled in the public mind with the fact that the Duchess remained in London and was residing only a short distance from Carlton House; the result was a rumor that the Duchess was having an affair with the Prince, who, it was alleged, had cleverly arranged for her husband's absence by sending him abroad. Less than three months after the appearance of these caricatures, the Duke suffered an agonizing death after being bitten by a rabid animal in Canada. George, *Catalogue*, 9: p. 900.

66   BMC 13231, published by E. Brooks, 12 May 1819.

67   BMC 13210, published by J.L. Marks, March 1819.

68   This notice was pasted on the back of the Library of Congress copy of the

print *Quite Well Again*, BMC 13691, published in March 1820.

69 BMC 13211, published by Sidebotham, March 1819, Robert Cruikshank, artist.

70 BMC 13215, published by T. Tegg, 9 April 1819, George Cruikshank artist.

71 A stupid fellow, according to [Frances Grosse], *1811 Dictionary of the Vulgar Tongue* (1811; reprinted, London: Bibliophile Books, 1984).

72 Ingram, 'Ridings,' 81; Tilly, *Popular Contention*, p. 215.

73 BMC 13220, published by M. Clinch, 20 April 1819, George Cruikshank artist.

74 This print was said to have been bought up and suppressed, but if this is so, the Regent failed in his purpose, for at least two imitations appeared. Layard, *Suppressed Plates*, p. 75.

75 This was related to a second issue: the growing belief that it was inappropriate for women to engage in politics. In 1809, *The Satirist, or Monthly Meteor* flatly stated, 'let women beware of *politics*, their eager discussion of which ... cannot possibly be productive of good, as they are effectually excluded from [it].' Another article in the same issue, 'Hints to Female Lecturers,' warns darkly that 'female Socrates' in public have undermined the 'traditional' education of women ('as to the old fashioned exercises of sewing, knitting, &c., they are totally unnecessary') and that 'As our English systems of education are become unfashionable, you must import one from our theoretic and philosophical neighbours [i.e. the French revolutionaries]...' *The Satirist, or Monthly Meteor* 4 (1 January 1809), pp. 20–21, 29–34.

76 BMC 11878, published by M. Jones, 1 May 1812, George Cruikshank artist.

77 BMC 11853, published by Walker and Knight, February 1812, Williams, artist.

78 BMC 11861, published by S.W. Fores, 30 March 1812, Williams, artist.

79 For a more complete examination of the caricatures surrounding the Queen Caroline agitation, see Tamara L. Hunt, 'Morality and Monarchy in the Queen Caroline Affair,' *Albion* 23 (Winter, 1991), pp. 697–722.

80 BMC 13850, published by J.L. Marks, *c.* September 1820, Marks, artist.

81 BMC 13897, published by S.W. Fores, 21 October 1820, Robert Cruikshank, artist. Such symbolism was not restricted to caricature. Thomas Wooler, editor of *The Black Dwarf*, suggested that the King establish an 'order of the golden horns' for the aristocratic husbands of the King's various mistresses. Thomas Laqueur, 'The Queen Caroline Affair: Politics as Art in the Reign of George IV,' *Journal of Modern History* 54 (September, 1982), p. 449.

82 Richard Rush, *Memoranda of a Residence at Court of London from 1819 to 1825* (Philadelphia: Lea & Blanchard, 1845), pp. 347–8. One government spy reported to the magistrates at Bow Street that several of the leading radical printers in London had employed men and boys to 'circulate in the metropolis, and for 50 miles round it, vast quantities of Bills, Placards and publications...' supporting the Queen. PRO HO 40/15, f. 65. The *Annual Register* of 1821 noted with disgust that 'Newspapers, placards, pamphlets, and caricatures of the most filthy and odious description were exposed to sale in every street, alley, and lane of the Metropolis, and circulated thence, though in less profusion, yet with great activity, to the most distant parts of the Kingdom.' p. 60.

83 Robert Peel to John Croker, 10 August 1820, *Croker Papers*, 1: pp. 176–7.

84 Quoted in E.A. Smith, *Whig Principles and Party Politics: Earl Fitzwilliam and the Whig Party, 1748–1833* (Manchester: Manchester University Press, 1977), p. 359.

85   HEH Pr. Box 212.8/115, published by John Fairburn, September 1820.
86   William B. Lighton, *Narrative of the Life and Sufferings of Rev. William B. Lighton*, rev. edn. (Boston: Samuel N. Dickinson, 1844), p. 59.
87   Laqueur, 'Caroline,' pp. 425–6. Undoubtedly, in some cases like these the targeted officials were already disliked for other reasons.
88   For other examples, see Laqueur, 'Caroline,' p. 454.
89   BMC 14122, published by G. Humphrey, February 1821.

CHAPTER 4

Political Aesthetics: British Army Fashion, 1815–55

Scott Hughes Myerly

Napoleon's private secretary, in describing efforts to win French political legitimacy in Egypt, noted that 'the art of imposing on mankind has at all times been an important part of the art of governing.'[1] Elaborate, ceremonial displays have long featured in the history of states, since 'the splendors of kings and princes [have] been universally proclaimed by pomp and circumstance.'[2] An essential element in royal shows is the ornamental display of force; as Bertrand Russell observed, 'the spectacular aspects of the army and navy,' are a form of 'propaganda ... employed ... for many centuries.'[3] In Great Britain the army was legally the monarch's possession (contingent on parliamentary funding), and literally still is in a narrow sense.

The early nineteenth-century British army embodied splendid images of disciplined, latent violence, with a resplendent display of brilliant trappings and precision drill, embellished by a preference for tall, handsome soldiers. Military parades, reviews, inspections and similar displays were considerably enhanced by martial music, and under the right circumstances they could exert an extraordinarily powerful, compelling charisma.

The costuming was a major factor in this show's visual appeal; an officer noted that 'the dazzling colour of the uniform, the variety of the facings [collars and cuffs], the contrasts of the different parts of the dress, the profusion of ornaments, namely, feathers, frisures ... and polished accoutrements, were singularly contrived to strike the admiring multitude,'[4] and this *gratis* show played wherever the army appeared throughout the realm and empire.

This era witnessed, however, a number of serious, internal political conflicts between elites and the populace. As the state's primary means of coercion, the army was probably the most controversial of all British institutions; it was traditionally feared and hated for constitutional tyranny and internal repression. Soldiers' behavior was notorious, and frequent, expensive wars claimed many lives. But Britons also strongly identified with this army which had defended the nation for more than 150 years, but especially after 1792 when so many served.[5]

Public attitudes were thus sharply ambivalent, and the context in which soldiers were displayed was crucial for audience reactions. Like other royal spectacles in which it was normally featured, the martial show was a significant point of interaction between the state and the people, and its collective reception was important as 'a sounding-board for public opinion.'[6] As a foreign spectator noted in 1810 London, "'It is not," as [William] Paley rightly observes, "by what the Lord Mayor feels in his coach, but by what the apprentice feels who gazes at him.'"[7]

Impressing civilians with an attractive uniform also dovetailed with regimental management; the more public admiration that a unit could win, the better for recruiting this volunteer force. Morale was thus aided by upholding the essential feeling of military honor – and the soldiers' presumption of believing themselves to be superior to civilians. Ridicule or other negative public reactions to the show tended to harm discipline. A pleasing appearance was so important for the dress in this era, that style normally superseded the significance of the clothing's physical utility for campaigning, combat and even health.[8]

But when it was appealing, the show's allure might even evoke the aesthetic appreciation of the state's enemies, who could respond with enthusiastic admiration. Chartist Thomas Cooper thought the 'varied costume of the English regiments mingled with the kilted Highlanders, and Lancers and Life Guards with the Scotch Greys, rendered the vision (Wellington's funeral) picturesque as well as stately.'[9] Even militants admired it; the Cato Street conspirator, William 'Black' Davidson, an ultra-radical and son of a Jamaican slave woman, had as much reason to loathe government coercion as anyone, but in preparing to do battle with the Lifeguards, he declared: 'I have not had the honour to wear a Red jacket.'[10]

As a charismatic entertainment, the spectacle's function was thus to mask its negative associations – or to offset them to the greatest possible extent – by fostering beliefs and imposing values on the public that served its rulers. Fundamentally the show promoted the notion that it was in the subjects' best interests to identify with and support the army and its masters, whose power was depicted as legitimate and omnipotent (and this advertising phenomenon long predates the modern proliferation of that purest form of propaganda). Thus, there were significant incentives to maximize the army's allure as both symbol and entertainment, because as Leigh Hunt observed, 'A bullet is of all pills the one that most requires gilding.'[11]

Design was thus primarily about fashion and having the right look, and the aesthetic goal was visually to embody in the most appropriate way, the sublime martial ideals of glory, honor, bravery, self-sacrifice, brotherhood, solidarity and defending the realm.

Inappropriate – and thus unpopular – designs were quickly noticed and condemned, oftentimes most strongly by soldiers themselves. An officer noted in 1814 that the generals' 'distinguishing mark [of] an edging or fringe of white feathers on the cocked hat ... was universally deemed to have originated in bad taste' because it 'was hallowed by no elevated *prestige*,' and consequently 'was a ... short lived regulation.'[12] But when designs succeeded, soldiers might be compared to gods.[13]

But for the styles of this era to be 'hallowed' by 'elevated prestige,' they had to embody 'Truth' visually. Artist Benjamin Haydon believed that 'beauty of form is but the vehicle of conveying ideas, but truth of conveyance is the chief object ... beauty is but a means.'[14] These Romantic era-values were deemed so inseparable, that beauty was considered to be intrinsically truthful. John Keats was 'certain of nothing but of the holiness of the Heart's affections and the truth of Imagination – What the imagination seizes as Beauty must be truth,'[15] and elegance – so imperative in uniforms – was only attained when these were united. As Oliver Goldsmith wrote, 'Nothing is truly elegant, but what unites truth with beauty,'[16] and as William Hogarth observed, 'we do not laugh at what is elegant, and do laugh at what is not.'[17] But as a Londoner in the theater trade repeated the old adage, 'there is only one step from the sublime to the ridiculous,'[18] a careful eye was needed to prevent the gaudy designs from backfiring, especially in an age when symbolic dress was taken so seriously.

Aesthetic qualities were thus critically scrutinized, and outlandish, old-fashioned or inappropriate uniforms provoked criticism; the 29th Foot in 1807, for example, 'had too much of the antique about them.'[19] Condemnations could also be startlingly harsh; Harriette Wilson thought a friend's bright yellow regimental facings 'the ugliest, most vulgar-looking things which could well be imagined,' with a 'frightful' shako.[20] It was therefore especially important that the style looked right when paraded before the traditionally fickle British public, and changes were frequent; one critic noted that 'nothing is so short lived as a good uniform.'[21] As an evolutionary process, design involved an immense variety of elements in clothing all ranks for well over a hundred units – each visually unique in some way – and much care was devoted to the army's dress.

The traditional view is that this exalted royal genre reflected the personal taste of a German dynasty's monarchs (George IV had a mania for it) and the army's leaders: 'A good uniform varies with the taste of a commander-in-chief, or [his] toady; or the fancy of some royal favorite.'[22] But the ultimate criterion for what becomes fashionable does not depend on the designer. A contemporary journalist observed the fashion truism that 'the laws of ... taste, rest on no settled authority, and depend entirely on the feeling of the world, which is necessarily a very capricious, fluctuating kind of tribunal.'[23]

Thus, in exercising this traditional command prerogative, there were significant, practical reasons for monarchs and army leaders to uphold a fashionable look. However, dignity required avoiding any appearance of pandering to mere civilian taste. When Lord Cardigan court-martialled an officer in 1833, one charge included addressing his troop in an 'irregular and unofficer-like manner' in stating after an inspection that some 'strangers or civilians' had remarked on their soldier-like appearance, which was 'highly improper.'[24] It was therefore in the best interests of those who controlled the styles to express in them, as nineteenth-century artist John LaFarge observed, 'the needs of others who have been looking in the same ways, and yet have had no voice.'[25] Such 'needs' can be traced in the changing designs over time, which reveal the evolution of public aesthetic taste in martial styles, and a distinct pattern appears during this era of transition between the *ancien régime* and the modern world.

Yet, fashion history has all too often been viewed by scholars as 'an area impervious to reason and analysis,' as Aileen Ribeiro has pointed out.[26] Roland Barthes echoed others' views by asserting that 'history does not produce forms ... Fashion remains outside history.'[27] But many scholars have shown that politics are intrinsic to broad fashion trends; Daniel Roche states that the logic of latter seventeenth-century French fashion 'is that of politics,'[28] Ribeiro argues that 'In a period of volatile political upheaval ... clothing was in many ways the visualization of political concepts and social change,'[29] and notes that 'with the French Revolution ... we begin the modern world,' and that its 'intrusive politics [and] greater awareness of class differences, and a restless need for change and for self-expression,' were all 'reflected in dress, that most sensitive of social barometers.'[30]

Richard Bienvenu's preface to Philippe Perrot's *Fashioning the Bourgeoisie; A History of Clothing in the Nineteenth Century*, noted that this book 'exploded ... the myth that it is futile for historians to study inconsequential things [specifically clothing], or things that *seem* inconsequential and trivial.'[31] This builds on Fernand Braudel's work in material culture, where he noted that 'little facts' which by 'indefinite repetitions' cannot be understood in isolated contexts, but rather 'add up to form linked chains ... [which with] history in the "long term" provides the horizons and the vanishing-points of all the landscapes of the past. They introduce a kind of order, indicate a balance, and reveal to our eyes the permanent features, the things that in this apparent disorder *can* be explained.'[32]

But in what ways can this be articulated for the history of fashion? This subject has a strikingly labyrinthine complexity; Ribeiro noted that *Fashion in the French Revolution* was not intended to be 'anything more than a preliminary study of what is a most complex subject,'[33] and not every scholar has approached this subject with such prudence. Roche noted that 'it is by no means easy to interpret these superficial changes' of fashion.[34]

The political significance of fashion was enhanced in the conflicts that accompanied the first phase in the transformation of the state from *ancien régime* Europe to the modern era. Philip Mansel notes for this period that 'the function of [European] clothes was particularly important,' since politically charged dress acted as a 'cutting edge' of revolutionary conflict by accenting symbolic, visual differences which evoked 'status conflict where there was no ideological conflict whatsoever.'[35] Henry Cockburn noted that in 1790s Britain, civilian dress became a 'curious' test of loyalty; conservatives labeled trousers and gaiters as 'Jacobinical,' and 'in nothing was the monarchical principle more openly displayed or insulted than in the adherence to, or contempt of, hair powder.'[36] As the visual representation of state power, the intrinsically political symbolisms of military dress thus tended powerfully to reinforce the incentive for the designers to create styles which appealed to public taste.

But in the later 1820s and early 1830s, the tone of British society underwent a significant transformation, signified by a series of dramatic political reforms. This was accompanied by a sea change in the evolution of militaria design, away from the elaborate regency style, towards a more subdued approach. But the immediate cause of this transformation was not just the fact that the styles symbolized and were emblematic of unpopular, *ancien régime* political values; such styles had been criticized for years. Rather, this connection was more complex: the shift in taste occurred because ultimately, the public sense of what looked appropriate was changing in a fundamental way. This strongly suggests that the public aesthetic sense for the abstract patterns of design was itself politically charged – and that the abstractions of taste in martial fashion were thus intrinsically political. Furthermore, the monarchs were pivotal in the change, managing this break with their own stylistic tradition to the best advantage of the crown and state.

The Evolutionary Transformation of Martial Styles: 1815–55

Army fashions after 1789 underwent much development and change, made more complex because style and combat conditions often pulled the modes in different directions. [See Plate 14].[37] But the post-Waterloo occupation of France was a significant factor in the genesis of a new British style. The allies, especially fancy units re-equipped with the latest modes, made a brilliant display in Paris, while British veterans in their campaign uniforms, were 'strange figures ... in dirty red coats, and ugly shaped caps ... our army made the worst appearance of all those assembled in and around the capital.'[38] This was humiliating; an English hussar sergeant was even invited into a Parisian haberdasher's, solely for the proprietor 'to hold up to ridicule the shape of a cocked hat worn by the staff-officers of the British army ...

Plate 14: "Types of the British Army 1812-1815"

left for him to renovate! ... I must admit that the upper gear of the British officer looked mean and contemptible in comparison [with continental martial headdresses].'[39]

British styles soon followed this trend of elevated levels of splendor; W. Y. Carman wrote that the brilliance and magnificence of martial finery blossomed as never before in this era, 'to beautify the soldiers' dress' with 'an elaborate appearance.' A few examples include making the post-1815 Regency infantry coat 'more splendid,' hussar dress became 'more elaborate and expensive' with a 'glorious appearance,' and four light dragoon units were converted into exotic, Polish-style lancers.[40]

A major feature in this fancier phase in design was the increase in headgear ornament, including the adoption of flashy brass chinscales for shakos in 1816 (replacing plain straps), but especially in their acquiring larger dimensions and bigger plumes. Descriptions of the more extravagant examples are sometimes hard to believe, but if these accounts were exaggerated, this merely illuminates the visual power of the designs; such enormous shakos were nick-named 'sky scrapers.'[41]

The increased headgear ornamentation and larger proportions were especially emblematic of this, the era of the European Reaction. Of all dress elements, headgear was the most associated with the potential for the wearer to be perceived as awe-inspiring, but also as dominating and threatening; a military manual author thought that these huge hats were designed so as to convey 'a fiercer and more martial appearance,' and likewise, flashy military uniforms also enhanced the potential for menace.[42]

Styles which increased the imposing and threatening qualities of martial dress factored into domestic political conflict, and the new tone in martial designs is merely one aspect of a broader shift in royal/civic public display. Roger Sales noted,

> All evidence suggests that the establishment very self-consciously waged a ritualistic offensive at both the local and national levels during this period. Social attitudes which might have been implicit in [political and religious] rituals before the 1790s became much more explicit. The counter-revolution was first and foremost a psychological war ... being fought for control, discipline and containment. No psychological quarter was given.[43]

Royal spectacle thus became more controversial in the Regency era; a thinly disguised satire (allegedly on the king of Hawaii) describes the Prince Regent using dazzling ornament and show as stratagems to delude: 'In peace he was immensely gay,/ And indefatigably busy;/ Preparing gewgaws every day,/ And shows to make his subjects dizzy.'[44] In 1816, radical MP Henry Brougham was more harsh, denouncing the show of London's royal Household troops as 'vicious ... childish and contemptible [and] dangerous to the Constitution.'[45]

Such criticisms carried some weight, especially since British martial spectacle was uncomfortably close to that of old enemies. William Hazlitt noted that 'The French, under the old regime, made the glory of their *Grand Monarque* a set-off against rags and hunger, equally satisfied with *shows* or *bread*; and the poor Spaniard ... looks up once more with pious awe, to permanent oppression ... the Holy Inquisition.'[46] In 1814 Restoration Paris, Benjamin Haydon thought that 'everywhere a sense of despotism pressed on your mind. There was in everything a look of gilded slavery and bloody splendor ... a polished fierceness in the soldiers.'[47]

Yet British military shows continued to draw large crowds of spectators; radical William Lovett later asked: 'By what powerful spell [do the masses] glory in the means which keep them slaves?'[48] Hazlett thought he had the answer. For him, the spectator was the oppressed, a degraded inferior fascinated and beguiled by show.

> The slave, who has no other hope of consolation, clings to the apparition of royal magnificence, which insults his misery and his despair; stares through the hollow eyes of famine at the insolence and pride of luxury which has occasioned it, and hugs his chains the closer, because he has nothing else left ... . As the herd of mankind are stripped of every thing, in body and mind, so are they thankful for what is left; as is the desolation of their hearts and the wreck of their little all, so is the pomp and pride which is built upon their ruin, and their fawning admiration of it.[49]

While opposition satires and caricatures pounded away at British military splendor throughout the Regency and beyond, the late *ancien régime* martial style remained fashionable – because it continued to look aesthetically appropriate to Britons – thus outweighing its negative associations.

But the increased political controversies of the Regency tended to sharpen and intensify the emotionally charged reactions of the audience, which could be either that of thrilling, heady enthusiasm, or harsh condemnation, depending on the context in which the military was displayed. While Waterloo was celebrated for decades on the stage and in literature, Britons could not forget that soldiers were also used to enforce harsh repression. The Spa Fields riots, Britain's first peacetime suspension of Habeas Corpus, the Peterloo massacre and the Six Acts, were forcible reminders of the government's willingness to utilize sweeping repressive powers.

The political context of spectacle was thus becoming more volatile; in 1820 the sensational Queen Caroline affair provided reformers and radicals with the strongest focus for political opposition in a generation.[50] The King fought back to regain public acclaim with the most expensive coronation in British history, which included many soldiers, and for this occasion the

entire Household Cavalry were furnished with new cuirasses.[51] Successful
royal visits to Ireland, Hanover and Scotland followed, all of which helped
to buck up his popularity.

The depth of emotion which Britain's most flamboyant monarch could
excite as royal showman is reflected in diplomat Philipp von Neumann's
reaction to the coronation: 'I went with the idea of seeing a theatrical show,
and I came away filled with a religious feeling.'[52] *The Times* noted that
young people who had gone expecting to see just a show were surprised,
and 'affected in a manner they never dreamt of.'[53] Whig Benjamin Haydon
was moved in a clearly political way: 'my imagination got so intoxicated
that I came out [of the abbey] with a great contempt for the pleb[eian]s,'
and even Christianity ['sacred subjects'] seemed 'insipid' in comparison.[54]
Yet at deeper levels opposition was growing, and the public's taste in
ostentatious royal shows was approaching a metamorphosis.

Previous condemnations of regency royal spectacle emphasized political
symbolism, but in these years, it appears that more objections were being
expressed on the purely abstract grounds of aesthetics, especially in the
degree of ornament. Thomas Hood and his wife declined taking a young
girl to the Lord Mayor's show (which included many soldiers) 'for fear that
it should give her a taste for gaudy and vulgar fripperies.'[55] In this era of so
much anxiety about the 'spread of luxury,' William Hazlitt linked old regime-
style splendor with immorality, asserting that the Lord Mayor's elaborate
gilt coach 'in all the glory of gold and scarlet, [was] like the naughty lady
of Babylon.'[56] The poor were also becoming less patient with their lot, and
it appears that their reaction to the show was shifting from admiration and
awe to contrasting it unfavorably with their own misery; a half-penny
broadside asked: 'Why look with insolent disdain/ On those not decked
with pomp and state?'[57]

Such attacks on ornament and splendor provoked Tory responses:
journalist William Jerdan's 1817 poem 'The Highlandman's Pistol: A Fable
for the Present Time' includes a passage entitled 'Moral,' denouncing 'insane
Reform, Vision'd Perfection, and wild Change,' urging 'Believe not every
spot a stain,/ Nor every ancient form misspent,/ Nor useless each rich
ornament./ *Experience* proves, at endless length,/ *These* may be glory,
wisdom, strength.'[58]

For a few years more, martial fashion continued its ascent in imposing
ostentation. Michael Barthorp notes that in the 1820–1828 era, cavalry
uniforms 'reached heights of costliness ... never seen before or since.'[59]
An American visiting Manchester disapproved of seeing 'young [soldiers]
wearing the uniform of a footman ... their epaulets looking like two brass
stewing pans and a bonnet that might save the purchasing of an umbrella
[and] spurs full four inches in length,' all of which 'shocks the eye of the
unaccustomed stranger.'[60] (See Plate 15).[61]

Plate 15: '17th 50th and 84th Regiments'

By the late twenties, such towering military headgear looked increasingly inappropriate; Lieutenant.-General Sir Herbert Taylor complained: 'I consider [cavalry] helmets abominable from their weight and inconvenience, and also from their appearance, as they are out of proportion to the general size of the man.' This had 'the effect of taking from [one's] height and breadth instead of adding to them.'[62] The designs had thus backfired in part because their essential aesthetic function to impress and overawe came to be impeded by the very size. E.H. Gombrich defines 'image inflation' as

> competition for attention [that] can lead to the unintended consequence of simply lowering the value of what you have done before. This is particularly so where methods of emphasis are concerned, and emphasis is after all a special case of soliciting attention. Decoration is a frequent victim of such inflation ... a fatigue is aroused by forms that are seen so often that they are no longer noticed so that a stronger stimulus is required...[as] signals trying to outshout each other and blunting their own effect in the process.[63]

This phenomenon is part of what Geoffrey Squire characterized for the post-1815 era, as 'the Neo-classical spirit ... yielding to a more complete Romanticism, [and it] began to be undermined by overstatement.'[64]

The point of absurdity had thus been reached – and this image, both symbolically and literally – toppled over. In 1829, the Duke of Wellington was blown off his horse when the wind caught his huge 'giant' bearskin cap, topped by an enormous swan's feather. This happened at a grand review in London, in front of tens of thousands of spectators, and provided an extra flourish for caricaturists at a time of intensifying demands for political reform.[65] (See Plate 16).[66] Perhaps nothing else exemplifies so clearly the limits of image inflation in the era's enormous military headgear. From visualizing the exalted heights of the symbolic sublime, it fell into the abyss of the ridiculous. But changes in customs had already been undermining the army officer's splendor.

At the end of the French wars, military uniform was favored by the public, and 'infantry officers, when upon home service, made their extravagant appearance [in uniform] on all public occasions.'[67] Likewise, 'plain clothes were never heard of, nor did anyone dream of complaining of his uniform, which we wore constantly.'[68] But as the flashy, imposing qualities of full dress increased after 1815, the modes' becoming more controversial appears to have caused a decline in their use by officers. John Fortescue wrote that they were finally driven out of uniform altogether when off duty, because of its political connotations to the public: 'a general officer could not ride down Piccadilly in plain clothes followed by an orderly in uniform, but Parliament must cry out that a debauched soldiery was dragooning freeborn

Plate 16: 'Oh What a Falling Off There Was'

Englishmen ... the King's uniform [was] thus interpreted as a menace to liberty.'[69]

Many officers also avoided full-dress coats in favor of the plain, dark blue frock coat. This unofficial adoption reflected a growing tendency, especially amongst older officers, to avoid the heavy, tight and inconvenient full dress – even on duty. A spectator at an 1827 review noted that it was 'extraordinary ... to see the perfect ease with which fifty or sixty officers in plain clothes [took part in the review] – several General officers among them, some in undress jackets and top-boots, some in frock-coats and coloured cravats ... the Inspecting General, who with his two aides-de-camp were the only men in uniform, except the regiment.'[70]

One apparent deterrent was that on riot duty, officers with more ornate uniforms might become targets. A contemporary revolutionary handbook on street-fighting advised that 'smooth-faced youth, whose chest and shoulders are buried under those huge and gorgeous epaulettes, is not field marshal ... nor a captain, but only a lieutenant, or a cornet!! Spare him, good sirs! – but commend me to your straight-coated-cocked-hatted gentleman, with nothing but a sort of footman's shoulder-knot to decorate him, – *he* is a general, or a field-officer, – let him be attended to!!'[71]

By the latter 1820s, the King's designs decreased the extent of bullion lace and trappings, and in the size of some headgear. A few examples include the infantry shako being divested of its broad lace band in 1828, the Royal Horse Guards losing their sabretaches and officers' silk sashes in 1829,[72] and the replacement of the Regency shako by the shorter Bell-shako in 1829.[73] A complete description of all such alterations would be a study in itself, and there are important exceptions to this tendency, but even a casual examination of the era's graphics shows a broad, unmistakable trend. The most dramatic example was the king's abolition in 1829 of an especially opulent, elegant motif that W.Y. Carman has praised as 'a work of art,' the richly laced, officers' plastron coat front, worn by the fanciest laced regiments.[74] One factor was the high cost; an order prohibited 'Unauthorized deviations or expensive additions of embroidery or lace...[in order] to protect officers, and particularly infantry officers, from the weight of unnecessary expense.'[75] Apparently even wealthy officers found them to be too expensive, especially since a rain shower might ruin a uniform.

Yet this retreat was directly opposite to the King's lifelong taste in a genre so important to his dignity and on which he lavished so much attention. His love of overwhelming opulence, luxury and sumptuous, rich splendor was apparently insatiable; he liked to bestow 'artistic effect wherever he thought it possible,'[76] with an unmistakable style. A guest at a royal levee in 1811 noted 'the very expensive manner in which the apartments are fitted up, not a spot with[ou]t some finery upon it, gold upon gold ... so over done with finery.'[77] This style in part evokes Orientalism, which appealed to the era's European elites, and in a political context, symbolized absolute power. A lady-in-waiting noted that a line from a poem: "'I am monarch of all I survey,/ My right there is none to dispute" suited the king's taste precisely,' and he was frequently mocked as 'the Great Mogul' or 'the Sultan.'[78]

The antithesis of such style in men's civilian dress was the subdued, restrained, somber and sober aesthetic values which exemplified republican taste; John Harvey notes of nineteenth century male dress, the 'powerful direct influence' of 'bourgeois severities.'[79] This style was despised by George IV, who 'hates black,'[80] a color which visually symbolized those liberal and revolutionary political principles that he feared and loathed. In the context of that era, any diminishment of the bullion lace, huge hats and other trappings necessarily implied a concession to middle-class dress aesthetics.

It is difficult to believe that the king was not fully aware that his new militaria designs represented a significant change in direction, and he did this in old age, when most people have become set in their ways and dislike change. This was especially true of this uncontrollably self-indulgent monarch, who cherished art, could get almost whatever he wanted throughout his life – except more political power (and a divorce) – and had always been incapable of curbing his desires. Yet at the very end of his life, George IV adopted styles which reduced the ostentation of his favorite toy, the army.

In this period of aggressive political reform, fortified by ongoing fears of revolution, did the most ridiculed monarch in English history come to believe that it was his duty to the monarchy and state to exercise artistic discretion, even when it was contrary to his lifelong tendencies? Did the King come to accept the necessity of making a fundamental shift towards less opulent styles, because he recognized that they had reached their limit, and that further attempts to enhance ostentatious extremes were inappropriate, and counter-productive?

There is some evidence that he did; in his last year of life, the King appears to have concentrated his declining powers on these designs; in December 1829 he was 'employed in altering the uniforms of the Guards, and has pattern coats with various collars submitted to him every day ... and this is his principal occupation; he sees much more of his Tailor than he does of his Minister.'[81] These actions might well have been George IV's most significant last service to the monarchy.[82]

This fundamental shift in the direction of design was made when the old style no longer looked right, and it is significant that the final catalyst for this change was essentially a question of taste, because 'where decoration is seen as a form of celebration it can only become objectionable when it is inappropriate.' Thus, 'the pretensions of decoration [had become] unfounded,' when 'pomp becomes pomposity, decoration mere gaudiness.'[83]

The old style thus met a dead-end, and underwent a design sea-change that was the first major shift away from imposing splendor since the standing army was created in the mid-seventeenth century.

This trend was continued by William IV: after months of experiment, he enacted further, major reforms in militaria design in the summer of 1830, as the first significant public acts of the new reign. He abolished the officer's gorget, symbolically important as a last vestige of feudal armor, reduced the width and amount of lace, abolished officers' moustaches in most types of units, banned infantry officers' bullion lace cap lines and tassels, and enacted other reforms.[84] Mrs. Arbuthnot noted this flurry of activity: 'the King ... seems a little wild (like the rest of his family) upon *dress*.'[85] His 'Sailor King' image also went over well, and the caricaturists pounced fiercely, depicting rough-and-ready 'Sailor King Billy' ordering that the widely-hated, obnoxious, dandy hussar officers' moustaches be forcibly shaved by the Jack-tars of England's favorite service, who are also ordered to 'dowse the glitter of those landsmen's jackets.'[86]

At this time of ongoing political confrontation over the Great Reform bill, these actions encouraged the safe venting of reformist anger, and helped to foster public approval for the new king. John Rickman observed, that William IV 'may perchance keep the mob in huzzaing [sic] humour, which will be clear gain.'[87] For the bluff, simple soul that the King was, this acclaim amidst growing, persistent and alarming demands for the Reform bill must have been most encouraging. But not everyone welcomed the alterations; those younger officers who loved their fancy uniforms fiercely opposed these changes. Cornet Jack Spalding, 'the greatest dandy of the day,' left his regiment 'rather than accept the rape of all that he held most precious.'[88]

Yet other factors in this design shift tended to render the army more politically safe for the state, by increasing the initial cost for officers – which they paid for themselves – especially in the less opulent 'working regiments' of the heavy infantry (in fancy units it was presumed that officers were wealthy). Since all regular units now wore gold lace, officers in unlaced regiments now had to buy it, and those in silver-laced units had to replace both their lace and epaulets with gold. Ensigns and lieutenants serving in gold-laced units also had to acquire an additional epaulet (before, only captains and higher ranks wore two).

There were still Napoleonic veterans in the lower commissioned ranks who had never been able to purchase promotion, and lived on their pitifully meager army pay – and some had families. The increased financial pressure was a heavy burden on those without the outside income enjoyed by rich officers, and the lace was especially costly, since 'almost every Regiment of the Cavalry and the Infantry had its own particular epaulette [pattern]. The expense ... must have been considerable.'[89] These reforms thus tended to weed out poorer officers, and made the army more politically secure for the state at a time of increasing political tension.

Yet, while the fashions underwent a decisive shift in direction, they did not undergo a major transformation in appearance. The two monarchs' reforms primarily curbed the worst excesses of an overblown, decadent style, but essentially upheld high levels of dress opulence. For example, hussar dress remained 'expensive,' and each unit maintained its unique dress, but in 1831 the King established a single pattern for all hussar regiments. Yet 'upon representations to the King by the [hussar] colonels, His Majesty directed that the patterns of jacket and pelisse and laces, etc., should be continued as before.' He also instituted an additional change which further enhanced the showiness of hussar dress, by ordering that their dark blue pelisses be altered to scarlet.[90] Sir John Fortescue has noted that George IV's post-Waterloo modes 'continued, with slight modifications, until the Crimean War.'[91] This fundamental shift in the evolution of the styles was therefore not as decisive and dramatic as it appeared at the time.

But the styles continued gradually to decline in splendor over the next decades. A few examples include the abolition of sabretaches for lancer privates in 1834, the replacement of infantry shako plumes with ball tufts in 1835, the white lace on privates' coats, decorated with regimental patterns of different colored 'worms' (stripes), was made plain white for all units in 1836, and subsequent changes followed this trend. Headgear patterns also tended (with exceptions) to become less elaborate and imposing than before, and cavalry dress was somewhat simplified.[92] (See Plate 17).[93]

This trend towards a piecemeal reduction in ornamentation was thus gradual and occurred at a measured and stately pace, and it is important to note that this shift did not result from any concern amongst army leaders that soldiers had to be made less eye-catching as targets because of advances in weapons, since this technology had not changed much since 1815.[94]

It was therefore a dignified design retreat, and it was some twenty-five years before the old style's tone was transmuted into a notably different look by the uniform reform of 1855. This alteration had been under consideration from before the Crimean War began, and it is most significant that once again, it was due to the initiative of the monarch, Queen Victoria, who took a great personal interest in the army[95] (much assisted by Prince Albert) – and not the disasters suffered in besieging Russian Sebastopol – that brought it about.[96]

This decline in the army's sartorial ornamentation was noticed by contemporaries. An 1844 anti-military essay by radical journalist Douglas Jerrold targets the Grenadier Guards, telling a grenadier that 'the fingers of opinion have been busy at your plume – you are not the feathered thing you were.' In contrast to the earlier Romantic era notion that beauty is inherently truthful, Jerrold now rather pompously proclaims that 'glory cannot dazzle truth.'[97] This highlights the triumph of a middle-class aesthetic sensibility

Plate 17: "Types of the British Army in 1854"

in what was probably the most spectacular of all British clothing genres. The earlier Regency fashion for imposing, exotic opulence was clearly in retreat because its reactionary symbolism had become aesthetically inappropriate for a majority of spectators.

Yet a decisive factor in this change in taste was that Britons still liked an impressive military show, and did not want it to be subdued too much. Radical Leigh Hunt had criticized the old regime throughout the Regency and beyond, and was even imprisoned in 1812 for libeling the Regent. But in 1835, after the Reform bill heralded middle-class triumph, the changes from the previous generation made it easier to feel nostalgic for the old splendor. These represented an idealized symbol of traditional noble values, which contrasted so favorably with the widespread image of the heartless, grasping money-grubbers of the soulless industrial age. Hunt wrote: 'England [has] gone through the feudal reign [and] must now go through the commercial [but] I confess I like the colours and shows of feudalism, and would retain as much of them as would adorn nobler things [such] external beauty ... softens the heart, enriches the imagination, and helps to show us that there are other goods in the world besides bare utility.' In our day, Hunt's further musings seem especially prophetic:

> I would fain see the splendors of royalty combined with the cheapness of a republic and the equal knowledge of all classes. Is such a combination impossible? I would exhort the lovers of feudal splendor to be the last men to think so; for a thousand times more impossible will they find its retention under any other circumstances. Their royalties, their educations, their accomplishments of all sorts, must go along with the Press and its irresistible consequences, or they will be set aside like a child in a corner, who has insisted on keeping the toys and books of his brothers to himself.[98]

Thus, like English political evolution, the transition in militaria design was measured and gradual, and more apparent than consequential, yet it was a decisive stylistic shift, and reveals the intrinsically political dimension of aesthetic sensibility in martial fashions. As Edward Lytton Bulwer observed in 1833, 'in agitated times, the people rise into importance, and their sentiments become the loudest and most obtrusive; the aggregate of *their* sentiments ... is Opinion ... even in costume.'[99]

NOTES

1   'The French View of the Events in Egypt: Memoirs by Louis Antoine Fauvelet de Bourrienne, Private Secretary to General Bonaparte,' in *Napoleon in Egypt: Al-Jabarti's Chronicle of the French Occupation, 1798*, trans. Shmuel Moreh (Princeton: Markus Wiener Pub., 1993), p. 156. I wish to thank Donald Jeffery

Kissinger and Tamara Hunt for their advice in writing this essay.

2   E.H. Gombrich, *The Sense of Order: A Study in the Psychology of Decorative Art*, 2nd ed. (London: Phaidon Press, 1984), p. 17.

3   Bertrand Russell, 'Power over Opinion,' in *Power: A New Social Analysis* (1938; reprint, New York: Unwin Books, 1963), p. 96.

4   Insp.-Gen. Sir Robert Jackson, *A View of the Formation Discipline and Economy of Armies*, 3d edn (1804; reprint, London, 1845), p. 185. For more on this appeal, see Scott Hughes Myerly, *British Military Spectacle From the Napoleonic Wars through the Crimea* (Cambridge, MA: Harvard University Press, 1996), ch. 8.

5   For more on this, see Myerly, *British Military Spectacle*, pp. 115, 133–8, ch. 8 and the Conclusion.

6   Arthur Bryant, *The Age of Elegance, 1812–1822* (1950; reprint, London: Collins, 1975), p. 123.

7   Louis Simond, *An American in Regency England: The Journal of a Tour in 1810–1811*, ed. Christopher Hibbert (London: History Book Club, 1968), p. 52.

8   See Myerly, *British Military Spectacle*, chs 1, 3, 4 and 5.

9   Thomas Cooper, *The Life of Thomas Cooper* (New York: Humanities Press, 1971), p. 333.

10 'I may not live till to Marrow night it is therefore proper to be serious When a man is so near his last.' 7 December 1819, HO 42/199, p. 545. Quoted in David Worrall, *Radical Culture: Discourse, Resistance, and Surveillance, 1790–1820* (Detroit: Wayne State University Press, 1992), p. 191. Also see: Myerly, *British Military Spectacle*, ch. 8.

11 Leigh Hunt, 'Postscript; Containing some Remarks on War and Military Statesmen,' in *Captain Sword and Captain Pen: A Poem* (London, 1835), p. 111. For more on the show's propaganda function, see *British Military Spectacle*, pp. 139–42.

12 George Laval Chesterton, *Peace, War, and Adventure: An Autobiographical Memoir of George Laval Chesterton*, 2 vols (London, 1853), 1: p. 144.

13 Thomas Hardy utilized this; his trumpet-major 'blazed in the [sun's] rays like a very god of war.' *The Trumpet-Major* (1880; reprint, Harmondsworth, Middlesex: Penguin Books, 1986), p. 94.

14 1 January 1813, Benjamin Robert Haydon, *The Autobiography and Memoirs of Benjamin Robert Haydon (1786–1846)*, ed. Tom Taylor, 2 vols (London: Peter Davies, 1926), 1: p. 151.

15 John Keats to Benjamin Bailey, 22 November 1817, *Letters of John Keats* (London: Oxford University Press, 1954), p. 48.

16 Oliver Goldsmith, 'Letter XIV,' in *The Citizen of the world; or, Letters from a Chinese Philosopher, residing in London, to his friends in the East*, 2 vols. (Taylor & Hessey, 1809), 1: p. 50.

17 Quoted in John Steegman, *The Rule of Taste: From George I to George IV* (1936; reprint, London: Century, 1986), p. 10.

18 George Augustus Sala, *The Life and Adventures of George Augustus Sala*, 2 vols. (New York: Charles Scribner's Sons, 1895), 1: p. 32.

19 John Patterson, *The Adventures of Captain John Patterson* (n.p., 1837), p. 6.

20 Harriette Wilson, *Memoirs* (1825; reprint, New York: Minton, Blatch and Co., 1929), pp. 511–12.

21 'Aesthetics of Dress. Military Costume,' *Blackwood's Magazine*, LIX (1846), p. 115.

22 Ibid.
23 'Judicial Decision on the Seat of Honor; or, Park on kicks,' *Spirit of the Public Journals, for the Year MDCCCXXIV: Begin the Most Impartial Selection of the Most Exquisite Essays, Jeux d' Esprit, and Tales of Humour, Prose and Verse* (London, 1825), p. 406.
24 *Proceedings of the General Court Martial upon the Trial of Captain Wathen, Fifteenth King's Hussars* (London, 1834; reprint, London: Frederick Muller, 1970), pp. 3–4.
25 John LaFarge, *An Artist's Letters from Japan* (1897; reprint, London: Waterstone & Co., 1986), p. 103.
26 Eileen Ribeiro, *The Art of Dress: Fashion in England and France 1750 to 1820* (New Haven, Conn.: Yale University Press, 1995), p. 3.
27 Roland Barthes, *The Fashion System*, trans. Matthew Ward and Richard Howard (London: Jonathan Cape, 1985), pp. 295–6.
28 Daniel Roche, *The Culture of Clothing: Dress and Fashion in the 'Ancien Régime'*, trans. Jean Birrell (Cambridge: Cambridge University Press, 1994), p. 29.
29 Ribeiro, *Art of Dress*, p. 235.
30 Eileen Ribeiro, *Fashion in the French Revolution* (New York: Holmes & Meier, 1988), p. 19.
31 Richard Bienvenu, preface to *Fashioning the Bourgeoisie; A History of Clothing in the Nineteenth Century*, by Philippe Perrot, trans. Richard Bienvenu (Princeton, NJ: Princeton University Press, 1994), p. xi.
32 Fernand Braudel, *Civilization and Capitalism, 15th–18th Century*, vol. 1, *The Structures of Everyday Life: The Limits of the Possible*, trans. Siân Reynolds (New York: Harper & Row, 1981), p. 560.
33 Ribeiro, *Fashion in the French Revolution*, p. 7.
34 Roche, *Culture of Clothing*, p. 29.
35 Philip Mansel, 'Monarchy, Uniform and the Rise of the *Frac* 1760–1830,' *Past and Present* 96 (1982), pp. 128, 132.
36 Henry Cockburn, *Memorials of His Time*, ed. Karl L. Miller (Chicago: University of Chicago Press, 1974), p. 62.
37 'Types of the British Army 1812–1815. The Peninsula and Waterloo Epoch,' Anne S. K. Brown Collection; Richard Simpkin print, Todd album. Mounted figures from the left: officer, 2nd Royal North British Dragoons (Scots Greys), troopers 1st Dragoon Guards, 9th Light Dragoons, 1st Life Guards. On foot: Officers of the 3rd Foot (The Buffs), Coldstream Guards, 95th Rifle Corps, Royal Artillery (Field Battery), 10th Hussars, Royal Horse Artillery; Privates: 28th Foot (North Gloucester) and 42nd Royal Highlanders (Black Watch). Scarlet coats for officers, red for privates; the dark coats are dark blue except for the 95th's 'rifle green,' and field dress is shown.
38 Col. James Campbell, *The British Army as It Was, Is, and Ought to Be* (London, 1840), p. 80.
39 A Chelsea Pensioner [W. Tale], *Jottings from My Sabretache* (London, 1847), pp. 266–7.
40 For these and other changes, see W.Y. Carman, *British Military Uniforms From Contemporary Pictures*, new edn. (London: Spring Books, 1968), pp. 102–124. This topic includes endless details – and there is not space to treat them here, but it is important to note that not all changes were consistent in the sense of always tending towards the same direction in their degree of ornament.
41 Col. Montgomery Maxwell, *My Adventures*, 2 vols. (London: Henry Colburn,

1845), 1: p. 60.

42 A Corporal of Rifleman [Capt. Henry Beaufroy], *Scloppetaria: or Considerations on the Nature and Use of Rifled Barrel Guns* (1808; reprint, Richmond, Surrey: Richmond Publishing Co., 1971), p. 240. See Myerly, *British Military Spectacle*, pp. 127–9.

43 Roger Sales, *English Literature in History, 1780–1830* (New York: St. Martin's Press, 1983), p. 166.

44 'Epitaph on the Late King of the Sandwich Islands, Translated from the Original of Crqazee Rattee[sic], His Majesty's Poet Laureate,' *Spirit of the Public Journals, for the Year MDCCCXXIV: Being the Most Impartial Selection of the Most Exquisite Essays, Jeux d'Esprit, and Tales of Humour, Prose and Verse* (London, 1825), 370. The Hawaiian monarchs visited Britain in 1824.

45 Robert Stewart, *Henry Brougham, 1778–1868: His Public Career* (London: The Bodley Head, 1985), p. 105.

46 William Hazlitt, 'Man is a Toad-Eating Animal,' in *Selected Writings*, ed. Ronald Blythe, (Harmondsworth, Middlesex: Penguin Books, 1982), p. 378.

47 Haydon, *Autobiography*, 1: p. 181.

48 William Lovett, *The Life and Struggles of William Lovett* (London, 1876), p. 152.

49 Hazlitt, 'Man is a Toad-Eating Animal,' p. 378.

50 See Tamara L. Hunt, 'Morality and Monarchy in the Queen Caroline Affair,' *Albion* 23 (Winter, 1991), p. 702.

51 Carman, *British Military Uniforms*, p. 119.

52 19 July 1821, Philipp von Neumann, *The Diary of Philipp von Neumann, 1819 to 1850*, ed. and trans. E. Beresford Chancellor, 2 vols. (Boston: Houghton Mifflin, 1928), 1: p. 69.

53 *Times*, 20 July 1820.

54 Haydon, *Autobiography*, 1: p. 314. David Cannadine dismissed the 1821 coronation as 'desperate and unsuccessful … it simply did not work.' 'The Context, Performance and Meaning of Ritual: The British Monarchy and the 'Invention of Tradition,' *c.* 1820–1977,' in *The Invention of Tradition*, ed. Eric Hobsbawm and Terence Ranger (Cambridge: Cambridge University Press, 1983), pp. 117–18. He highlights some errors, but these were normal; see Jeffrey L. Lant, *Insubstantial Pageant: Ceremony and Confusion in Queen Victoria's Court* (New York: Taplinger Publishing Company, 1980). He also makes sweeping assertions about the supposed failure of the era's royal ceremonial. I strongly disagree with this oversimplification; although this is not the place for a full discussion, the question is not just about whether people liked the shows – each event's reception was different, and must be interpreted within a larger context depending on many factors, including the monarch's popularity. The issue is whether each rite's management did or did not enhance the desired effect. When, how and why did particular features and styles succeed or not? Such questions can reveal the political interactions between public opinion and the abstract aesthetics of design in service to the state, and in doing so reveal transformations in aesthetic taste as a cultural/political evolution.

55 Thomas Hood to Charlotte Reynolds, 9 November 1825, *The Letters of Thomas Hood*, ed. Peter F. Morgan (Toronto: University of Toronto Press, 1973), p. 67.

56 [William Hazlitt] 'Sketches of Manners; The Dromios in London. Smithfield in 1825.' Unidentified newspaper clipping, Pusey Library Theatre Collection, Harvard University; *Bartholomew Fair*, vol. 4. Officers who fussed over their

uniforms were frequently compared to women in this era.

57 Quoted in George Otto Trevelyan, *The Life and Letters of Lord Macaulay*, 2 vols. (1876; reprint, Oxford: Oxford University Press, 1978), 2: p. 44. The date is uncertain.

58 William Jerdan, *The Autobiography of William Jerdan*, 4 vols. (1852–53; reprint, New York: AMS Press, 1977), 2: pp. 363–4.

59 Michael Barthorpe, *British Cavalry Uniforms Since 1660* (Poole, Dorset: Blandford Press, 1984), p. 88.

60 John James Audubon, *The 1826 Journal of John James Audubon* (Norman: University of Oklahoma Press, 1967), pp. 141–2.

61 '17th 50th and 84th Regiments,' artist, D. Alexander, Alexander-Del Vecchio Prints, (London and Dublin: Jas. Del Vecchio, *c.* 1827), Brown Collection, Peter Harrington, *Catalogue to the Anne S. K. Brown Military Collection: The British Prints, Drawings and Watercolours* (New York: Garland Publishing, 1987), 465, #2141, #1. 'Sky-scrapers,' huge plumes and light infantry wing epaulets of the 50th (West Kent) light company officer, highlight the nadir of imposing display. But these working line infantry regiments do not have the army's most flashy dress by any means; all are silver laced, and the coat plastrons of the 50th and 84th are modestly decorated. Facings are white, black and yellow. The fanciest is the 17th (Leicester) captain (one epaulet, right shoulder) with a laced collar and swallowtails. The 50th officer has a hunting horn badge on the boss of his festooned shako; the 84th (York and Lancaster) officer is either a captain or staff officer. All have high collars, elaborate cap lines, crimson sashes, gloves, and silver gorgets (in front below the collar). Flared cuffs are typical of the late-Romantic era.

62 Lt.-Gen. Herbert Taylor to Sir Hussey Vivian, Inspector-General of Cavalry, 20 November 1829, 'Concerning the Accoutrements of the Cavalry' in *The Taylor Papers, Being a Record of Certain Reminiscences, Letters, and Journals in the Life of Lieut.-Gen. Sir Herbert Taylor, G.C.B., G.C.H.*, arr. Ernest Taylor (London: Longman, Green, and Co., 1913), pp. 285–6.

63 E. H. Gombrich, *Ideals and Idols: Essays on values in history and in art* (Oxford: Phaidon Press, 1979), p. 65.

64 Geoffrey Squire, *Dress and Society, 1560–1970* (New York: The Viking Press, 1974), p. 141.

65 M. Dorothy George, *Catalogue of Political and Personal Satires Preserved in the Department of Prints and Drawings in the British Museum*, 11 vols (London: Trustees of the British Museum, 1954), 11: p. 147, print # 15773.

66 'OH WHAT A FALLING OFF WAS THERE,' P. Pry, [W.[illiam] Heath], 29 May 1829, (London: T. M'Lean), Caption: 'All accou[w]—terd the Hero Lay.' The 'w' is crossed out and a 'u' written in over it, making the word 'accoutred' (as in 'accoutrements'). The inscription is intended falsely to suggest that Wellington fell into muck after being literally blown off his horse when a gust of wind caught his 'giant' bearskin cap.

67 Patterson, *Adventures*, p. 276.

68 De Ainslie, Col. C[harles] P[hilip], *Life as I have found it*, (Edinburgh, 1853), p. 180.

69 John Fortescue, *Wellington*, 3rd edn. (London: Ernest Benn Limited, 1960), pp. 231–2.

70 16 June 1827; Hermann von Pückler-Muskau, *A Regency Visitor: The English Tour of Prince Pückler-Muskau Described in His Letters, 1826–1828*, ed. E.M. Butler, trans. Sarah Austin (New York: E.P. Dutton & Co., 1958), pp. 219–20.

71 Francis Macerone, *Defensive Instructions for the People*, (London, 1832), p. 49.

72 Carman, *British Military Uniforms*, pp. 118–22.

73 The Bell-shako's loss in height was compensated to a degree by its being made wider. Alex R. Cattley, 'The British Infantry Shako,' *Journal of the Society for Army Historical Research* 60 (1982), pp. 188–208.

74 Carman, *British Military Uniforms*, pp. 111, 122. This is a large padded bullion lace ornament.

75 General Order # 439, Horse Guards, 2 September 1826, Adjutant-General's Office, *Addendum to the Orders and Regulations of the Army ... January, 1820–1830*, copied in the *Scots Guards Orderly Book*, p. 531.

76 Sacheverell Sitwell, *British Architects and Craftsmen: A Survey of Taste, Design, and Style during Three Centuries, 1600–1830*, 3rd edn. (London: B. T. Batsford, 1947), p. 188.

77 Joseph Farington, *The Diary of Joseph Farington*, ed. Katherine Cave, 16 vols. (New Haven: Yale University Press, 1981–1984), 11: pp. 3884–5.

78 Lady Charlotte Bury, *The Diary of a Lady-in-Waiting*, ed. Francis Steuart, 2 vols. (London: The Bodley Head, 1908), 2: pp. 162 , 239.

79 John Harvey, *Men In Black* (Chicago: University of Chicago Press, 1995), p. 34.

80 Princess Lieven to Lady Cowper, 25 December 1828, *The Lieven-Palmerston Correspondence, 1828–1856*, trans and ed. Lord Sudley (London: John Murray, 1943), p. 7. When dark 'rifle green' camouflage increased in the army from the 1790s (for a few rifle-equipped units) reactionary officers disliked both its somber hue and symbolic political implications, since riflemen were under less rigid control. See Myerly, *British Military Spectacle*, pp. 107–8.

81 1 December 1829, Charles C. F. Greville, *The Greville Memoirs: a Journal of the Reigns of King George IV and King William IV*, ed. Henry Reeve, 5th edn., 3 vols (London: Longmans, Green, and Co., 1875), 1: p. 250.

82 While he could not inspect every uniform, the court was the show's focal point, and the royals were 'noted for their quick perceptions in all matters of military uniform.' General A.[lexander] C.[avalie] Mercer, 'Military Reminiscences of the Latter end of the Eighteenth and Beginning of the Nineteenth Centuries,' in Capt. R. J. Macdonald, *History of the Dress of the Royal Regiment of Artillery, 1625–1897*, new edn. (Bristol: Crecy Books, 1985), p. 53.

83 Gombrich, *Sense of Order*, p. 17.

84 See *Gentleman's Magazine* (August 1830), p. 170.

85 8 July 1830, Harriet Arbuthnot, *The Journal of Mrs. Arbuthnot, 1820–1832*, ed. Francis Bamford and the Duke of Wellington, 2 vols. (London: Macmillan & Co., 1950), 2: p. 370.

86 William IV adds, 'Tis time these fooleries were at an end.' *The Nautical Shaver; or, Downfall of the Mustachios* [*sic*]. Henry E. Huntington Collection, Pr. Box 212.8/91. Hussars and the Household Cavalry kept their moustaches, which were then viewed as militaristic and un-English, but were considered part of the Central European-derived hussar uniform.

87 John Rickman to Robert Southey, 31 August 1830, quoted in Orlo Williams, *Life and Letters of John Rickman* (Boston: Houghton Mifflin Co., 1912), p. 265.

88 Philip Ziegler, *King William IV* (Wm. Collins, 1971; reprint, London: Fontana Books, 1973), p. 161.

89 Maj. N. Dawnay, *The Distinction of Rank of Regimental Officers, 1684 to 1855* (London: The Society for Army Historical Research, 1960), p. 48. Escalating costs had driven poorer officers out of the service after 1815, but some units had served for many years abroad where expenses were lower. In contrast, such middle-class men had risen in the revolutionary French army after 1789. See Myerly, *British Military Spectacle*, p. 45.

90 PRO W.O. 7/58, Board of General Officers Report, 1 June 1842. Hussar dolmans (jackets) were formerly dark blue, and these exquisite, gold-laced scarlet sartorial confections (with sable fur cuffs and collars) were most spectacular. Linda Colley's assertion for the Napoleonic era, that 'Never before or since have British military uniforms been so impractically gorgeous, so brilliant in colour, so richly ornamented or so closely and cunningly tailored' is a bit off the mark; *Britons: Forging the Nation, 1707–1837* (1992; reprint, London: Pimlico, 1994), p. 186. While the 1816–1830 dress was more splendid, most 1830s modes were more brilliant than the pre-1816 styles.

91 Fortescue, *Wellington*, p. 232.

92 Carman, *British Military Uniforms*, pp. 129–34.

93 'Types of the British Army in 1854. The Crimean Epoch,' Brown Collection, Simpkin print, Todd album. Mounted figures from the left: Troopers of the 17th Lancers, 4th Light Dragoons, 2nd Dragoons (Scots Greys), 1st Royal Dragoons and Col. Cardigan, 11th Hussars. On foot: corporal, 93rd (Sutherland) Highlanders; and privates of the 19th Foot 1st Yorkshire (North Riding) and the Rifle Brigade; officers of the Grenadier Guards, Royal Artillery, and 20th Foot (East Devonshire), and the Royal Horse Artillery. All officers' lace is gold except for the Rifle Brigade's black silk. The 1855 reform diminished decorativeness, reducing hussar lace, abolishing most infantry Other Rank's lace, and the 'Albert' shako was replaced by the shorter French kepi.

94 Rifles were not even approved for general use until 1851. Howard L. Blackmore, *British Military Firearms: 1650–1850* (London: Herbert Jenkins, 1961), p. 230; some units had smoothbores as late as 1855. Robert Beaufoy Hawley to Robert Toovey Hawley, 9 January 1855, in *The Hawley Letters: The Letters of Captain R. B. Hawley, 89th from the Crimea, December 1854 to August 1855*, The Society for Army Historical Research Special Publications, no. 10, (London & Aldershot: Gale & Polden Ltd., 1970), p. 21.

95 As Walter Arnstein has pointed out: 'The army ... played a central role in Victoria's life as monarch.' 'The Warrior Queen: Reflections on Victoria and Her World,' *Albion* 30 (Spring 1998), p. 3.

96 See: H. F. A. Strachan, 'The Origins of the 1855 Uniform Changes – An Example of Pre-Crimean Reform,' *Journal of the Society for Army Historical Research* 55 (1977), pp. 85–117 and 165–75.

97 Douglas Jerrold, 'The Folly of the Sword,' in *The Essays of Douglas Jerrold*, ed. Walter Jerrold (London: J. M. Dent & Co., n.d.), pp. 173, 178.

98 Leigh Hunt 'Remarks on War,' in *Captain Sword*, pp. 77–8. The contrast between greedy commercialism and martial glory appeared in higher circles too; after the victory at Inkermann – where the Queen's cousin, the Duke of Cambridge served bravely in the field – *The Court Journal* proclaimed that, 'Inkermann shed a halo of glory around the arms of Britain, which relighted the expiring rays of its most brilliant deeds in the days of chivalry, and we were rejoiced to feel that we had wiped off the stigma of being a sordid nation, bent solely on commerce.' No. 352, new series (16 December 1854), p. 852.

99 Edward Lytton Bulwer, *England and the English*, ed. Standish Meacham (1833; reprint, Chicago: University of Chicago Press, 1970), p. 108.

CHAPTER 5

Free-Trade Radicals, Education, and Moral Improvement in Early Victorian England

Richard F. Spall, Jr.

The work of Professor Walter L. Arnstein in the field of Victorian studies is very well known, not just to his professional colleagues but to generations of students – both graduate and undergraduate – as well. It has spanned the political and social history of the nineteenth century in Britain, and much of it has concentrated on the religious and cultural history of the period. Without jargon or sociological cant, Arnstein's work has considered, among a variety of topics, the relationships between what it is now fashionable to call 'ingroups' and 'outgroups' and the ways in which civil disabilities, which owed to religious belief or the rejection thereof, were often imposed on persons outside the fold of an established Church that was deeply imbedded in a profoundly class-ridden political and social system.[1]

This essay considers how early Victorian, middle-class, free-trade radicals, who may be considered an outgroup on the verge of being admitted to the mainstream of British public life, looked upon issues of educational reform and moral progress – two deeply intertwined political and social issues that were very much at the core of Victorian public discourse and controversy. It attempts to illustrate how the most visible and highly organized free-trade advocates, the members of the Anti-Corn-Law League (1838–1849) saw education and moral progress as inseparably linked and central to their perceptions about how British society was in need of improvement. Their own frequent declarations that they were a single-issue group devoted only to the cause of the repeal of the Corn and Provision Laws notwithstanding, the Anti-Corn-Law Leaguers managed, as will be demonstrated here, to articulate their views on issues of education and moral progress on quite a number of occasions and in a variety of ways, leaving little doubt that these issues were of significance to them, and illuminating how economic, social, and political issues resist facile compartmentalization in nineteenth-century England.[2] Not a few League members were Nonconformists; so it is true that some of their views on these issues had their roots in the sensibilities, and the anxieties, of the Dissenting tradition. And, with so many Nonconformists among their number, the League could hardly afford, politically or financially, to offend or ignore the views that Dissenters held on education or morality. While Leaguers perceived these issues through the spectacles of free-trade ideology, they often articulated them with an evangelical tone and zeal that must have been familiar to those who attended chapel rather than church.

Apart from the question of Ireland, perhaps no issue occupied more attention or generated more controversy in the Victorian era than that of state provision of education. The need for broader access to education was clear, as was the necessity that it include instruction in moral values; but moral values were perceived as inseparable from religious instruction, and religious instruction would almost certainly be denominational. This was the central dilemma of Victorian education, and the matter was further complicated by the fact that there was an established state church, which would almost certainly have a substantial role in any provision of education by the state.

Education was at issue when the League was getting organized, and the debate concerning it became quite prominent when the government put forward an education scheme in 1843–44. The free-trade radicals of the League resented this scheme because it placed the burden of state-supported education upon factory owners, but as middle-class manufacturers, many of whom were Dissenters, they continued to maintain the need for moral improvement and education of the working classes.

Since 1833, Parliament had provided rather modest annual grants of 20,000 pounds for purposes of education, grants that had been administered by the National Society and the British and Foreign School Society. In 1839, the Melbourne government proposed to increase this amount by 5,000 pounds and to change almost entirely its method of distribution by establishing a Board of Education. The new board was to be composed of five Privy Councillors and was to be charged with the responsibility of establishing both normal and infant schools where it saw the need to do so. This proposal launched a debate on the subject of national education that lasted for decades. At issue, as it would be for at least the next forty years, was whether the schools to be established should be under control of the state or administered by voluntary societies. There was general agreement that religious and moral instruction should form part of the curriculum, but there was great controversy, particularly among Dissenters, as to how rights of conscience and the religious identity of Nonconformists could be preserved in such a system.[3]

The middle-class manufacturers of the Anti-Corn-Law League did not take much part in the debate on education in 1839 as they were just getting organized themselves, but they did print in their official organ, *The Anti-Corn-Law Circular,* part of a sermon by the Rev. W.J. Fox on the subject of a general system of education for the laboring classes. William Johnson Fox, a Dissenting minister of some prominence in the League, took the position that a national system of education could not be brought into effective or fruitful operation until the material condition of the working classes had been substantially improved, and he asserted that Britain would not see such an improvement in material life until the Corn Laws had been removed.[4] This, in a nutshell, was the position of the Anti-Corn-Law League, and it appeared repeatedly in the League newspapers as they proclaimed that the education of the hungry and ill-clothed children of the nation's operatives and mechanics was by itself no solution to their deplorable moral or intellectual condition.[5]

Four years later, the Peel ministry proposed a plan for the establishment of district schools for the instruction of pauper children in large towns, which were to be under the superintendence of the clergy of the established Church. Sir James Graham, the Home Secretary, proposed a Factory Education Bill, which was intended to limit employment of factory children between the ages of eight and thirteen years to six and one-half hours per day and require them to attend school for three hours daily. Under the provisions of Graham's plan, millowners would be prohibited from employing any child who could not present a certificate stating that he or she had attended classes, as specified in the provisions of the bill, for at least five days during the preceding week. Graham's education proposal further provided that the schools, which would become subject to inspection, would be financed by a combination of local rates, grants from the central government, and mandated contributions from the factory owners. Moreover, the schools were to be administered by the employers themselves. The mill owners' contributions were set at three pence per week, or one-twelfth of the standard weekly earnings of each child. Graham's plan also contained provisions for religious instruction under the direction of the local clergyman of the Church of England, but it allowed for the children of Dissenters to be excused from religious instruction, except for required scripture reading, if their parents objected. The bill also provided for oversight of the new factory schools by boards of trustees, which were to be chosen in such a fashion as would ensure that they would be almost completely dominated by the adherents of the Church of England.[6]

Middle-class millowners and manufacturers, the bulk of whom were Nonconformists, could hardly have been pleased with Graham's education proposal. It implied that the children who worked in their mills were in the greatest need of education, but it did not address the needs of the children of agricultural tenants and day-laborers of the landed aristocracy and gentry who controlled Parliament and enjoyed the monopoly conferred by the Corn Laws. It proposed limiting hours of employment, always a sticky issue for employers even when it involved children. It required establishment of factory schools, made continued work in the mills contingent upon proof of attendance the previous week, and made the schools subject to inspection by potentially hostile authorities representing a government dominated by the landed interests. The proposal also required the mill owners themselves to pay the bulk of the local costs for education, and the schools would be, for all practical purposes, under the control of members of the established Church with the local Anglican clergyman in charge of religious and moral instruction, effectively marginalizing the religious beliefs of the very millowners, many of whom were Nonconformists, who were to be forced to provide the schools. No issue, other than Church rates, was more certain to engender the opposition of Dissenters, and factory owners resented being singled out and feared not only the cost of the schools but also the potential expense of hiring additional labor to make up for the lost hours while children were in class.

Given this context of Nonconformist ire, it is rather remarkable that the Anti-Corn-Law League remained fairly consistent in its articulation of support for the general principle of education for working-class children; like the whole of Victorian society for most of the century, however, they simply could not agree on specific proposals for the creation of a system of publicly provided education. The particulars of Graham's Factory Education Bill were as insulting as they were threatening, and the League opposed them on several grounds.

First, the Anti-Corn-Law Leaguers resented deeply the fashion in which the proposal, in their view, seemed to single out factory children as those most in need of intellectual development and moral improvement. They perceived it as another attempt by the landed monopolists – the same group who, in the free traders' opinion, controlled the nation's religious life, politics, and economy – to impugn the morals, social responsibility, and intelligence of middle-class manufacturers and traders. The League made the case, but only in general terms, for a more universal system of education, one that would include the laborers of the landed artistocrats and gentry and perhaps share the cost more evenly. Writing in unmistakably religious and moral terms in their newspaper, the *Anti-Bread-Tax Circular*, they asserted that 'The factory people are singled out as sinners above all people that dwell in Jerusalem. Their districts [the agricultural districts of the landed proprietors] must be invaded and conquered, and made to pay tribute for their own progress in civilization.'[7]

Second, the Anti-Corn-Law Leaguers believed, as they had been asserting since the education controversy commenced in 1839, that the provision of mere education without material improvement in the lives of the working classes would be of little value or effect. Leaguers argued that the means of subsistence were already deficient and that placing further limits on hours of employment would only compound that fundamental problem of destitution owing to restrictions on trade and labor. Not surprisingly, the League called for full employment by means of removing the Corn Laws. Addressing the landed interests who controlled virtually every aspect of national policy, the League newspaper said, 'Let them give us full employment; and therefore high wages for these children, and we will pay it willingly; but do not let them thus doubly diminish that fund which is to provide for the wants both of the mind and the body, and thus preclude us with one hand, from obtaining that of which, with the other, they dispose.'[8]

The third and most frequent League criticism of the bill was the degree of control that the plan afforded the established Church, particularly pertaining to the religious instruction of the children of Dissenters. It is fair to say that Dissenters, who made up a quite considerable proportion of the leadership of the League, were outraged at the prospect of the Church of England being given general superintendence over the education of the nation's children. An extraordinary notice was carried in the *Anti-Bread-Tax Circular* under the heading, 'Subsistence, not without, but Prior to Education,' and called for rejection of the education clauses of Graham's bill. Nearly 200 prominent gentlemen of Manchester affixed their names to it.[9] The list contained the names of a great many well-known contributors (or subscribers as they were called) and members of the Anti-Corn-Law League's governing council. In the by-elections of 1843, parliamentary candidates who were associated with the League, including most prominently John Bright, made known on the hustings their outright and unequivocal opposition to the government's Factory Education Bill.[10]

Edward Baines, a well-known Anti-Corn-Law Leaguer and editor of the *Leeds Mercury*, blasted Graham's proposal in *The Social, Educational and Religious State of the Manufacturing Districts*. Baines provided a lengthy and detailed analysis of the bill that was directed to Dissenting clergymen, superintendents and teachers of Sunday schools, and what he called all friends of religious liberty. He argued that the government plan ultimately would: 1) put an end to all Sunday Schools in factory districts; 2) bring virtually all education under control of the Church of England; and 3) make every ratepayer contribute to Church schools. Baines characterized the attempt to enact the plan as a manifestation of the spiritual and ecclesiastical despotism of Anglicans, and in the unmistakable language of free-trade radicals called it an example of the 'spirit of monopoly' so much associated with the landed interests. According to Baines, the effort of the landed ruling class and their Church to impose Graham's education scheme not only threatened religious liberty but made second-class citizens of Dissenters while seriously misrepresenting the spiritual condition of the industrial north of England.[11] Baines also wrote a pamphlet, the publication of which he helped to finance himself, that dissected Graham's bill, criticized it clause by clause, and explained that it posed a serious threat to Sunday Schools.[12]

W.J. Fox, the Dissenting clergyman whose sermon had at first been used by the League to articulate their position that material improvement was the key to moral improvement, frequently lectured on behalf of the Anti-Corn-Law League and wrote for its newspapers. He expressed his personal opposition to Graham's Factory Education Bill on many of the same grounds as Edward Baines in his own pamphlet, *On the Education Clauses in the Bill Now Before the House of Commons*. Fox, however, recommended some changes in the proposal that might make it more acceptable to Dissenters in the industrial districts. He proposed that school trustees be elected by ratepayers, rather than by parish vestries as called for in Graham's plan, and that these locally elected trustees should have oversight of both instruction and overall management of the schools. He proposed that a specific time be reserved for religious instruction, so that 'opting-out' by parents was more practical and possible. He suggested further that religious teachers be approved by the parents of those attending the schools. Fox also proposed that the privileges under the bill be extended to cover already existing voluntary schools and that the 'certificate of attendance' required for employment, which was called for in Graham's proposal, be made instead a 'certificate of achievement' to help ensure that educational progress – and not mere attendance – was the genuine object of the schools.[13] Clearly, this prominent League spokesman was giving support to public provision of education in principle, while remaining opposed to the particulars of the government's plan.

In April of 1843, at the very height of the public debate over Parliament's consideration of Graham's Factory Education Bill, the *Anti-Bread-Tax Circular* reprinted an article from the *North of England Magazine* that endorsed the action of the government in awakening to the responsibility of providing education. It was a common League practice, as it was in many nineteenth-century newspapers, to reprint articles from other publications in order to praise or condemn them, depending on whether the views expressed in them were in line with League opinion. In fact, there is reason to suggest that the League even subsidized other publications for this purpose, but the great bulk of the particular evidence for this in the League's financial records was destroyed by the League President, J.B. Smith, when he moved his household on one occasion. The *North of England Magazine* was a publication that had received the endorsement and praise of the Anti-Corn-Law League as being a consistent advocate of free-trade doctrines, and the article that they reprinted on the subject of the Factory Education Bill contained some mild criticism of the bill's particulars and recommended that the proposed Boards of School Trustees be elected by all ratepayers, as Fox had suggested, as well as advocating that schools be financed by local rates, rather than mandated employer contributions. The article went a little further, however. It accepted, for example, the principle of central inspection, and, while acknowledging that 'the cultivation of the religious sentiment [was] the most important branch of education,' argued that public education should only be a supplement to the pulpit, the Sunday School, and the Christian home. It urged liberals and Dissenters not to oppose the bill on this issue alone or force the government to withdraw it altogether.[14]

It is obvious that this particular bit of indirect advocacy in the League newspaper was a source of consternation to many of its own members. In the very next issue of the *Anti-Bread-Tax Circular* the League took the highly unusual step of expressing its regret over the publication of the article, and even went so far as to claim that its printing had been a complete mistake, saying that they had published the wrong article and that another one, on the subject of medical statistics and the Corn Laws, had really been intended for publication.[15] It seems doubtful, though not impossible, that publication was an outright mistake. More likely, someone at League headquarters in Manchester, possibly Richard Cobden who, as an Anglican, was something of a rarity in the League's upper echelon, had underestimated the depth of Dissenter feeling on the issue and included an article that contained a good many of Fox's suggestions without appreciating that many League members, and more importantly contributors, found their resentment at government intrusion, dominance of the established Church, and unfair financial burdens of the bill more than they were willing to risk having to endure. In the next few issues of their newspaper, the League found it necessary to back-pedal.

It is clear that this flap over publication of the article from the *North of England Magazine* led League headquarters to develop a greater appreciation of the sensitivity of the many Dissenters in their ranks on the issue of state-sponsored public education. The education clauses in Graham's bill were withdrawn after taking the sense of the House of Commons on the matter, and by that time the League not only proclaimed the withdrawal a success for the Dissenters, but it also held up the determination of Nonconformists to oppose it as an example to the League itself in their common struggle for repeal of the Corn Laws.

When Graham introduced a similar bill the following year, it was far less comprehensive and did not go a very long way in attempting to set guidelines for instruction. The discussion of the second bill centered on the limits to be imposed on hours of labor rather than on education or religious instruction. The government, it seems, had gotten the message too – that education was, to use a late twentieth-century expression, the 'third rail' of Dissenter political sentiment – and the measure was withdrawn in the Commons.[16] The League returned to its original appeal, that the material progress, which would result from repeal of the Corn Laws, was the necessary precondition for the success of public education and moral improvement. This position was safe. It put repeal ahead of the potentially divisive issue of education while still allowing it to be supported in principle. Cleverly, the Anti-Corn-Law League argued that opponents of sectarian education could not also be friends of the bread tax. Praising the success of Dissenters in blocking Graham's education proposals, the League newspaper linked the emerging cause of 'voluntary' education with that of repeal. It implied, rather optimistically, that it would be the material improvement of the working classes – brought about by nothing less than adoption of free trade – that would allow them to afford an education, and an education of their choice too, for their children. While this view seems too optimistic and perhaps even cynical in the early twenty-first century, it illuminates much about the confidence and optimism of early Victorian, free-trade radicals. Convinced, as they were, that free trade was the solution to virtually every problem, they could argue that repeal and working-class education were linked. The *Anti-Bread-Tax Circular* proclaimed, 'To a large extent it is, indeed, the same cause; take off the poor man's bread-tax, and his children will be educated, in thousands and tens of thousands of instances; educated at his own charge and his own choice; educated, where they will neither be exposed to the superciliousness of charity nor to the devices of proselytism.'[17]

Nonetheless, the support of a good many leaders of the Anti-Corn-Law League for broader availability of education was steadfast, if not always entirely consistent in the form or particulars of its expression. In many cases such support antedated participation in the free-trade movement itself, and many Anti-Corn-Law Leaguers were later active in the Lancashire Public School Association, which eventually evolved into the influential National Public School Association. Richard Cobden, for example, was an early supporter of a national system of public education, serving as treasurer of the Friends of National Education in Manchester in the late 1830s.[18] In fact, it was through his activity in the education movement that he met both J.B. Smith and John Bright, two of his closest partners in the repeal movement.[19] In the early months of 1839, when Cobden was busy trying to find an editor for the just-proposed Anti-Corn-Law League newspaper, he wrote a series of letters to J.H. Burton in which he described the proposed League organ as intended to be, among a variety of things, an advocate for national education.[20] Cobden continued his interest in national education during the period of the agitation against the Corn Laws, and saw their repeal in 1846 as leaving the path clear for enactment of some form of national educational system.[21]

Though he was a voluntaryist, John Bright's interest in universal education went back to 1833, when he helped to found the Rochdale Literary and Philosophical Society.[22] George Wilson, the influential Chairman of the League Council, on the other hand, served as secretary of the Friends of

National Education in the 1830s, and several other prominent Leaguers, including Henry Ashworth, Edward Brotherton, and Thomas Spencer, were openly supportive of national education before or during the period of the agitation for the repeal of the Corn Laws. It was Leaguer James Heywood who, with the aid of Richard Cobden and one of Manchester's MPs, Mark Philips, formed the Manchester Society for Promoting National Education in 1837. Many members of the Manchester Statistical Society, including R.H. Greg and William R. Greg, were also members of this group.[23] W.J. Fox lectured frequently on the topic of education in the 1840s, emphasizing that instruction should be both general and spiritual in nature and stressing the need for children of all denominations and social classes to be mixed.[24]

Thus there is evidence that a good many prominent leaders of the Anti-Corn-Law League favored broader provision of education and that they were particularly interested in instruction for the children of the working classes. They were, of course, in agreement that the Corn Laws were the fundamental obstacle to this goal, but they seemed to be unable to develop a consensus as to just how education was to be brought to the masses. At the heart of this difficulty were two related issues. The first was the principle of voluntaryism, and the second had to do with the nature of religious instruction and the belief that moral education could not take place outside this context. If the Anti-Corn-Law League was unable to come together on these issues, it reflected English society as a whole. Those who favored a national system of education, such as Cobden, Fox, Wilson, and the Gregs, were more willing to accept a situation in which the state might endow schools that would be charged with providing religious instruction in some form. Voluntaryists, such as Edward Baines, Edward Miall, Joseph Sturge, and John Bright, were unwilling to countenance such an approach. In a society with an established Church, state endowment of schools with provision of religious instruction was bound to favor the Church of England and thus alienate the Dissenters. An organization like the Anti-Corn-Law League, with so many Non-conformists in its ranks, could not endorse a national system of education because it was such a sore point with Dissenters, who already felt marginalized, resented Church rates, and remembered many previous years of civil disabilities because of their religious beliefs, disabilities that Parliament had, until 1828, suspended only annually.

The League could advocate the provision of broader education in general terms; it could even afford to criticize specific educational proposals such as Graham's bill, but it could not advocate any specific educational plans of its own without risking a major split in its own organization, which would cost it political support as well as much-needed financial contributions. The League came perilously close to doing just this with the publication of the article supporting Graham's bill from the *North of England Magazine* in the spring of 1843; thus it very quickly backed away from any appearance of supporting Graham's bill, saying publication of that article had been a mistake. Not until the Corn Laws were safely repealed did the considerable support by some of the former members of the Anti-Corn-Law League for a national, secular, rate-supported system of public instruction coalesce into the National Public School Association.[25]

The issue of education shows very well how difficult it was for the Anti-Corn-Law League to develop consensus on any issue apart from repeal. To the extent that the members of the League discussed other reform issues in specific terms they ran the risk of fragmenting their own organization, yet it was difficult for the League and its members to remain altogether silent about issues for which there was considerable support within the ranks of the organization. This internal tension helps explain how and why the League, as an organization, remained general and superficial in its support for broader education while talking about it fairly often.

Nonetheless, much of the interest of the Anti-Corn-Law Leaguers in education was related to their individual concerns with the moral and religious condition of the working classes, which, as mill owners, many of them were in a position to know only too well. In the minds of many leaders of the League, there was a close connection between material improvement and moral progress, and this view was frequently reflected at League meetings, in publications, and in public speeches.[26] The League headquarters even collected data on the state of the poor, and the issue was often discussed in the context of concern, not just for the physical condition of the people, but for their moral, intellectual, and religious states as well. Much of this interest and concern seems quite earnest, despite misgivings in our own time about the class interests of the mill owners, and the considerable body of moralists among the many devoutly religious Dissenters in the League tends to enhance such an appearance. Still, the fact remains that appealing to feelings of charity and moral concern on the part of the League itself could also have been just an effective or clever tool used to attract precisely such support.

It seems to have been the belief of a great many free-trade radicals in the League that material progress was an essential precondition for widespread moral improvement, and such thinking permeated their views on poor relief, factory acts, and education. The League newspaper proclaimed, 'The amelioration of the condition of the people as the grand object contemplated by the Anti-Corn-Law League.'[27] It was the position of the League that material improvement brought about by the prosperity that would undoubtedly follow the repeal of the Corn Laws would be more effective in promoting moral improvement than any number of social institutions that might be established for that purpose. The *Anti-Corn-Law Circular* asserted, 'Churches, schools, libraries, mechanics' institutes with their systems of lectures, & c., are excellent in their proper places; but to trust merely to the

agency of those for the redemption of the masses from blank inanity, or
what is worse, from profligacy and sensuality, is to begin at the wrong end.'[28]

Among those members of the Anti-Corn-Law League who emphasized
most prominently the connections between moral and material progress was
Richard Cobden. Cobden had long held this view; in one of his earliest
pamphlets, *Russia and the Eastern Question*, published in 1836, he asserted
such a connection, and suggested that only by labor and personal
improvement could nations achieve greatness.[29] Writing for the *Anti-Corn-
Law Circular* in 1840, Cobden argued that the material progress of the Swiss,
which he admired, was primarily a result of their application of the principles
of Adam Smith, and in a speech to a League meeting at Drury Lane in
1843, he made known his belief that Britain stood at the threshold of a
great era of moral improvement, which would proceed from material
progress as soon as the Corn Laws were swept away.[30]

The theme of the connection of material and moral progress was also
prominent in the tale, *Dawn Island*, which Harriet Martineau produced for
sale at the Anti-Corn-Law League Bazaar in May of 1845. *Dawn Island*
was a parable about a small tropical island in the Pacific, which had been
plagued with poverty, rebellion, war, and pagan morality until European
merchants visited the place and transformed its economy from mere
subsistence to thriving production for export trade. Not only did material
life get significantly better on Dawn Island as a result of adopting an
economy based upon free trade, but, as the material condition of the natives
improved, they abandoned infanticide, eliminated war, gave up pagan
sacrifices, and made rebellion completely unnecessary and obsolete.[31] Here
was the optimism and confidence of free-trade radicalism in parable form:
British trade, unfettered, was *the* solution to *all* the problems of the age.
This was what made the unrestricted capitalism of the Anti-Corn-Law
Leaguers a fighting inspirational creed. That such a view was naive or that
it failed to take account of the great disparity of power and wealth between
owners and producers in an emerging capitalist system does not change the
fact that such views were genuinely or deeply held or that the confidence in
free trade and British institutions of those who held such opinions was
considerable. The ideas of Marx had not yet gained currency, and to free-
trade radicals it was the class of landed aristocrats that had to be overcome
for material and moral progress to be made. Free-trade radicals perceived
the battle lines of class conflict as being between monopolist landed interests
and the 'productive classes' of the emerging industrial economy.

Writing for the *Anti-Bread-Tax Circular* under the pen name, 'One Who
Has Whistled at the Plough,' League writer and lecturer Alexander
Somerville emphasized what he perceived as the loose morality in rural
districts among paupers, peasants, and even the landed aristocrats and gentry
as well, but this sort of concern with morality was also attributed to the

Anti-Corn-Law League's campaign to discredit landed monopolists at the time of the debate over Graham's Factory Education bill.[32] Nonetheless, the League organs carried articles that made abundantly clear their position that poverty itself was the principal cause of moral degradation, and that destitution together with the idleness that was inherent in unemployment were overpowering temptations to what they termed 'unchristian behavior.'[33]

The League's insistence on an essential connection between morality and material conditions was proclaimed in the circular section of the *Anti-Bread-Tax Circular*, in which official statements of League policy were frequently announced, when they stated:

> It is since the working classes have been unable to obtain 'a fair day's wages for a fair day's work,' that their downward progress has been perceptible. Enforced idleness is of itself the parent of almost every crime. Unrenewed exertion and fruitless energy cannot long continue to exist. The poor may struggle for a time against the tide whose power is overwhelming him, but he succumbs at last; and when despair takes place of hope, he surrenders himself to some of the many temptations which beset him ...[34]

At meetings of the League, it was not uncommon to hear speakers discuss the agitation for the repeal of the Corn Laws as if it were a moral crusade. Dr John Bowring spoke of the 'mission' of free trade and identified the cause of unfettered commerce with that of Christianity itself in a speech before the Anti-Corn-Law League at Drury Lane in 1843.[35] W.J. Fox proclaimed the Leaguers as convenanters at another such meeting, concluding his speech by saying,

> We take this solemn League. (*Loud cheers.*) We pledge ourselves to it as a religious covenant; (*enthusiastic cheering;*) and we swear by Him who liveth for ever and ever, that this egregious folly of the corn laws, this foul wrong, this atrocious iniquity shall be entirely abolished. (*Tremendous cheering, and the audience rising as one, waving hats and handkerchiefs.*)[36]

There is considerable evidence that free traders often emphasized religious and moral elements in their agitation for repeal, and, while a good deal of this feeling was, no doubt, genuine, it is also likely that some League leaders were aware of the extent to which religious imagery and moral sentiment could be utilized to promote their cause. The cadence and tone of Fox's speech before the League at Drury Lane, for example, must have seemed familiar to evangelicals. In the spring of 1840, Cobden, through his colleague, P.A. Taylor, sought to obtain the services of W.J. Fox as a publicist or paid lecturer for the League. In a private letter, Cobden instructed Taylor to have the Reverend Fox approach the issue from a moral and religious point of view, not as a capitalists' or manufacturers' question but, as he put it, on the 'primitive ground of right and justice.'[37] Cobden wrote,

> Then the religious and moral feelings must be appealed to, and the energies of the Christian world must be drawn forth by the remembrance of the Anti-Slavery, and other struggles, and by being reminded that the cause of truth and justice must prosper in the end, ... Then the people should be told that the country's salvation must be worked out at the hustings and the polling booths.[38]

In April of 1846, *The League* publicly asserted that many within the ranks of the organization were primarily motivated by religion and morality rather than by commercial or political sentiments: it observed that 'There are those who seek the total abolition of the Corn Law, as logically implying and practically necessitating the extinction of the whole of the protective and restrictive system – and there are those with whom it is an affair of conscience and religion to protest against a tax on food as intrinsically oppressive and iniquitous.'[39]

In a religious age, the utility of portraying one's opponents as the enemies of the deity cannot be denied, and Anti-Corn-Law Leaguers, it seems, understood this. Quotations from the Bible implying that the proponents of protection were behaving in a fashion that was clearly contrary to the will of God were a frequent feature in League newspapers, and occasionally articles would be printed that advanced a converse, though in some respects more intense view, that the Corn Laws were a tool of Satan himself.[40]

The Anti-Corn-Law League organized a conference of what they called 'ministers of religion' to enhance the moral and religious dimensions of their cause, and they were eager to generate publicity for repeal agitations in which religious groups or clergymen were involved.[41] The League asserted over and over again that repeal of the Corn Laws was at its core a moral question and, therefore, almost by definition a religious question. They argued that it was the duty of all Christians, on grounds of humanity, patriotism, and religion, to oppose protection as inimical to the progress of both religion and morality.[42] The religious and moral character of their deeply held free-trade principles were strikingly extolled in the lyrics of a song that were published in the *Anti-Bread-Tax Circular* in 1843:

> Free Trade, like religion, hath doctrines of love,
> And the promise of plenty and health;
> It proclaims, while the angels look down from above,
> The marriage of Labour and Wealth.

Free Trade, like religion, hath doctrines of peace,
Universal and God's vital air;
And throned o'er doomed evil, he hails its increase,
While his enemies only despair.

By all who their blood on Truth's altar resigned,
To enfranchise a sin-fettered race!
Our sons shall be freed from the curse of the blind,
And redeemed from the bonds of the base.[43]

With so much emphasis on the moral elements of opposition to the Corn
Laws it was not difficult for Leaguers of religious conviction to see the
economic principles of free trade as part of a system of natural and divine
law established and ordained by Providence itself. As adherents to the new
doctrines of classical economics, natural-law arguments were not new to them.
Thus, the League tended to regard all monopolies and all interferences on the
part of government with the fair and regular course of commerce and trade as
contrary to the designs of nature and of nature's God. In the *Anti-Bread-Tax
Circular*, they characterized any such government attempt as, 'nothing more
and nothing less than an attempt to interfere with the laws of [H]im who
framed society, who placed man where he is, who made him what he is, who
created all the relations amongst men; they were an attempt to amend and
alter natural arrangements, which sprang out of the Great Supreme ... .'[44]

The League also advanced the argument that free trade would do much
to spread Christianity throughout the world so that opposition to the Corn
Laws appeared to contribute to the fulfillment of the Great Commission to
spread the gospel.[45] It was, therefore, no less than the work of God.

Whether by conviction, by the desire to bind religious (particularly
Dissenting) opinion to their cause, or both, a good many distinctions between
religious and moral issues on the one hand, and economic and political
ones on the other, appear thus to have been melded, confused, and sometimes
blurred. For example, the *Anti-Corn-Law Circular* carried reports of
meetings of sabbatarians, which, while not directly endorsing stricter
observance of the sabbath, nonetheless implied a fairly clear sympathy with
that cause and went on to suggest explicitly that the repeal of the Corn
Laws would promote more faithful and widespread observance of the
sabbath.[46] The moral issue of slavery and of duties on the importation of
slave-grown sugar were of great concern to the members of the League.
Reports in their newspapers linked American slave-owners to British
protectionists, but the issue of the importation of slave-grown sugar was a
difficult one for the free-trade advocates.[47] The Anti-Corn-Law League
had considerable sympathy for the objectives of the Anti-Slavery Society,
and not a few Leaguers were members of both organizations. While the
League naturally took a dim view of any restrictions on trade, this position

was not always entirely compatible with the desire of the opponents of slavery to restrict or prohibit the importation of slave-grown products, and of sugar in particular.

During the summer of 1844, the Anti-Corn-Law League became indirectly involved in an internal debate of the Anti-Slavery Society and attempted to head off a major split in the ranks of that organization over the issue of government sanctions against slave-grown produce. The League favored the abolition of the sugar monopoly for reasons of free trade, but many in the Anti-Slavery Society argued that the exclusion of slave-grown sugar, or at the very least restrictive duties upon it, would raise the moral standard of Britain and demonstrate to slave-owners that Britain would rather suffer economic loss than be on friendly terms with them.[48] Anti-slavery is another example of an issue to which the Anti-Corn-Law League could give general support, but on which taking a specific position could only undermine its own consensus – a consensus more delicate than historians have been apt to think.

The contemporary moral issue that received the most attention from Anti-Corn-Law Leaguers was temperance. It is no surprise to discover that there were teetotalers among the supporters of the League inasmuch as Dissenters and moralists were well-represented in its ranks, yet abstinence from alcohol was hardly a *sine qua non* for either of those groups.[49] What is surprising is the use that the Anti-Corn-Law League made of this issue apparently without alienating those who did drink alcohol. At League banquets separate teetotal sections were set up for those who abstained from drink.

The League encouraged the formation of abstinence societies in 1842, when Peel brought forward his proposals for revision of tariffs, but, cleverly, it did so as a way of protesting that policy. The League reported on a meeting in Birmingham at which it was recommended that there be an abstinence from alcohol as a means of bringing pressure to bear on the government and the landowners. It was emphasized that there was no need for teetotalism, but that reductions in the consumption of beer and ale would reduce revenue by perhaps as much 10 million to 11 million pounds annually.[50] The *Anti-Bread-Tax Circular* carried an article from Archibald Prentice's *Manchester Times* that reported that many members had resolved to use no excisable articles, but suggested that 'Others may resolve to disuse beer, wine, spirits, tobacco, tea, sugar, &c. to a greater extent, and make the *direct* loss to the exchequer equal to the amount of his income tax.'[51] It must be said that the Anti-Corn-Law League did not specifically endorse this plan of action, but by discussing it in such detail and explaining the rationale for such a course in such explicitly free-trade terms they certainly did not discourage it.

The League maintained a variety of connections with the Temperance Society as well. One Anti-Corn-Law League lecturer, George Grieg, even after the council had sacked him for apparently being too political in his agitation on their behalf, wrote to the League office several months after his dismissal requesting instructions and an endorsement from the council for a new series of lectures, which he intended to give at Leeds.[52] Sidney Smith, the Secretary of the League from 1839 onwards and the editor of the *Anti-Corn-Law Circular*, directed George Wilson, Chairman of the League Council, to see to the insertion of articles on Temperance Society meetings in the League organ as the discussion of them on the lecture tour in which he was then engaged was having such a good effect.[53] It has not been possible to determine precisely which articles pertaining to temperance may have been inserted in response to this request, but several articles on temperance and Temperance Society meetings were reported in the *Anti-Corn-Law Circular* during 1840, including one that directly and explicitly expressed approval of teetotalism.[54]

All in all there seems little doubt that the free-trade radicals of the Anti-Corn-Law League were indeed interested in education and moral improvement; it is also certain that they regarded them as linked. Naturally, they also perceived these issues through the lens of free-trade ideology, and they articulated their views on them frequently, usually in general terms, and often with a tone and enthusiasm that was familiar – and appealing – to persons of religious conviction, especially those in the Dissenting tradition. The considerable number of Nonconformists in their ranks already felt they were outsiders or second-class citizens and resented the monopoly of the established Church as much as they opposed the monopoly in corn. State provision of education, which would undoubtedly involve the state Church, was a 'hot-button' issue for them. The emphasis on education, which was a part of the Dissenting tradition, assured that broader provision of or access to education would be valued, but how to provide it was a very thorny issue indeed. This helps explain the paradox inherent in free-trade radical support for education and opposition to specific educational proposals. Moreover, the dynamics and occasional back-pedaling of Anti-Corn-Law League articulation of support of such views illustrates how fragile the consensus among the ranks of freetraders could be.

As manufacturers, free-trade radicals feared government intrusion and resented the suggestion that the factory children employed in their mills were in the greatest need of moral improvement. They were also still smarting from the reimposition of the income tax. When free-trade perceptions, middle-class interests, and Dissenter resentments and anxieties combined, the feeling could be intense. The League reflected all these sensibilities, tried to harness them, and worked assiduously to avoid conflict amongst them. The safest course was articulation of general support in free-trade terms, based on the assumption that material advances were necessary to moral improvement. By emphasizing the end result, rather than specific proposals, differences in opinion could be minimized and the primacy of repeal – the very issue for which they had organized themselves as a League – could be most readily promoted.

The politics, society, and economic life of the early Victorian era are particularly illuminated by such issues and events. The early years of the 'age of improvement,' we are reminded, involved much more than the high parliamentary politics of political and social reform. The significance of the use of political symbols, articulation of key issues, and performance of public political rituals in out-of-doors political life has in recent years become plain, and a good bit of what free-trade radicals did with respect to articulating support for education and moral improvement can be explained in these terms. Interest-group politics and perhaps even 'out-group' politics may be more revealing as interpretative tools than the politics of class *per se,* but neither are they unrelated. The perceptions, concerns, and activities of free-trade radicals illustrate too some of the ways in which politics, social issues, and economic matters resist facile compartmentalization and the dogmas of class conflict. The perceptions and sensibilities of free traders were shaped by the legacy of being religious outsiders as well as by laissez-faire economics, and they seem not to have been knee-jerk opponents to every imaginable manifestation of social reform. If they were divided on how to bring about greater access to formal education, they still managed to share the assumption – and the confidence – that material progress would lead to moral improvement. In both these elements they reflected Victorian society as a whole.

NOTES

1   The author wishes to acknowledge the support of a Thomas E. Wenzlau Grant and an Eli Lilly Faculty Development Grant in support of some of the research for this essay.
2   The Anti-Corn-Law League agitated for the repeal of the Corn and Provision Laws from the late 1830s until Peel suspended import duties on foreign cereal grains in 1846. Archibald Prentice, himself a member of the League, was the first to recount its history in *History of the Anti-Corn-Law League*, 2 vols. (London: Cash, 1853). The best-known study of the League as an organization is by Norman McCord in *The Anti-Corn-Law League, 1838–1846* (London: Allen and Unwin, 1958), which concentrates on organization and methods of the League rather than upon free-trade ideology or its implications. The most recent study is a popular one, Norman Longmate's *The Breadstealers: The Fight Against the Corn Laws, 1838–1846* (London: Temple Smith, 1984), which does a fine job of recapturing the rhetoric of the League. A variety of biographies of League leaders provides another approach to the subject; the most recent ones include Wendy Hinde's *Richard Cobden: A Victorian Outsider* (New Haven: Yale University Press, 1987); Nicholas Edsall's *Richard Cobden: Independent Radical* (Cambridge: Harvard University Press, 1986); and Keith Robbins's *John Bright* (London: Routledge and Kegan Paul, 1979). For a much broader discussion of the implications of economic reform

and the political climate in which free traders opposed what they regarded as the enormously unfair economic and other privileges of the landed aristocracy, see Philip Harling's *The Waning of 'Old Corruption': The Politics of Economical Reform in Britain, 1779–1846* (Oxford: Clarendon Press, 1996).

3   *Annual Register, 1839* (London: Ribington, 1840), 81: pp. 140–72. *British Almanac, 1840* (London: Knight, 1840), pp. 198–205.

4   'N.T.', *Anti-Corn-Law Circular,* 25 June 1839. Fox had begun as a Unitarian but shifted religious affiliation after being censured by his original denomination.

5   'Lord Ashley and the Corn Law,' *Anti-Bread-Tax Circular*, 23 May 1843; 'Education *versus* Food,' 4 April 1843; 'Metropolitan Anti-Corn-Law Association,' 18 April 1843; 'Morals of Restriction,' 13 June, 1843.

6   *Annual Register, 1843*, 81: pp. 52–60. *British Almanac, 1844*, pp. 94–200. See also Eric Midwinter, *Nineteenth-Century Education* (Harlow: Longmans, 1970). For the origins of this sort of plan and the denominational controversies that it created, see Donald Akenson's *The Irish Education Experiment* (Toronto: University of Toronto Press, 1971).

7   'The Factory Education Question,' *Anti-Bread-Tax Circular*, 11 April 1843; and 'Agricultural Morals,' 27 June 1843.

8   'Subsistence, not without, but Prior to Education,' *Anti-Bread-Tax Circular*, 7 March 1843.

9   'Borough of Manchester,' *Anti-Bread-Tax Circular*, 25 April 1843. The same notice appeared in the following issue as well.

10 'Durham Election,' *Anti-Bread-Tax Circular*, 1 August 1843; 'To the Electors of the City of London,' *The League*, 14 October 1843.

11 Edward Baines, *Social, Educational and Religious State of the Manufacturing Districts with Statistical Returns on the Means of Education and Religious Instruction* (London: Simpkin and Marshall, 1843), pp. 61–71.

12 Edward Baines, *Effect of the Government Education Bill on Sunday Schools Shown in a Letter to the Parents of Sunday Scholars* (Leeds: Baines, Newsome, & Knight, 1843), pp. 1–2.

13 W.J. Fox, *On the Education Clauses in the Bill Now Before the House of Commons* (London: Charles Fox, 1843), pp. 1–30. Fox suggested criteria for achievement as well, such as the ability to read the gospels by age nine, ability to write by age ten, and knowledge of the rules of arithmetic by age eleven, etc.

14 'North of England Magazine, December No. XI,' *Anti-Bread-Tax Circular*, 1 December 1842; 'Strictures on the Government Plan of Education,' 4 April 1843.

15 'To Readers and Correspondents,' *Anti-Bread-Tax Circular,* 11 April 1843.

16 *Annual Register, 1844*, 82: pp. 107–133.

17 'Success of the Dissenters Against the Factories' Bill,' *Anti-Bread-Tax Circular*, 20 June 1843.

18 Cobden may also, as has already been suggested, have been responsible for the publication of the *North of England Magazine* article.

19 'Announcement of a meeting of the Friends of National Education.' George Wilson Papers, Archives Department, Manchester Central Reference Library. The precise year of this announcement cannot be determined, but 183_ is clearly legible. A note on the reverse side signed by Cobden requests Wilson to forward additional 'begging petitions' to potential contributors. Wilson is identified as secretary of the organization, and contributors are instructed to pay Cobden as treasurer. H. Dunckley to Cobden, 10 November 1837, Cobden

Papers, West Sussex Public Record Office. Cobden also outlined his admiration for the American use of public lands to finance an educational system in his pamphlet, *England, Ireland, and America* (London: Simpkin, 1835), pp. 33–34. See also Cobden to Tait, 5 May 1837, and 17 August 1838 in which Cobden expresses his admiration for American education and his belief that a national system of education in Britain would be the first step towards genuine radicalism. Cobden Papers, British Library Add. MSS. 43,665. Cobden was also an admirer of Prussian education; Cobden to Neild, 30 September 1838, Neild Correspondence, John Rylands Library. 'My First Acquaintance with Cobden,' a handwritten memoir by J.B. Smith in J.B. Smith Papers, Archives Department – Manchester Central Reference Library, mentions Cobden's early interest in the subject. For John Bright's interest see R.A.J. Walling, ed., *Diaries of John Bright* (New York: Morrow, 1931), pp. 52–53; and G.M. Trevelyan, *The Life of John Bright* (London: Constable, 1919), pp. 29–30. For J.B. Smith's early and consistent support of national education see 'To the Electors of the Borough of Blackburn,' and 'The Stirling Burghs Nominations of Candidates,' in J.B. Smith Papers, Archives Department – Manchester Central Reference Library.

20   Cobden to Burton, 23 March 1839 and 25 March 1839, J.H. Burton Papers, National Library of Scotland.

21   G.M. Mackensie to Cobden, 18 September 1841, Cobden Papers,West Sussex Public Record Office. Cobden to Combe, 'confidential', 14 July 1846, Cobden Papers, British Library Add. MSS. 43,660. See also Donald Read, *Cobden and Bright: A Victorian Political Partnership* (New York: St. Martin's Press, 1968), pp. 177–180, 209–218; John Morley, *The Life of Richard Cobden* (London: Chapman and Hall, 1879), pp. 410–411; and Paul Leroy-Beaulieu, 'Richard Cobden: His Work, and the Outcome of His Ideas,' pp. 77–128 in Henry Dunckley, et al. *Richard Cobden and the Jubilee of Free Trade* (London: Unwin, 1896).

22   Read, *Cobden and Bright*, p. 74 and William Robertson, *Life and Times of the Right Honourable John Bright, M.P.* 2 vols. (London: Cassell, 1877), pp. 70–74, 209–210. See also an undated fragment of a letter in Bright's hand and signed 'J.B.' in George Wilson Papers, Archives Department, Manchester Central Reference Library.

23   Ashworth to Wilson, 26 October 1837; Brotherton to Wilson, 21 October 1837; and Urquhart to Wilson, 28 November 1837, all in George Wilson Papers, Archives Department – Manchester Central Reference Library. Thomas Spencer, *Remarks on National Education* (London: Gilpin, 1844), pp. 1–16. Spencer outlines a mixed system of lectures and private study to insure a moral education. He advocates a national and comprehensive system. See also Thomas Southcliff Ashton, *Economic and Social Investigations in Manchester 1833–1933: A Centenary History of the Manchester Statistical Society* (London: King, 1934), pp. 1–33, and p. 64. Robert Hyde Greg, *The Factory Question Considered in Relation to Its Effects on the Health and Morals of Those Employed in Factories* (London: Ridgway, 1837), pp. 122–38.

24   W.J. Fox, 'On Public Education,' pp. 226–50, and 'On the Duties and Rights of a Society as to Education,' pp. 262–76, in *Lectures Addressed Mainly to the Working Classes*, 4 vols. (London: Charles Fox, 1845–1849). Fox was a great admirer of Mann and proposed an education bill in 1850 providing for establishment of secular education funded by ratepayers. See Richard Garnett and Edward Garnett, *Life of W.J. Fox, Public Teacher, and Social Reformer,*

1786–1864 (London: John Lane, 1910), pp. 300–306.

25   'Crime & Corn Laws,' *Anti-Corn-Law Circular*, 6 August 1839; 'Influence of the Corn Laws on Popular Education,' 10 December 1839; 'Commercial Restrictions,' (reprinted from *Tait's Magazine*), 10 December 1839; 'Fifth Letter from a Member of the Anti-Corn-Law League on the Continent,' 27 August 1840. This letter from Cobden praises the Swiss system of education. 'Chartism and the Late Strikes,' *Anti-Bread-Tax Circular*, 28 February 1843; 'Popular Education in England,' 7 March 1843; 'Free Trade Meeting in Barnsley,' *The League*, 23 December 1843.

26   See, for example, 'Monopoly and Marriage,' *Anti-Corn-Law Circular*, 3 September 1839; 'Street Walking,' 12 November 1839; 'Distress and Crime,' 31 December 1839; 'Address of the Metropolitan Anti-Corn-Law Association,' 26 March 1840; and an untitled report of a lecture by Sidney Smith, 9 July 1839. 'The Gathering of the League' (Circular Section), *Anti-Bread-Tax Circular*, 20 December 1842; 'Statistics of the Corn Law Question,' 17 January 1843. See also Alexandrina Peckover, *Life of Joseph Sturge* (London: Sonnenschein, 1890), pp. 54–62.

27   'Necessaries and Luxuries,' *Anti-Corn-Law Circular*, 30 July 1840. This was the leading article in the issue.

28   Ibid.

29   Richard Cobden, *Russia and the Eastern Question* (Edinburgh: Tait, 1836), pp. 30–32. Cobden's thought on the connections between moral and material improvement may have been influenced by his association with the noted phrenologist, George Combe, with whom Cobden was a frequent correspondent for many years. See George Combe's book, *The Constitution of Man in Relation to External Objects* (Edinburgh: Chambers, 1836), esp. pp. vii–viii. See also Morley, *Cobden*, pp. 93–4.

30   'Fifth Letter from a Member of the Anti-Corn-Law League on the Continent,'*Anti-Corn-Law Circular*, 27 August 1840. Though Cobden is not identified in the League newspaper as being the author of this letter, the date on the letter is consistent with the timing of Cobden's visit to Zurich, and the tone of the letter is quite similar to others that Cobden sent back to Leaguers on that journey. *Anti-Bread-Tax Circular*, 9 May 1843. See also William H. Dawson, *Richard Cobden and Foreign Policy* (London: Allen and Unwin, 1926), p. 103.

31   Harriet Martineau, *Dawn Island: A Tale* (Manchester: Gadsby, 1845), *passim*. Gadsby, it is worth noting, was the League's printer. For a discussion of how material progress was presumed to improve with repeal of the Corn Laws and how even aristocratic families would be reformed by the diminished temptation to profligacy and villainy, which the anticipated prosperity of free trade would bring, see Joseph Barker, *Blessings of Free Trade, ... and How They May be Increased and Made Lasting* (1846), pp. 1–24. Barker's pamphlet carries no reference to the Anti-Corn-Law League but does demonstrate the currency of such notions by the time the Corn Laws actually were repealed.

32   'Notes from the Farming Districts,' *Anti-Bread-Tax Circular*, 16 May 1843.

33   'Lecture by Mr. J.C. Fitzgerald, A.B.,' *Anti-Bread-Tax Circular*, 14 March 1843.

34   'Morals of Restriction,' *Anti-Bread-Tax Circular*, 13 June 1843; 'Free Trade Meetings in Barnsley,' *The League*, 23 December 1843.

35   'Weekly Meeting of the Anti-Corn-Law League,' *Anti-Bread-Tax Circular*, 18 April 1843; 'Another Great Fact,' *The League*, 2 December, 1843.

36   'Weekly Meeting of the Anti-Corn-Law League,' *Anti-Bread-Tax Circular*, 4 April 1843.

37   Cobden to Taylor, 4 May 1840, cited in Garnett, *Fox*, pp. 258–259.

38   Ibid.

39   'Why Compromise Is Impossible,' *The League*, 11 April 1846.

40   'Corn Laws,' *Anti-Corn-Law Circular*, 23 October 1840, (reprinted from the *Examiner*); 12 October 1839; 15 October, 1839; 26 November 1839. For a complete discussion of League opposition to the Church establishment and the 1841 Conference of Ministers of Religion see Richard Francis Spall, Jr. 'The Anti-Corn-Law League's Opposition to English Church Establishment,' *Journal of Church and State* 32 (Winter 1990): 97–123 *passim* and especially pp. 102–103.

41   'Correspondence,' *Anti-Corn-Law Circular*, 3 December 1840; 'Corn Laws a Religious Question,' *Anti-Corn-Law Circular*, 16 June 1841; 'Commencement of the Movement Against the Bread Tax by Ministers of Religion,' 29 July 1841.

42   'Natural Law of Wages,' *Anti-Corn-Law Circular*, 11 March 1841; 'Repeal of the Corn Laws a Religious Question,' (a letter of T. Spencer from *The Patriot*), 26 November, 1839; 'Weekly Meeting of the Anti-Corn-Law League,' *Anti-Bread-Tax Circular* 2 May, 1843; 'Corn Laws a Religious Question,' 19 May 1841; 'Corn Laws a Religious Question,' 5 May 1841; 'Conference of Anti-Corn-Law Deputies at Manchester,' 21 April 1841; 'Gainsboro,' 29 August 1843; 'Weekly Meeting of the League,' 3 November 1842; and of particular interest is the speech of Rev. Cox at the seventh Drury Lane meeting in 1843, 9 May 1843. The theme of Cox's speech was '*Homo sum-humani nihil a me alienum puto.*', which he translates as, 'I am a man, and I think nothing foreign to my purpose that is connected with the welfare of my country and the interests of the world.' Rev. T. Spencer wrote a pamphlet in 1843 that urged religious men to be politically active, and that gave Biblical examples and admonitions to do so. Rev. Thomas Spencer, *Religion & Politics; or, Ought Religious Men Be Political* (London: Green, 1843), pp. 1-16.

43   'Song,' *Anti-Bread-Tax Circular*, 7 March 1843.

44   'Great Free Trade Meeting in the Music-Hall, Liverpool,' *Anti-Bread-Tax Circular*, 7 March 1842; 'Weekly Meeting of the League,' 27 December, 1842; 'Laws of Man Opposed to the Law of God,' 21 October 1841; 'Thoughts on the Corn Bill, Free Trade, & c,' 14 March 1843.

45   Lecture by Sidney Smith, *Anti-Corn-Law Circular*, 9 July 1839; 29 October 1839; 'Physical Improvement Must Precede the Spread of Christianity Among the People,' 14 May 1839. 'Gainsboro,' *Anti-Bread-Tax Circular*, 29 August 1843.

46   'Rev. Mr. Allen, of Bury, and the Corn Laws,' *Anti-Corn-Law Circular*, 25 June 1839; 'Meeting of the Hand-loom Weavers,' 7 January 1840.

47   'Unholy Alliance Between the Slaveholders of America and the British Bread-Taxers,' *Anti-Corn-Law Circular*, 25 February 1841. 'The Crisis,' *Anti-Bread-Tax Circular*, 5 May 1841; 'Anti-Slavery Society,' 19 May 1841; 'Mr. Sturge in America-White and Black Slaves,' 29 July 1841.

48   Anti-Slavery Society and the Sugar Question,' *The League*, 1 June 1844; 'Zeal Unguided by Wisdom. The Sugar Monopoly and the Anti-Slavery Society,' 4 January 1845.

49   For a discussion of this issue with regard to John Bright and the Quakers see J. Travis Mills, *John Bright and the Quakers*, 2 vols. (London: Methuen,

1935), pp. 71–72.

50   'Movement and the Sliding Scale,' *Anti-Bread-Tax Circular*, 24 March 1842.

51   'Passive Resistance,' *Anti-Bread-Tax Circular*, 24 March 1842. Similar suggestions had earlier been made during the fall of 1841; *Anti-Bread-Tax Circular,* 21 October 1841 and 4 November 1841.

52   Grieg to Wilson, 20 October 1840, ACLL Letterbook, Archives Department, Manchester Central Reference Library.

53   Sidney Smith to Wilson, 8 May 1840, ACLL-Letterbook, Archives Department – Manchester Central Reference Library.

54   'Success to Teetotalism,' *Anti-Corn-Law Circular*, 5 November, 1840; 20 February 1840; 'Why is Employment Scarce?,' 10 September 1840; 'Teetotalism and the Corn Laws,' 3 December 1840. Thomas Milner Gibson wrote to Wilson in the autumn of 1841 – after the elections – asking how much he should contribute to the Temperance Society, and reporting that Mark Philips had already subscribed a sum to that organization. Gibson to Wilson, 9 September 1841, George Wilson Papers, Archives Department – Manchester Central Reference Library.

An ACLL handbill in the collection of eighty circulars and tickets of the ACLL in the Social Sciences Library of the Manchester Central Reference Library poses a series of 'Questions for the Times,' of which 'What is Drinking?' was one. The answer is as follows: 'The taking of that excellent fluid provided by the Almighty for our first parents in Eden; and its various modifications for the sustenance and health of man; or the absurd suction of alcohol and alcoholic drinks at births, weddings, funerals, bargain makings, &c. &c. to drown care, and generate false spirits and false strengths, by which the mind is shattered, the character wrecked, the estate wasted, body and soul destroyed – a practice, from which flows more sorrow, and in which we see a more amazing amount of present and continuing insanity and woe, than can be traced to any other habit, to which rational creatures are prone.' ACLL Circulars and Tickets, Social Sciences Library – Manchester Central Reference Libary. See also Spencer, *Parson's Dream*, p. 11.

CHAPTER 6

Chartists After Chartism: *Reynolds's Newspaper* and Mid-Victorian Political Reform

Michael H. Shirley

Until recently it has been common historical currency that Chartism essentially breathed its last in 1848, having outlived its usefulness.[1] Chartism as a political movement had been the product both of a specific moment and of received ideas. The Chartism of the 1830s and early 1840s had been a movement of both ideology and action, with public demonstration and petition its most visible activity. The demonstrations and petitions of 1848, inspired in large measure by the example of continental radicalism, truly did mark an end to what is best described as the method of Chartism. As both Gareth Stedman Jones and Jon Lawrence have pointed out, the underlying assumption of the Chartists had been that significant social reform could not be won from an aristocratic Parliament; the actions of Sir Robert Peel's Conservative administration from 1841 to 1846 had undermined that assumption.[2] Peel's ministry had been responsible for several significant reforms, ranging from the strengthening of the currency to the abolition of the Corn Laws. To the Chartists, however, all such changes were irrelevant without real political reform. The ideology of Chartism was certainly not dead, nor would it die. Radicals continued to maintain the six points of the Charter as goals for years after the disappointments of 1848. The methods they espoused changed, but their ideology remained essentially the same. They concentrated, however, on obtaining the franchise, without which, they asserted, no further reform could come.

As Trygve Tholfsen has shown, Chartism must be understood not merely as a militant working-class movement, but also as a visible expression of previously nascent radical traditions. Chartists, he writes, 'were not the passive creatures of forces that determined their 'being.' They chose values and principles from the legacy of the past and adapted them to their needs and aspirations.'[3] The movement itself was diverse, but was centered around the idea that class domination should cease. That idea of democratization was the essence of Chartism, while the implementation of the Charter itself was seen as the means to that end. Dorothy Thompson, in her invaluable book *The Chartists,* gives credence to the success of the working classes' self-help movement, among other things, as a reason for Chartism's decline. 'The strength of Chartism,' she writes, 'had lain in the participation of whole communities and of whole trades. It had also lain in an unquestioning belief in the efficacy of political change to bring about social improvement. In the late forties many of these ideas were no longer so potent.'[4]

While Thompson is correct that self-help movements among the working classes did provide a way for them to better their lives, self-help movements alone could not create the change that radicals sought. This essay will argue that the idea that political change was the means necessary to bring about social improvement was still just as potent after 1848 as it had been before. It will show that the great public demonstrations and petitions of the 1830s and 1840s, so often seen as the most significant aspect of Chartism, were simply the method used to attempt to implement the Charter. It will demonstrate that while the failures of 1848 marked the beginning of a change of that method, the ideology of Chartism remained strong in radical circles for years thereafter. As Chartism had grown from the soil of native English radicalism, so it would nourish subsequent radical activity and thought. This continuity of Chartist ideology can be seen most clearly in the pages of *Reynolds's Newspaper,* the most popular radical newspaper of the so-called 'post-Chartist era,' under the editorship of its founder, G.W.M. Reynolds. It was *Reynolds's Newspaper* which acted as the 'mass public meeting' after the era of mass public meetings had ended. It is thus on Reynolds and his *Newspaper* that this essay will concentrate, focusing especially on *Reynolds's Newspaper's* response to reform legislation of the 1850s, 1860s, and 1870s in order to illustrate the continued potency of the Chartist ideal.

Reynolds's Newspaper, which began publication in May of 1850, was a Sunday weekly whose main appeal lay in its professed radicalism.[5] While any number of periodicals might have been read for their sensational stories and fiction – *Lloyd's Weekly Newspaper* or *Reynolds's Miscellany,* for example – *Reynolds's Newspaper* was the most overtly political and polemical newspaper widely available in Britain in the mid-Victorian era.[6] Reynolds's readers read the *Newspaper* precisely because they agreed with the political and social philosophy which lay at the heart of its polemic, and because they wished to read the news of the day in a paper whose opinion and progressive orthodoxy they could trust. Thomas Wright, 'The Journeyman Engineer,' writing of the *Beehive* and *Reynolds's Newspaper,* insisted that 'These two papers are accepted and looked up to by the political division of the working classes as their special guides, philosophers, and friends; they believe in, admire, and are materially influenced by their political teachings.'[7] 'The believers in

Reynolds's – ,' he added, 'and their name is legion – have caught the style of their organ.'[8] As F.A. Collier, a third-generation subscriber, wrote in 1950, 'Both my grandparents, being Chartists and pioneer co-operators, had *Reynolds* from its first issue. In those days it was the bible of advanced thinkers.'[9] It should be kept in mind that, although the *Newspaper*'s actual reading audience was largely working-class in nature, it was directed at anyone of radical republican inclinations.[10] Radicalism had, by the 1840s, become the *de facto* property of the working classes, but it was not a class-specific ideology. Radicalism, and the literature which espoused it, were based on political and social exclusion.[11] Radical newspapers, *Reynolds's* in particular, were directed not only at those who were excluded, but also at those members of the reading public who wanted to include them.[12]

That reading public was a large one. Ellegard estimates that *Reynolds's Newspaper* sold approximately 50,000 copies a week in 1855, a figure which increased to 60,000 by 1860, 150,000 in 1865, and 200,000 in 1870.[13] The only other figures available are from the *Newspaper* itself; they must obviously be treated cautiously. Reynolds was certainly no stranger to self-promotion, and the circulation figures often appeared under the heading 'Notice to Advertisers.' Some inflation in the figures was likely. Despite the disadvantages inherent in using such information, however, they do lead to some useful conclusions about the size of the audience of the *Newspaper.* In 1870, when Ellegard claimed that it sold 200,000 copies per week, the *Newspaper* also claimed a guaranteed circulation of 200,000, but noted a steady increase in actual circulation: it claimed sales of 220,000 in March; 230,000 in April; 240,000 in May; 250,000 in July; 280,000 in August; and 300,000 in September.[14] Even assuming that Ellegard was reasonably accurate in his estimations, and that the *Newspaper* was overly enthusiastic, it is clear that *Reynolds's Newspaper* had a very large circulation.[15]

Raw circulation numbers alone, however, do not tell the entire story of the size of *Reynolds's* readership. Working-class newspapers of the nineteenth century had an audience considerably larger than bare sales figures alone would indicate. Reading for the working classes, far from being a solitary activity, was essentially communal in nature.[16] It was common for one man to read a newspaper aloud to others. Reynolds himself estimated that each copy of a weekly newspaper was read by at least five people.[17] Old readers of the *Newspaper*, on the occasion of its 100th anniversary, wrote in to describe its place among those who could not read, or who could not afford to purchase a personal copy. Mary Orton, of Old Lenton, Nottingham, writing on behalf of her eighty-six-year-old husband, recalled that 'He never had a day's schooling in his life, and it was from *Reynolds' News* that he learned to read seventy years ago. In those days the old men of the village used to gather at my father-in-law's house to have the paper read to them.' Walter T. Webb, eighty-two, remembered that his parents used to invite a few elderly people in to hear him read the *Newspaper* every Sunday. This practice was not limited to England. David Reilly, of Longwood, Huddersfield, wrote that when he was a boy in Ireland, his home was a gathering place for those villagers who could not read; his mother would 'read *Reynolds News*' reports of speeches in Parliament on the then vital issue of Home Rule.'[18]

Workers might even pool their resources for a subscription to a newspaper and commission one among them to read aloud while the others worked, although this practice depended somewhat on the stability of the local job market. John Cassell, publisher of *The Freeholder*, told the Newspaper Stamp Committee in 1851 that 'Five working men will each be subscribing their penny a week to take in [*The Freeholder*]; two of that number, perhaps, or three, may be agricultural labourers, and remove, and the consequence is that those remaining cannot afford it ... and they cannot continue the paper any longer ... .'[19] Coffee houses, public houses, and barbershops often subscribed to newspapers and magazines, which a patron could read for a price.[20] Working-class political clubs, too, purchased newspapers, of which *Reynolds's* was one of the most popular; the *Newspaper* claimed in 1855 that it was 'taken by all the political club houses.'[21] Indeed, Sunday weeklies as a whole were more popular than daily papers, especially among members of the working classes. Raymond Williams asserts convincingly that Sunday weeklies were popular among the working classes as that was their only day of leisure, and they preferred to read journals in a timely fashion.[22] That so many members of the working classes chose to read *Reynolds's Newspaper*, as compared to the many other periodicals which were available, is telling. If reading was a social activity, it was also a political one.

Readers of the *Newspaper* were not passive recipients of information. Natalie Zemon Davis, in her essay about sixteenth-century France, 'Printing and the People,' points out that, as a solitary reader interacted with the text, so too did groups of readers; they also interacted with one another.[23] As Elizabeth Long notes, echoing Zemon Davis, group readings often form the basis for conversation and debate, and have done so for centuries.[24] For readers of *Reynolds's Newspaper*, that conversation centered around politics. The 'Tramp Socialist,' a peripatetic radical who had first seen the *Newspaper* in 1850, described in 1906 the catalytic role it had played in the shop in which his father had worked:

> In those days few of advanced age among that class could read.
> Yet they were the keenest of politicians. Having the paper read
> daily kept them always abreast of the times. To secure one of
> their shop mates who could read would cost them what he could
> make – all work being done by piece ... . If the services of a boy
> could be obtained, it would be quite a saving. So many days
> have I sat on a high, three-legged stool in the centre of that

shop, shouting at the top of my young voice the Parliamentary speeches of those whose tongues have long been silent. It was only after the lapse of years that I realized the spirit of the hot debates that took place on the floor of that shop. Who can doubt that whatever of advanced thought is manifest among the workers of Dundee is the result of the efforts of those truly patriotic men, who regarded *Reynolds's* as their Holy Writ, and who were fully alive to the cant and hypocrisy by which they were surrounded.[25]

With a circulation of at least 200,000 by 1870, and a readership far greater than that, it is the best indicator available of radical working-class opinion of the so-called 'post-Chartist' era.

Reynolds, a well-known journalist and popular novelist who remained the guiding force behind the *Newspaper* until a stroke incapacitated him in 1877, had never been involved in Chartist demonstrations before 1848.[26] He was a republican, and had been so since his youth. The excitement of 1848, however, caused him to embrace the Charter in a very public way. As he himself declared on the twenty-fifth anniversary of his newspaper, 'Although a Republican, and so proclaiming myself, I had cheerfully accepted the Chartist programme as a means to the attainment of the end which I desired.'[27] His activity in Chartist politics from 1848 on was significant, not because he was a committed Chartist, but because that activity is indicative of the fluid nature of post-1848 radicalism.

Margot Finn, whose book *After Chartism* is indispensable to an understanding of mid-Victorian working-class politics, has brought together and clarified recent strands of scholarship about the course of radicalism and liberalism after 1848. Class allegiances in Marxist terms, she notes, were less important in the mid-Victorian period than were national identities. The idea of the English 'people' or 'nation' resonated with radicals far more than did any conscious self-identification as the 'working class.'[28] While the rhetoric of post-1848 radicalism in the pages of *Reynolds's Newspaper* often used terms such as 'working class' and 'middle class' when discussing economic relationships, the term 'the people' appeared with greater frequency, usually when describing the vast majority of British subjects who were disenfranchised. The latter concept was inherent in Reynolds's discussion of economic relationships. The term 'working class,' as he used it, did not describe a simple economic group, but a political group as well.

R.C. Gammage, in his early history of Chartism, wrote that, in the eyes of the masses, the economic might of the ruling classes arose from their monopoly of political power, and that the exclusion of the working classes from political power was the cause of their overall economic and social misery.[29] This view, as Gareth Stedman Jones has noted, has been forgotten by most historians.

Stedman Jones asserts that, to the Chartists, 'Political Power [was] the cause, Opulence was the effect. But to subsequent historians, whether liberal, social democratic or Marxist, it has been axiomatic that economic power is the cause, political power the effect.'[30] Neville Kirk would seem to agree with those subsequent historians, stating that 'in his stress upon the political nature of Chartism, Stedman Jones greatly underestimates the influence exerted by economic and social factors upon the political ideas of the movement.'[31] Trygve Tholfsen echoes this assertion when he says that Chartists, unlike middle-class liberals, saw that the problem of justice and progress was centered on the question of class.[32] Neither of these scholars is entirely convincing. Jon Lawrence, in a very perceptive article, does convince. He 'rejects both the determinist straitjacket of the traditional emphasis on standards of living … and the countervailing tendency to focus purely on the interplay of political ideas or the conjuring tricks of high politics.'[33] To Reynolds, and to the radical working classes who were his readers, economic wealth rested on the past and present monopoly of political power, and vice versa. The monopoly of both wealth and political power were of long-standing duration, and had been sanctified by time; both of them required reform. Such reform, which to Reynolds and his readers meant moving toward a republic, required that universal manhood suffrage – the first point of the Charter – become a reality.

At the heart of Reynolds's political philosophy was a dichotomous view of the English social and political system: on the one side stood the 'toiling millions' and their enlightened republican allies; on the other stood everybody else. The enemies of the people sided entirely with the prevailing system of privilege and status based on birth, which existed solely to rob the many for the benefit of the few. He declared his attitude succinctly in *Reynolds's Political Instructor:*

> The Peers of the Realm belong to that Aristocracy which has monopolized all the honours and all the lands of the State, and actually made them hereditary in their own families. The Members of the House of Commons belong to that branch of the legislature which boldly, insolently, and arrogantly denies the right of all the people to be represented, and which has adopted the style and behaviour of the people's masters instead of the people's servants. The Clergymen belong to an Establishment which possesses larger revenues than all the other State-Churches in the world put together, but which is nevertheless ever crying out for 'more, more!' And the Merchants belong to the class of employers who fatten on the labour of the employed, who thrive by that very competition which ruins the masses, and whose constant endeavour seems to be to screw up the human machine to do the greatest possible amount of work at the lowest possible remuneration.[34]

This vision of a rapacious upper order fattening on the collective body of the masses was the idea around which *Reynolds's Newspaper* was organized; an understanding of Reynolds's conception of society as it existed is central to an understanding of his, and his newspaper's, editorial stance.

Although the hereditary aristocracy had sprung from the monarchy, it was the aristocracy which now held – in the name of the Queen – most of the real political power. That power which they now possessed they used for two purposes: first, to maintain their social and political positions, so that they might run the country for their own benefit; second, to steal as much money from the people as possible, while contributing nothing to the country's welfare. As the front-page leader proclaimed in 1856, 'The House of Lords is knavery and imbecility, organized, consolidated, and perpetuated.'[35] It was self-perpetuated, the *Newspaper* stated frequently, for the sole purpose of maintaining the wealth of its members. And in this effort it was not alone; the House of Commons was a willing accomplice.

Parliament, as the *Newspaper* presented it, was not bicameral, but essentially unicameral; the House of Commons was actually a 'lower House of Lords,' existing for no other reason than to conserve and protect the interests of the aristocracy.[36] 'The aristocratic and moneyocratic interests,' Reynolds wrote in 1854, 'constitute the basis on which the social system is built; and whatsoever Reform measure emanates from the House of Commons can have no other object than to strengthen that basis.'[37]

The political parties themselves were presented as being nothing more than factions of the upper classes.[38] 'The occupants of the Treasury and Opposition benches,' the columnist Northumbrian wrote in 1863, 'are but two rival gangs of place-hunters. Their policy is popular plunder; their object personal and family aggrandizement; their professions instruments of popular delusion; their denunciations of foreign wrongs winning devices to put the people off the track of domestic abuses.'[39] Those domestic abuses were myriad, but were essentially of one character: they deprived the toiling millions of the fruits of their labor, and enriched the idle upper classes.[40] The *Newspaper* stated that the Great Exhibition of 1851, for example, had been devised by the upper classes to put money in their own pockets, to provide themselves with amusement, and to distract the working classes from their own misery.[41] The 'titled paupers' were not allowed to remain paupers for long; there was always a sinecure available for them, given by their better-positioned relatives and friends, 'who can put their hand into the pocket of the nation and rob without fear of check ... .'[42] This greediness continued even after death. Even those nobles who were wealthy were often buried at state expense; the Duke of Wellington, Reynolds claimed, had probably always planned to have the public purse pay for his funeral, as it had paid for everything else in his life.[43]

The poor, Reynolds maintained, were robbed of everything by the upper classes, including things which could not be measured in pounds, shillings, and pence. Even food, which was God's gift, was taken away. The aristocracy's practice of hiring wet nurses, the *Newspaper* claimed, caused poor women to neglect their own infants, and was the leading cause of infanticide in England.[44] The children of the poor were condemned so that the rich would not be inconvenienced. 'The [crocodile],' cried the *Newspaper,* 'may be assumed to reason thus – 'Men must die, that crocodiles may dine.'[45] The allusion to the upper classes was clear. Their privileges were derived from the wretchedness of the underprivileged.[46] The latter was necessary to the former. The social system – which depended on birth, property, and appearance – kept the working classes in perpetual servitude. For their bonds to be broken, the entire system had to be changed. This single principle was the essence of Reynolds's and the *Newspaper's* political philosophy.

Reynolds's republicanism, which was not based on a concept of class but on a fundamental idea of justice and democracy, provided his newspaper with a firm base from which to comment on political issues of the day. His desire was not for a working-class government, but for a government in which all of the people had a voice:

> We have no objection to the representation of people who are landowners and holders of stock; we admit the expediency of having those acquainted with trade and commerce in parliament – not because they are landowners or millionaires, or great employers, but because they are Englishmen, and we desire to see the English people represented as a people with a great national interest at stake. We object to class representation, because landowners are only too likely to legislate for the benefit of land, and moneyed men for the protection of usurious profit, unless they are checked by the presence of men drawn from the order of labour – the true source of wealth. We should deprecate a House of Commons exclusively composed of working men, and for exactly the same reason we deprecate a house exclusively composed of rich men.[47]

Reynolds often placed his discussion of English radicalism and republicanism in the context of European radicalism as a whole. As the *Newspaper* was born in the aftermath of the revolutions of 1848, he continued to draw attention to the recurrent republican impulses which arose in the monarchies of Europe. He decried the 'royal and immoral despotism' of Spain, and looked to France for proof that the entire social and political system must be changed for real reform to occur.[48] The rise of Napoleon III was a crushing disappointment to him, but he assured his readers that 'French liberty ... is not dead, but sleepeth, and will one day awake, arise, and overcome the tyrant by whom she has been crucified, mangled, and entombed.'[49] The Greek Revolution of 1862 came as no surprise, he wrote, for monarchy was abhorrent to the freedom-loving Greeks. 'Monarchy,' he asserted, 'was the nursery of revolutions.'[50]

His delight in the revolutionary impulse in other countries, however, did not cause him to urge a similarly violent revolution in England. Sufficient progress had taken place at home to make such a revolution unnecessary. Further peaceful change at home was possible. In a speech to the Literary Association in 1850 he predicted further violent revolutions in Europe, but noted that 'There would be no necessity for physical force here, because, from the enlightenment of the people, the exercise of their moral influence would be sufficient to obtain the fulfillment of all their demands.'[51] The mission of Chartism, he had proclaimed earlier in the *Political Instructor*, was a

> peaceful, legal, and constitutional change in those systems which are invested with too much of ancient feudalism to suit modern civilisation. Chartism does not contemplate a bloody revolution – does not want it: its very votaries would be the first to suffer by such an insane course. Chartism does not intend spoliation and general plunder: its leaders and its adherents are too honest and too humane, too just and too generous, to entertain such a barbarous idea. Chartism does not seek to upset society: its apostles and disciples are intelligent philanthropists whose object is to remodel and not destroy.[52]

Nor did he advocate a violent international class revolution, or any war of intervention against a despotically governed country. The hardships of such a war, he stated in 1864, would fall most heavily on the working classes. The nation should reform itself first, before it sought to reform others.[53] Despite the frequent violence of his rhetoric and his goal of complete political reform, his was in many ways a conservative vision.

Rather than attacking Parliamentary attempts at political reform in the 1850s and 1860s from an idealized position of working-class privilege, the *Newspaper* analyzed such efforts according to their practical results, with the ultimate goal of universal manhood suffrage and complete representation. The battles over the various reform efforts of the 1850s and 1860s, and the reform bills of 1866 and 1867 provide a fairly clear picture of the *Newspaper*'s attitude towards reform in general and towards Parliamentary reform in particular.[54]

Reynolds had written in 1850 that 'twenty years hence, the principles we at present advocate, and which are now considered ultra, red, and republican, will be looked upon as tame and extremely conservative.'[55] While this vision of the future proved to be overly optimistic, the increasing clamor for electoral reform in the 1860s did indicate that the *Newspaper*'s principles were not seen as being as outlandish as they once had. Harold Perkin has asserted that, by 1867, the relative calm among the working classes had led upper- and middle-class leaders to believe that the working classes had accepted the idea of an entrepreneurial class society based on competition, and that the more well-to-do of them could thus be trusted with the vote.[56] Rejection of an entrepreneurial society, however, had not been at the heart of the reform Reynolds wanted, nor had his rhetoric abated. The franchise was the first step on the journey to a republican form of government, wherein class government, at least as it had been practiced, would no longer keep the masses in a position of economic disadvantage. The argument that the position of the working classes had improved substantially since the Reform Act of 1832, and that they should therefore cease agitating for drastic reform, held no weight with the *Newspaper*. What mattered was that their relative position had not improved. In 1857, Reynolds noted that, because the 1832 Reform Act had increased county representation, it had actually increased the power of the House of Lords, as the peers controlled the counties.[57] Any political influence which the middle classes had gained in 1832, the *Newspaper* asserted, had been offset by the power retained by pocket boroughs. Andover, it pointed out, which had only 247 electors, sent two representatives to Parliament, as did Birmingham and Manchester, with 10,000 and 20,000 electors respectively.[58] No matter how well the middle classes had done, the aristocracy had done better. In comparison, the working classes had lost ground. 'I do not allege that the condition of the working classes has not materially improved during the last thirty years,' wrote the columnist Gracchus in 1865, 'but I do contend that the governing orders have taken good care that whenever the workman makes one step towards the bettering of his position, those above him shall take half a dozen.'[59] Reform bills which changed things 'bit by bit' were next to useless; real reform required drastic change.[60]

Reform efforts in 1859 and 1860 provoked mixed reactions. The government-sponsored reform bill introduced by the second Derby Ministry in 1859 was praised with faint damns. Although it did make concessions to the working classes, the *Newspaper* said, it gave away too much to the landed interests. Only universal manhood suffrage, the front-page leader concluded, would bring real reform.[61] The Liberal government's 1860 reform bill, which was introduced (and would later be withdrawn) by Lord John Russell, the *Newspaper* announced, would be a sham. 'The betrayal which we believe to be in store for the working classes,' proclaimed the front-page leader,

> is attributable to their own apathy and credulity – to the cunning of the aristocracy – the faithlessness and faintheartedness of the middle classes – the treachery or incapacity, or both, of the self-elected leaders of the reform movement ... . The credulousness of the working classes has been manifested in their reliance on

members of the now enfranchised orders to work out their emancipation.[62]

Parliamentary negotiations over the bill brought mostly negative reactions. The amount of aristocratic opposition to the bill, claimed the first leader in April, proved that it had some elements of justice in it.[63] Those elements, however, were so minute as to constitute less progress than even the enemies of the working classes might accept. By the next month, the *Newspaper* sounded a frustrated warning, reminding its readers that they had been promised a reform bill by so many successive administrations that further delay might lead to violence by the working classes.[64] The possibility of agitation, however, had no effect, as in June the frontpage leader mourned, 'The Tories have triumphed. The people are slaves. The Reform Bill is withdrawn.'[65]

The *Newspaper*'s rhetoric about battle over the reform bills of 1866 and 1867 varied from hopeful to downcast. The frontpage leader declared that Gladstone's proposed bill of 1866 was, at best, a weak attempt to enfranchise only those members of the working classes who were most under control of the middle classes.[66] The 'Liberal hypocrisy' had advanced so far only because Gladstone was the spiritual leader of the party. The Liberals, as Reynolds put it, 'resembled a pirate ship with the image of a saint for its figure-head.'[67] The measure did have the benefit, however, of providing a good litmus test: given that it was so weak, those who opposed it as too radical could never be friends of the masses.[68]

The dissolution of Russell's government, and Disraeli's subsequent reform bill, caused the *Newspaper* to become rather more agitated than it had been hitherto. In a bit of hopeful hyperbole, it declared that 'The struggle is becoming exciting. We are evidently on the eve of a great national crisis. Old political parties are in a state of rapid decomposition.'[69] The real prospect of the possible redistribution of seats was cause for celebration, but the *Newspaper* cautioned that the situation would not be satisfactory until 'that point of the People's Charter known as "equal electoral districts"' was made into law. Until the Conservatives were converted to Chartism, the paper warned, 'it will be the bounden duty of the reformers to do all in their power to prevent the further aggrandisement of the political power of the landed interest through the impending apportionment of parliamentary seats.'[70] The *Newspaper*'s focus on the aristocracy and their land-based wealth remained central to its political rhetoric throughout the reform bill debates. A general election, it proclaimed, was supposed to be an appeal to the entire country; what it was in reality was 'an appeal to the cheque-books of wealthy candidates.'[71]

Disraeli's reform bill, although an improvement over Gladstone's, still left a substantial portion of the working classes without the vote. That the electorate had doubled at a stroke was good; that so many of the working

classes were still without the vote was evil.[72] Before the rest of the people
could be enfranchised, noted the *Newspaper* in its front-page leader, the
House of Commons would have to change its character entirely, and a new
reform bill of 'a far more radical and righteous' nature must be passed.[73]

The general election of 1868, held under the provisions of the new Reform
Act, dominated the opinion columns of the *Newspaper* in that year. Readers
were warned that the future would depend on the kind of candidates returned
to the House of Commons. 'This is the giant folly – ,' the first leader declared
in August,

> the monstrous crime and iniquity of our country – that the toiling,
> industrious, wealth-creating millions should be destitute of the
> necessaries of life, while the most idle, the most worthless and
> contemptible part of the community are wallowing in a sea of
> superfluous luxuries. But this stupendous scandal is certain to
> be continued, if not extended, unless the next House of Commons
> contains a band of resolute democratic members, who will
> fearlessly maintain that the rights of the people are as sacred as
> the rights of royalty, and that the poorest man or woman in the
> Kingdom is as well entitled to life and liberty, food and raiment,
> decent dwelling and mental and moral development, as any of
> the sons or daughters of Queen Victoria.[74]

The *Newspaper* promoted certain candidates who were seen as solid friends
of the people. Charles Bradlaugh, an iconoclastic radical standing for
Parliament for the first time, was, not surprisingly, a particular favorite.[75]
Up until the election itself, the *Newspaper* urged its readers to use the
opportunity they had been given, inadequate though it was, to affect the
composition of the next Parliament. The *Newspaper*'s rhetoric had not
abated: Gracchus warned readers that

> The industrious bees are being destroyed by the drones. Royal,
> clerical, and aristocratic leeches are all at one time busily sucking
> at the veins of the people, and, vampire-like, drawing their life-
> blood. Let the working classes, then, bestir themselves at once,
> and endeavour to return for their representatives, not your milk-
> and-water Liberals, who are loud in their protestations of
> devotedness to the throne, the constitution, and other such
> antiquated institutions, but men devoted to the welfare of the
> commonwealth; and who would not hesitate to sweep away, like
> cobwebs, all those abuses that militate against its best interests.[76]

The people now had the chance to send men to Parliament who would
represent them, rather than rob them: 'The people have been robbed with
the sanction of law, and by permission of legislation up till now; but now
they have the means of making just and equitable laws, and if they do not

use the opportunity, they will be robbed again by their own consent.'[77] Although only a fraction of them were now enfranchised, the people should organize into a national electioneering league, with the sole purpose of advancing republican candidates.[78] Unless twenty such candidates be elected, the *Newspaper* warned, the reform bill would turn out to be a failure and a farce.[79]

But the outcome of the election was an extreme disappointment. 'Whenever the working class have put up a candidate,' the *Newspaper* noted sourly, 'they have been thwarted by so-called Liberals.' While some members of the growing middle classes might be true Liberals, and so true friends of the people, most were not.[80] The people might have some friends whose honor and loyalty had been proven over time, but they could trust no one but themselves.[81]

The Reform Act of 1867, an advance though it might be, had been proven insufficient to bring about real change. Too much power was still in the hands of the aristocracy and landowners. The secret ballot proposal of 1871 was therefore greeted with real joy. The ballot was necessary, the *Newspaper* stated, because it 'will destroy the power of the landlords and creditors to coerce, and it will defeat the corrupt desires of the man willing to buy a place in the House of Commons.' It would still, however, be inadequate to make the representatives of the people truly *of* the people. For that to come about, payment of members would be required.[82]

The Secret Ballot Act of 1872 was hailed as a real advance toward republicanism, but the *Newspaper* continued to press for payment of Members of Parliament. Until a bill authorizing such payment was enacted into law, no working-class representatives could afford to stand for election; the House of Commons could not, therefore, be a truly representative body. That was what Reynolds and his *Newspaper* had been pressing for from the beginning; they would continue to do so until their goal was reached.

On the twenty-eighth anniversary of the last great Chartist demonstration in 1848, The *Times* noted with pleasure that there had been no great public ceremony to mark the date; there were, it seemed clear, no more Chartists. The *Newspaper* scoffed at The *Times*'s foolishness. The tenth of April, it proclaimed, was still an auspicious date, for it marked the beginning of a period of agitation which had led to great reform. If there were no more Chartists as a recognizable body agitating for reform, that was because most Chartist reforms had been achieved.[83] Now that most of the means of societal change had been realized, change itself was the goal. It was true that there were no more Chartist agitations, but that did not mean that the philosophy which had taken the name of Chartism had ceased to exist. Chartists, noted the *Newspaper,* were now called republicans, but, whatever they were called, they sought the same thing: equal representation, equal justice, and equal opportunity before the law.[84]

Reynolds's political outlook had remained essentially consistent over the preceding decades. If there had been significant changes over that time, as he acknowledged there had, the underlying idea behind those changes had been that the extension of the franchise to portions of the working classes was the extension of a privilege, rather than of a right. Reynolds rejected this idea absolutely. If the working classes had to be educated to exercise their vote more intelligently, so be it. He and the *Newspaper* had been educating them, and would continue to do so. But however well or poorly informed they were, the franchise was their right as human beings. That idea of the necessity of universal manhood suffrage remained at the core of Reynolds's and the *Newspaper*'s public discourse. *The Times* might proclaim that there were no more Chartists, but that was because they misunderstood the word. A Chartist, in Reynolds's eyes, was more than a member of a body which took that name. He was, more broadly, a human being who tried to bring about political equality for all. To Reynolds, Chartism and republicanism were convenient names given to a common political philosophy of equality. In the narrowest practical political sense, Chartism as a formal movement might be dead; in its truest essence, however, at least as Reynolds presented it, and his readers understood it, Chartism would never die.

NOTES

1   Chartism is less the name of a coherent political movement than it is a term of convenience applied to the various protest movements of the 1830s and 1840s which espoused the People's Charter, a petition which Chartists presented – or attempted to present – to Parliament on a number of occasions. Its six points set out much of the radical agenda of the mid-Victorian era: annual parliaments, universal manhood suffrage, abolition of the property qualification for members of the House of Commons, the secret ballot, equal electoral districts, and payment of MPs.

2   Gareth Stedman Jones, *Languages of Class: Studies in English Working Class History, 1832–1982* (Cambridge: Cambridge University Press, 1983), pp. 102–3, 176–8; Jon Lawrence, 'Popular Radicalism and the Socialist Revival in Britain,' *Journal of British Studies,* 31 (April 1992): p. 167.

3   Trygve R. Tholfsen, *Working Class Radicalism in Mid-Victorian England* (New York: Columbia University Press, 1977), p. 23.

4   Dorothy Thompson, *The Chartists: Popular Politics in the Industrial Revolution* (New York: Pantheon Books, 1984), pp. 319–20.

5   Reynolds tested the waters before beginning the *Newspaper* with *Reynolds's Political Instructor,* which ran from 10 November 1849 to 11 May 1850. The final issue of the *Political Instructor* began with the following announcement: 'THE POLITICAL INSTRUCTOR was intended as the pilot-balloon sent forth to test the political atmosphere, preparatory to a more important venture. The experiment has met with an unexampled success; and I am therefore emboldened to embark at once upon the grander venture. ... [T]hose who have admired the spirit in which [the *Political Instructor*] has been conducted and the varied democratic talents that were united in the supply of its contents will find the same recommendations in the columns of my WEEKLY NEWSPAPER.' RPI, 11 May 1850.

6   The *Beehive* was political in its focus, but it was neither as widely distributed as was the *Newspaper,* nor did it print such a wide variety of news.

7   Thomas Wright, *Our New Masters* (London: Strahan, 1873), p. 334

8   Ibid., p. 346.

9   RN, 7 May 1950.

10 In 1871, this group included at least one Cambridge undergraduate, who wrote to say that all of the Cambridge working classes and seven-eighths of the student body opposed any grant of public monies to the Princess Louise. RN, 2 July 1871.

11 Stedman Jones, 'Rethinking Chartism,' in *Languages of Class:* p. 104.

12 Of course, it is likely that, while Reynolds certainly welcomed readers from the 'establishment,' he recognized that the bulk of his readership came from the ranks of the politically disadvantaged.

13 Alvar Ellegard, *The Readership of the Periodical Press in Mid-Victorian Britain* (Göteborg: Göteborgs Universitets Årsskrift, 1957), p. 20.

14 RN, 27 February, 27 March, 17 April, 22 May, 24 July, 28 August, 11 September 1870.

15 Circulation continued to increase into the next century, reaching a maximum of over 1,000,000 just before the First World War. It experienced a slow decline thereafter, falling to 730,000 in its hundredth year. *Co-Operative News,* 22 April 1950.

16 Elizabeth Long, 'Textual Interpretation as Collective Action,' in Jon Cruz and Justin Lewis, eds., *Viewing, Reading, Listening: Audiences and Cultural Reception* (Boulder: Westview Press, 1994), p. 196.

17 RN, 13 July 1862.

18 RN, 7 May 1950.

19 *Newspaper Stamp Committee Report,* 1851, Q.1364.

20 R.K. Webb, *The British Working Class Reader, 1790–1848: Literacy and Social Tension* (London: George Allen and Unwin, 1955), p. 34; Raymond Williams, *The Long Revolution,* rev. edn. (New York: Harper, 1966), p. 193. Some members of the clergy did not consider the habit of reading in pubs to be a beneficial one. The Reverend Thomas Spencer, testifying before the Newspaper Stamp Committee, claimed that it led to alcoholism: 'I know, myself, the cases of men who never would have been drunkards but for going to the public-houses to read the newspaper ... that is the case with the working-classes all over the kingdom. They go to the gin-shop, or the beer-shop, or the public-house; they have no [other] opportunity, generally, of getting at the news, and besides that, there are other inducements to make the news pleasanter there; there is a good deal of society, and lighted rooms, and the bribe of the news of the day, which news comes to them in a most garbled form; and when they are in liquor, and have spent their money and made fools of themselves, and angry with society, and are ready to entertain the most desperate feelings against any class, and against any government, and therefore all pot-house politics are the most dangerous of all.' *Report of the Newspaper Stamp Committee,* 30 May 1851, Q.2364.

21 Charles Booth, ed., *Life and Labour of the People in London,* vol. 1, 2nd edn (London: Williams and Norgate, 1899), p. 99. RN, 4 March 1855. At least one Welsh political club later in the century preferred *Reynolds's* to a local publication: in 1891 the Aberystwyth Junior Radical Club discontinued their subscription to the *Baner ac Amserau Cymru* in favor of *Reynolds's Newspaper.* Aled Jones, *Press, Politics and Society: a History of Journalism in Wales,* (Cardiff: University of Wales Press, 1993), p. 111. For a discussion of pubs as

centers of working-class political debate, see Brian Harrison, 'Pubs,', pp. 179–80, in H.J. Dyas and Michael Wolff, eds, *The Victorian City: Images and Realities*, Vol. 1 (London: Routledge and Kegan Paul, 1973), pp. 161–90.

22   W.H. Smith, when testifying before the Newspaper Stamp Committee in June, 1851, said that the total circulation of the morning and evening London newspapers combined was roughly 60,000 daily, as compared to a total Sunday newspaper circulation of 275,000. *Newspaper Stamp Committee Report*, 1851, Q.2935–6. Raymond Williams estimated that in 1850, while one adult in eighty might read a daily paper, one adult in twenty would read a Sunday paper. Raymond Williams, *Communications*, rev. edn (London: Chatto and Windus, 1966), p. 23. Given a total adult population of nine million in England and Wales in 1851, Williams's estimate was low, especially if each paper sold had five readers. In any case, the Sunday newspapers remained popular among the working classes. Edward G. Salmon, writing for the journal *The Nineteenth Century* in 1886, said 'The working classes concern themselves little about any newspapers save those issued on the Sabbath.' *The Nineteenth Century*, 20 (July 1886): 109.

23   Natalie Zemon Davis, 'Printing and the People,' *Society and Culture in Early Modern France* (Stanford: Stanford University Press, 1975), p. 192.

24   Long, 'Textual Interpretation as Collective Action,' p. 196.

25   RN, 29 April 1906. The Tramp Socialist's description of the reading aloud of *Reynolds's Newspaper* as one might read 'Holy Writ' mirrors the role played by the psalms in monastic worship. As Kathleen Norris has noted, 'To say or sing the psalms aloud within a community is to recover religion as an oral tradition, restoring to our mouths words that have been snatched from our tongues and relegated to the page, words that have been privatized and effectively silenced. It counters our tendency to see individual experience as sufficient for formulating a vision of the world.' Kathleen Norris, *The Cloister Walk* (New York: Riverhead Books, 1996), p. 100. Interpretation of the text of the *Newspaper* was very much a collective action, in which the readers and listeners reinforced and refined their understanding of the world and the word.

26   For a general treatment of Reynolds, his *Newspaper*, and his politics, see Michael H. Shirley, *On Wings of Everlasting Power: G.W.M. Reynolds and Reynolds's Newspaper, 1848–1876*, Ph.D. diss., University of Illinois, 1997. The best strictly biographical information about Reynolds is contained in Louis James and John Savile, 'G.W.M. Reynolds' in Joyce Bellamy and John Saville, eds, *Dictionary of Labour Biography*, vol. 3 (London: Macmillan, 1976), pp. 146–51. See also the entry on Reynolds in the *Dictionary of National Biography*, written by Ramsay MacDonald. The most valuable short discussions of Reynolds in terms of his politics are Rohan McWilliam, 'The Mysteries of G. W. M. Reynolds: Radicalism and Melodrama in Victorian Britain' in Malcolm Chase and Ian Dyck, eds., *Living and Learning: Essays in Honour of J. F. C. Harrison* (Aldershot: Scolar Press, 1996), pp. 182–98; Anne Humpherys, 'G.W.M. Reynolds: Popular Literature and Popular Politics,' *Victorian Periodicals Review* XVI (Fall & Winter 1983); pp. 79–89; and Humpherys, 'Popular Narrative and Political Discourse in *Reynolds's Weekly Newspaper*,' in *Investigating Victorian Journalism*, ed. Laurel Brake, Aled Jones, and Lionel Madden (New York: St Martin's Press, 1990), pp. 33–47.

27   RN, 11 July 1875.

28   Margot C. Finn, *After Chartism: Class and Nation in English Radical Politics, 1848–1874* (Cambridge: Cambridge University Press, 1993), pp. 6–7. See also *Patrick Joyce, Visions of the People: Industrial England and the Question*

of Class, 1848–1914 (Cambridge: Cambridge University Press, 1991), p. 11.
29 R.G. Gammage, *History of the Chartist Movement, 1837–1854* (London: Merlin Press, 1894; Facsimile Ed., 1976), p. 9.
30 Stedman Jones, *Languages of Class*, p. 100.
31 Neville Kirk, 'In Defence of Class: a Critique of Recent Revisionist Writing Upon the Nineteenth-Century English Working Class' *International Review of Social History* XXXII (1987): p. 5.
32 Tholfsen, *Working Class Radicalism*, p. 86.
33 Lawrence, 'Popular Radicalism', p. 186.
34 RPI, 5 January 1850.
35 RN, 13 July 1856. This statement was a bit more restrained than was a headline of 1864: 'Hereditary Incapables as Rulers – England Endangered by Royal and Aristocratic Noodles.' RN, 24 July 1864.
36 RN, 17 April 1859, 26 July 1857.
37 RN, 26 February 1854.
38 RN, 18 April 1852.
39 RN, 7 June 1863. Northumbrian was one of two regular columnists – Gracchus was the other – for the *Newspaper.*
40 In response to several train crashes, Reynolds did suggest one use for 'spare princes and nobles'. He proposed that they ride excursion trains on a regular basis, which would inspire the government to make sure the trains were safe. RN, 18 June 1865.
41 The 'sybarites of the west-end', Reynolds claimed, needed a new 'sensation.' RN, 15 June 1862.
42 RPI, 16 February 1849.
43 RN, 5 December 1852.
44 RN, 2 October 1859.
45 RN, 3 June 1860.
46 RPI, 12 January 1850. 'The power and grandeur of the British aristocracy is founded upon the degradation of the rest of the community.' RN, 5 March 1854.
47 RN, 30 August 1868.
48 RN, 6 August 1854, 15 June 1851.
49 RN, 7 June 1863. Gracchus would later write that the 'triumph of Republicanism in France would foreshadow its triumph over nearly all Europe.' RN, 9 January 1870.
50 RN, 2 November 1862. The fact that Greece chose to continue as a monarchy in 1863 was not a cause for celebration.
51 RN, 28 July 1850.
52 RPI, 17 November 1849.
53 RN, 26 June 1864.
54 This paper will not discuss the *Newspaper*'s attitude toward the reform bills of 1884 and 1885, as Reynolds died in 1879.
55 RN, 12 May 1850.
56 Harold Perkin, *The Origins of Modern English Society, 1780–1880* (Toronto: University of Toronto Press, 1969), p. 319.
57 RN, 9 August 1857.
58 RN, 28 October 1866.
59 RN, 22 January 1865. Gracchus was the pseudonymous author of a weekly opinion piece which appeared in the *Newspaper* almost from its inception. Samuel Kydd was the first Gracchus, but soon left and was at some point

replaced by G.W.M. Reynolds's younger brother Edward. Edward Reynolds continued to write the Gracchus column until his death in 1894.

60 RN, 6 March 1864.
61 RN, 23 January 1859.
62 RN, 5 February 1860.
63 RN, 15 April 1860.
64 RN, 13 May 1860.
65 RN, 17 June 1860.
66 RN, 28 January 1866.
67 RN, 28 April 1867.
68 RN, 1 April 1866.
69 RN, 14 April 1867.
70 RN, 9 June 1867.
71 RN, 30 August 1868.
72 Rohan McWilliam is correct when he states that Reynolds and the *Newspaper* 'welcomed' the 1867 reform bill, but it should be noted that welcoming something does not mean being content with it. Reynolds welcomed the reform bill as a step on the road to complete reform, and not as a final destination. McWilliam, 'The Mysteries of G.W.M. Reynolds,' p. 191.
73 RN, 21 July 1867. The rate-paying clause came in for heavy criticism. Under the reform bill, tenants would have to pay at the full rate, whereas before they might have been compensated. This regressive clause, the *Newspaper* noted, was designed to impoverish those in the working classes who might wish to exercise their newly granted right. While the increase in the number of working-class voters looked good, the rate-paying clause might result in a decrease in that number, as workers sought to move to poorer lodgings to keep from paying such rates. RN, 8 December 1867.
74 RN, 2 August 1868.
75 For a discussion of Charles Bradlaugh's career, see Walter L. Arnstein, *The Bradlaugh Case: a Study in Late Victorian Opinion and Politics* (Oxford: Oxford University Press, 1965). A paperback and hardback reprint with a new postscript chapter was published as *The Bradlaugh Case: Atheism, Sex, and Politics Among the Late Victorians* (Columbia, MO: University of Missouri Press, 1984).
76 RN, 13 September 1868.
77 RN, 20 September 1868.
78 RN, 28 June 1868.
79 RN, 14 June 1868. Reynolds himself thought of standing, and announced that he would pay his own expenses if he did so, but he finally decided not to do it. RN, 1 March 1868.
80 RN, 1 December 1867.
81 RN, 1 November 1868.
82 RN, 26 February 1871.
83 Reynolds was overstating the case, as he was wont to do. While the electorate had been expanded, only two of the six goals of the Charter had been achieved by 1876: the secret ballot and the end of property requirement for MPs. With these goals achieved, however, and with reform seemingly moving forward, he likely felt that he had cause to be optimistic.
84 RN, 23 April 1876.

CHAPTER 7

'A Whig Private Secretary is in itself fatal': Benjamin Disraeli, Lord Derby, Party Politics and Naval Administration, 1852

John Beeler

Accounts of the brief Derby Ministry of 1852, Benjamin Disraeli's first taste of public office, have typically stressed the precariousness of the government's existence, his patch-work Budget for 1853–54, and the epic debate which greeted the latter, a debate which, in Lord Blake's words, marked 'the beginning of the great parliamentary duel which for twenty-eight years was to be a feature of English public life ... .'[1] In this context, his relations with the Admiralty during the Government's eleven-month existence appear relatively unimportant. Yet just as the budget debate marked the emergence of the 'great rivalry' with Gladstone, so would Disraeli's problems with the Navy's administration in 1852 set the tenor for his subsequent dealings with the service in 1858–59, 1866–68, and, to a lesser extent, 1874–80.

Most obviously, Tory attempts to manipulate Admiralty political patronage in the dockyards soured Disraeli's relations with the officers who oversaw those establishments–in particular Surveyor of the Navy Sir Baldwin Wake Walker–and instilled in him a deprecatory attitude towards naval professionals which persisted for the rest of his life. Ancillary to this situation, inklings of the clash of political and service motives subsequently surfaced in Parliament and the press and, following the fall of the Tories, generated a House of Commons inquiry which ruined the political career of Admiralty Parliamentary Secretary Augustus Stafford and subjected Disraeli and Derby to public embarrassment.

The 1852 struggle with the Admiralty, however, is illustrative of several larger issues of policy and partisanship faced by British politicians, especially the Conservatives, during the 1840–90 period. Indeed, the events of 1852 provide a paradigm not only for Disraeli's own attitudes towards the Navy and national/imperial security issues, but also for the conflicting impulses which helped shape Conservative naval policy during the next three administrations, and beyond them, into the Salisbury era. Finally, the dockyards patronage scandal furnishes a valuable lens through which to view the difficulties which confronted the Conservatives in constructing the 1852 Ministry and the extent to which party affiliations, whether based on ideology or family connections, still pervaded the Civil Service.

To address the last of these points first, the Board of Admiralty which served during the 1852 Ministry was a recalcitrant body, one which, if the surviving evidence is indicative, rarely bent to the will of Prime Minister Derby and Chancellor of the Exchequer and Tory Commons leader Disraeli. The root of the problem was the First Lord, the Cabinet member responsible for naval administration. Derby's choice for the office fell on Algernon Percy, fourth Duke of Northumberland (1792–1865), whose interests were more scientific and antiquarian than political.[2] His chief claim to office, indeed, lay in his background as a naval officer, although he had seen no active service since 1815. Derby and Disraeli appear to have regarded the Duke as a cipher, a figurehead for the Board who would furnish the necessary appearance of gravitas but remain their compliant tool.

The Duke did not play along. Derby gave him a free hand in choosing the naval officers who would comprise the professional element of the Board, specifying only that any M.P.s among them support 'the general policy of the Govt.'[3] The Duke selected Rear Admiral Sir Hyde Parker (First Naval Lord), Rear Admiral Phipps Hornby (Second Naval Lord), Captain Sir Thomas Herbert (Third Naval Lord), and Captain Alexander Milne (Junior Naval Lord). Of the four, Hornby and Herbert were reliable Tories. Milne, however, had served on the Board since 1847, having been appointed by Lord John Russell's Government. He came to the Admiralty on the specific understanding that he be excused from dealing with party political matters.[4] Yet, as an anonymous memorandum to Disraeli stressed, Milne was 'on most friendly terms' with Whig former First Lord Sir Francis Baring and 'leans strongly to their views.'[5]

Even more fraught was the situation regarding Parker who, like Milne, 'professe[d] to have no politics,' but all of whose 'associates [were] Whigs.'[6] These associates included Parker's brother-in-law, Captain Henry Eden (1797–1888), a cousin of the Whig First Lord of the Admiralty Lord Auckland (1784–1849), whose Private Secretary Eden had been from 1846 to 1848. Parker's own private secretary, moreover, was a son of Admiral Maurice Frederick Fitz-Hardinge Berkeley (1788–1867), himself one of seven sons of the high Whig Frederick Augustus, fifth Earl of Berkeley, three of whom in addition to Maurice were MPs during the early and mid-nineteenth century. All but one of the three, and Sir Maurice as well, were self-described 'Reformers' or 'Liberals;' the remaining brother was a 'Protectionist Whig.'[7] Northumberland's own Private Secretary, Captain

Frederick Thomas Pelham (1808–61) was a brother of the moderate Whig third Earl of Chichester, and Northumberland himself was married to Lady Eleanor of the Whig Grosvenor family, a sister of Hugh, third Marquis and first Duke of Westminster.[8] Last, but by no means least, Surveyor Walker, like Milne, was a Whig appointee and, again like Milne, his friends–among them Sir Francis Baring and Sir Maurice Berkeley–were Whigs.[9]

This unpromising political situation greeted Stafford on his appointment as Parliamentary Secretary to the Admiralty in early March 1852, and it was most likely he who drafted the memorandum to Disraeli on the party affiliations of the Board members and their secretaries, a memorandum which ended with the unmistakable warning that those affiliations, 'coupled with a host of subordinates both at the Admiralty, & holding situations at the various Dock Yards, adverse to & very active against, the present Government, is seriously undermining their legitimate influence, & decisive steps should be taken to put an end to it without loss of time.'[10]

By the end of March circumstances had persuaded Derby to intervene with Northumberland. The Prime Minister claimed he was 'the last man who would desire to interfere with the exercise' of the Duke's patronage and even further deprecated the idea that the First Lord should 'again introduce that system of political jobbing for which the late Board of Admiralty was so eminently distinguished.' Still, he was obliged to remind Northumberland that however much he 'may desire the strictest impartiality in the distribution of Naval employment,' it was impossible to ignore protests from the party faithful in the House of Commons that even minor positions 'have been given to our political opponents.' Hence, the Prime Minister lectured, 'we cannot ... conceal from ourselves that the exercise of the Patronage of the Admiralty is an instrument which according to our form of Govt. is expected to be used, & *must* be used, to a certain degree, in furtherance of Political objects ... .' Although Derby admitted he knew of no specific cases to support the charges of Tory MPs, he added that the Duke must not leave them out of his calculations, and closed with the admonition 'that the doctrine of political impartiality *may* be applied to an extent dangerous to the party which adopts it and (*without reciprocity*) ultimately prejudicial to the interests of the Country.'[11] Northumberland's reply to this homily does not survive, but it prompted from Derby a further missive, assuring the First Lord that he 'had no wish to *taboo* any officer or convert the Admiralty promotion into a Political Engine ... .' Yet again he stressed that 'a turn is due to political connexion,' less for the sake of the appointees themselves, than for 'those whom his appointment gratify [*sic*].' To make his point unmistakable, Derby also passed along two patronage requests from a Tory MP.[12]

Stafford was working in the same direction at the same time, for according to Walker the former's private secretary approached him at the end of March attempting to block promotions in Devonport Dockyard 'as Mr. Stafford's Political Friends were dissatisfied, [and] he wished to promote some of their party ... .'[13] Walker was central to the bestowal of dockyard patronage because a Board Minute of 1849 mandated that recommendations for advancement in the yards be sent by the superintendents to the surveyor, in order that promotions might be made on the basis of merit alone, a principle established by an earlier Admiralty circular. Stafford's response to the impasse presented by the surveyor's refusal to 'commence jobbing' on behalf of the Tories was first to write a private letter to him (3 April 1852) reiterating Tory complaints that 'there is a general impression that all those things [i.e., dockyard appointments and promotions] are dispensed among political opponents' and threatening to 'resume the system which existed previous to September 1849.'[14] His second act was to issue a circular on 19 April directing dockyard superintendents to forward 'all Reports and Correspondence on the subject of vacancies, promotions or changes of the Officers and Workmen of the Dock Yards' to the Secretary of the Admiralty–Stafford–rather than to the Surveyor. This action was taken in the name of the Board, but was in fact done without the knowledge of a single Naval Lord or, for that matter, Walker, who only learned of it through the superintendents to whom it had been sent directly.[15]

A man of touchy pride, Walker took the circular as a personal reproach and, on 21 April, wrote a letter of resignation addressed to the Secretary. Before delivering it, however, he showed it to First Naval Lord Parker, his immediate superior, who promised he would bring it before the Board. Instead, he apprised Northumberland of its contents. Accounts vary as to what happened next, but the upshot was that Stafford met Walker privately in an attempt to smooth the latter's ruffled feathers. The former subsequently issued a further circular (26 April 1852) which stated that 'no imputation' was 'intended to be cast...upon the Surveyor of the Navy' by the Minute of 19 April. Walker remained in his job and Parker destroyed the letter of resignation without ever having brought it before the whole Board.[16]

Stafford's clarification mollified the Surveyor's sense of honor but, as subsequent events revealed, it left unresolved the underlying issue of dockyard appointments. The Secretary had already (5 April) overruled the superintendent of Chatham dockyard by promoting one Joseph Ridgway at the behest of Sir Frederic Smith, Tory candidate for the borough who 'represented ... that Ridgway was kept out of his just promotion on account of his political opinions ... .' [17] Moreover, according to Sir Benjamin Hall, who pushed for the appointment of the Select Committee to investigate the matter, between 19 April and 30 June some fifty-seven men were added to the dockyard work force, whereas only seven had been entered in the three preceding months. Hall also charged that several men had been 'discharged without any reason' from the dockyard establishments in order to make room for Tory partisans.[18] Such actions prompted Walker to write to

Northumberland on 10 May. The Surveyor adduced to numerous evils which he claimed followed from the cancellation of the 1849 Minute, among them the fact that 'vacancies have been filled up which were not necessary, and men advanced not for merit, but by political influence,–and in one instance a person [Ridgway] has been promoted who is not competent to fill the situation to which he has been appointed ... .'[19]

Yet at the same time Northumberland was being urged by Walker to adhere to the system of merit promotion, partisan pressure was being brought to bear by others. Stafford complained to Derby on 3 May that he had repeatedly tried to get the Duke to sign a paper authorizing the transfer of patronage disbursements 'from his hands to mine as I am in the H. of C. and in daily ... communication there with the friends of the present Government.'[20] Northumberland had thus far refused to sign Stafford's paper, and the Secretary maintained 'that the present dispensation of Admiralty patronage is exceedingly unsatisfactory, I must add irritating, to your [Derby's] political adherents ... .' Were this warning not sufficient, Stafford added that 'the elections of your supporters in some instances are [im]perilled' and closed with the admonition 'that one political favour conferred now is worth a dozen a month later and that in a short time it will be too late to do anything.'

This missive prompted Derby to address himself to Northumberland a third time. Again he stressed the 'great dissatisfaction' which existed among Tories 'at the manner in which Admiralty patronage has been exercised since we came into office.' Again, too, he expressed the pious wish 'that in conducting the affairs of a Government, there was no such thing as Patronage ... .' Yet 'I fear we must take the world as we find it, and be content, more especially just before a General Election, to make use of the power of giving appointments for the purpose of gratifying and strengthening our political supporters ... .' Derby also made clear that he considered the Duke's closest advisor suspect. 'I have no doubt that Captn Pelham[,] your Private Secretary[,] is a highly honorable man, but I hear that his political opinions are decidedly Whiggish and that unconsciously to him they may bias him in the cases which he has to lay before you[.]' Such being the case, and since he was 'sure' the First Lord had neither time nor inclination to deal with such matters, 'I must be permitted to express a hope that as far as possible you will allow Stafford to deal with these petty appointments, and to seek for the means of gratifying and encouraging our supporters[.]'[21]

Again, Northumberland remonstrated with his superior. Since coming to the Admiralty, he informed Derby, he had awarded five cadetships, appointed one clerk and one messenger, and promoted two commanders.[22] Four of the first had been recommended by or were related to Tory supporters and the fifth had been passed to a Captain Davis via Civil Lord Arthur Duncombe. Furthermore, Stafford 'expressed his satisfaction' at the man chosen for clerk, and one of the two commanders was 'son of Sir J Hope well known to be Conservative.' Thus, 'I think your informant has been unjust.' On the subject of dockyard appointments the Duke was openly defiant:

> Mr. Stafford tried the appointment of a Political appointment in Chatham Dockyard; and as I feared that a continuance would do injury to the Service, and damage the Government in the public estimation if the principle of reward for merit was abandoned, and reward for political votes substituted, that I offered to give up my patronage [naval cadets and promotions, and the Admiralty office staff] to Mr. Stafford as a substitute.

According to the First Lord, Stafford accepted his offer, and even produced a memorandum 'to say what Patronage he wished, & thus the matter was concluded.'[23]

If so, there was a decided misunderstanding between First Lord and Parliamentary Secretary as to the terms of the bargain, for Stafford neither ceased making appointments and promotions in the dockyards on the basis of partisanship, nor ceased complaining that Northumberland continued to use the remaining patronage at his disposal to appoint Whigs.[24] On 2 July Stafford wrote both Derby and Disraeli inveighing against the appointment of Captain Stephen Lushington to a ship's command, claiming the Captain's 'politics are those of his family and his past services nothing. in [sic] short he is reckoned an inefficient officer.'[25] Worse still, he had, Stafford charged, previously served under Baldwin Walker and was the son-in-law of Admiral Henry Prescott, 'A Whig Lord of the Admiralty and now a strong opponent of ours as Superintendent at Portsmouth.' In short, '[s]uch an appointment at such a moment is about the worst thing that could have happened,' and he urged Derby to write the Duke to postpone announcing the appointment until after the General Election. To Disraeli, Stafford added that the appointment, if publicized, 'would spread like wildfire thro' our dockyard towns' and would 'exercise considerable influence upon the elections there as elsewhere.' 'As this is the way of patronage,' he concluded plaintively, 'all I can do is hopeless ... . All the old clerks in the office are laughing at us ... .'[26] Disraeli was sufficiently alarmed by Stafford's news to write Derby himself, warning it would be 'quite impossible to secure a single dockyard return' in the impending election: 'We shall lose Devonport and Greenwich, as we have already lost Portsmouth.'[27] But Northumberland, when queried about the appointment, replied that Lushington had been chosen 'principally because I was told that he was a sure Tory.' The First Lord's information came from Tory Board members Herbert and Hornby, 'and was said to be certain, otherwise Captain Lushington is not an officer I would have selected.'[28] Indeed, the Duke stressed that he had chosen the Captain over 'every strong remonstrance against him by Captain Pelham,' prompting Derby to complain to Disraeli 'Stafford ought to be quite sure of his facts before he asks for interference.'[29] Derby's 'interference,' whether misdirected or not, apparently had a salutary effect, at least from Stafford's perspective, for within a few days of the fracas over Lushington the Parliamentary Secretary cryptically informed Disraeli that he had extracted what he wanted and that there was no longer any nonsense from the Duke 'about regulations &c but that—'the wine he drinks is made of grapes' like other peoples and that what Lord Derby and you did is working admirably ... .'[30]

The respite was short-lived. By the end of July Stafford was again writing Disraeli to complain that although he had submitted to plans to ensure the Conservatives winning Devonport and Plymouth in the next election, he was 'afraid Pelham and the Surveyor of the Navy will be too much for me.'[31] In this assessment Stafford evidently saw eye-to-eye with the Prime Minister, for the latter remarked to Disraeli in the midst of the Lushington incident, that although he had written to the Duke he doubted beneficial results 'as long as his entourage is such as it is. A Whig Private Secretary is in itself fatal, and Sir Baldwin Walker, I am afraid, exercises a very mischievous influence.'[32]

The situation deteriorated still further as summer gave way to fall. Stafford spent much of August and September inspecting naval facilities in the Mediterranean, but upon his return he discovered that First Lord Parker had 'been ordering some appointments in the Dockyards' which, if implemented, would 'supplant and at all events appear to deceive our staunchest supporters at Woolwich and Chatham.'[33] Any attempt to block appointments, however, would antagonize the First Naval Lord, who 'swears and damns that he will not give way and is going to appeal to Alnwick [Northumberland's country seat] where our Doge [Stafford's nickname for the Duke] is to be for the next ten days.' A few days later Stafford alerted Disraeli to a lengthy missive he had sent to Northumberland protesting at his treatment by the Naval Lords.[34] The Secretary's covering letter bore alarming news. Not only he but Herbert and Duncombe sought a joint audience with Disraeli to present their message: 'Pelham must go.'[35] Disraeli in turn repeated the news to Derby following his meeting with the Board members:

> I am very harassed about the Admiralty, [and] have come up to town today in consequence of a most serious [situation] there. Stafford, Duncombe, & now Herbert, alike announce that the system can go on no more, & that if Pelham does not resign, they must.
>
> Worse than all this, the mischief to the government is very great. I have soothed them, by coming up & seeing them but something must be done.[36]

Derby quite agreed that the impasse was likely to 'give us much trouble;

for the Duke will not like to give up his private Secretary, and we cannot afford the loss of our House of Commons men [Herbert and Duncombe].'[37] It was, however, 'a matter to be settled only in conversation,' so there is no means of discovering the method of its resolution. Certainly it was smoothed over without recourse to extreme measures, for on 9 October Stafford was able to report to Derby that 'affairs here are not quite as bad as they were' and that the Duke had even consented to having Pelham leave the room while Stafford was conversing with him.[38]

With the General Election past and the opening of Parliament approaching, the significance of patronage dwindled, only to be replaced with other worries.[39] Stafford was troubled by the Admiralty's relations with the Commander-in-Chief of the Mediterranean Squadron, Rear-Admiral James Deans Dundas (1785–1862), a former Liberal MP (1832–34, 1836–38, 1841–52) and Naval Lord (1841, 1846–52).[40] 'The Board,' Disraeli was informed in late September, 'seems inclined to teaze [sic] Adml Dundas into resignation.'[41] Were this course to be maintained, Stafford warned that Dundas 'will send all his papers to Lord John Russell and I assure you the correspondence of this precious Board ... will not bear day light.' The Secretary was thus 'anxious' to speak with Disraeli on the matter 'as soon as you come to town.' Slightly less than a month later Stafford alerted both Disraeli and Derby to the Board's orders that Dundas split up his squadron between Malta, Gibraltar, and Lisbon.[42] With Louis Napoleon having recently declared himself Emperor, and with '[t]he French Naval Force ... collecting at Toulon,' Stafford was convinced that 'our Fleet ought not to be divided' and that the Board's action 'seems to me so objectionable that I am obliged to trouble you on it[.]' He hoped, therefore, that Derby might nudge Northumberland back to his senses by 'expressing a hope that in any orders he may send out he will keep the Medn Fleet as much as possible together and as near Malta as possible.' Again he warned: 'if a blow up should come between Adml D[undas] and this Board, it would be most disastrous to us as we are clearly in the wrong.'

But the government's chief concern was money. In late August Northumberland informed Derby that he was 'anxious to have an enquiry into the Steam Engines of the Ships of the Navy, in order that we may keep pace with the times.'[43] Derby, presumably thinking it an innocuous request, approved appointment of a committee to examine mercantile steamships in the major commercial ports. On learning of the inquiry upon his return from the Mediterranean, Stafford immediately warned Disraeli that its cost, although officially estimated at £1,500, was more likely to be about £4,000, adding that he had written independently to Treasury Secretary George Hamilton in an attempt to withhold that department's sanction for the expense.[44] Hamilton obligingly followed Stafford's lead. The Parliamentary Secretary then proudly confessed to Derby his part in the scuttling operation, stressing that the Navy's

Accountant General 'tells me we have a very small margin of surplus and ought to be *most* careful for the remainder of the financial year.'[45]

Far larger financial problems soon appeared, however. Shortly after the Ministry's formation, Queen Victoria forwarded Derby 'a Memorandum respecting the necessity of attending to our national defences on a systematic plan.'[46] In late October she again prodded the Prime Minister on the subject, 'wish[ing] to hear how far we have advanced in this important object since that time' and asking for reports from the service chiefs. Three weeks later the Queen again urged that the Government's financial statement to Parliament stress 'our defenceless state, and the necessity of a *large* outlay, to protect us from foreign attack ... .'[47] Disraeli, in turn, had to assure the monarch that his budget contained 'a very large margin,' which would 'permit the fulfillment of all your Majesty's wishes with respect to the increased defence of the country ... .'[48] To this reply the Queen expressed 'much satisfaction,' but she reiterated that the need for adequate defensive arrangements was '*very* urgent.'

Nor was Victoria content to wait. Around 20 November Derby asked to meet with Disraeli 'on the subject of *immediate* Naval preparation, about which the Queen is very urgent.'[49] What the Queen and Prince Albert had in mind as regards the Navy was an immediate increase of 5,000 seamen and 1,500 Marines; personnel who would, of course, have to be paid, outfitted, and fed. Derby thought 'we want them, and might have them,' but wished to know whether the Chancellor of the Exchequer had assented to this 'immediate augmentation ... .' Disraeli quickly assured the Prime Minister that he had

> agreed to ... carry into effect the complete wishes of Her Majesty and the Prince ... with reference to defence ... I promised to do this, and, as far as I am concerned, I have done it. These arrangements include five thousand seamen and *two* thousand artillerymen ... . I have promised nothing about the Marines; the Prince never mentioned them or included them in his written memoranda.[50]

Derby, however, overruled Disraeli, insisting on the additional Marines.[51]

This confusion was exacerbated by the situation at the Admiralty, where Stafford complained to Northumberland that he was being kept in ignorance of the complexion of the Navy Estimates.[52] Despite being 'the person responsible in the House of Commons for every act of the Board and for the whole state of the Navy ... there seems some notion ... that there are some subjects upon which I ought to know nothing ... .' Hence, when the First Lord dispatched to Disraeli a 'comparative list of the English and French Navies,' Stafford, who learned from the Duke of this 'wonderful paper,' warned that 'I have never seen it' and thus the Chancellor of the

Exchequer 'must *not hold me responsible* for one word it contains.'[53] Nor did he, presumably still in the dark, give any intimation of the tenor of the Estimates until 30 November when the news gave Disraeli–on the verge of presenting his Budget in Parliament–a terrible shock: 'we have had no explanation from Stafford,' he wrote Derby, 'as to his letter ... that the navy Estimates for 1853–54 will be increased nearly one million.'[54]

To appreciate properly Disraeli's shock, it must be made clear that an additional £1 million would increase the Navy's budget some twenty percent over the previous year's £5 million.[55] The entire government, for that matter, spent only £54 million in 1852. 'I fear we are in a great scrape,' Disraeli warned his chief, 'and I hardly see how the Budget can live in so stormy a sea.'[56] He admitted that the Government 'was pledged to the Queen, as far as the seamen and Marines are concerned ... but I think you must exert your utmost authority that there shall be retrenchment, no matter at what inconvenience ... .' Derby wasted no time. The same day that Disraeli appealed to him he spoke with Stafford, 'and ... told him that ... the Navy Estimates for next year must not present an increase of more than £350,000, which is, in point of fact the expense of the addition we have made of 5000 Seamen and 1500 Marines ... .'[57] Moreover, the Prime Minister warned Disraeli 'we must back him against his Board, in cutting down extra expense,' again suggesting the divide at the Admiralty between Stafford and the Naval Lords, and between Stafford and Northumberland, as subsequent events revealed. On 3 December the former wrote Derby that the First Lord was '*furious* with me this morning and told me I had no business to cut down the Estimates without consulting him.'[58] But when Northumberland 'brought my conduct before the Board,' Stafford informed it 'that I had acted in obedience to your directions.' After that revelation the Lords 'listened very well ... .' Nonetheless, the Secretary hoped that Derby would "stand by me' when you next see him [the Duke] for I assure you I have much to put up with and while Pelham is here perpetually poisoning [his] mind against me I am almost in despair of being able to hold on.'

Thus in the end, the Estimates showed an increase of less than one-half million rather than double that figure, but there is no doubt that this augmentation figured heavily in the 'last-minute demands for increased expenditure on the armed services [which] caused [Disraeli] twice to recast his [Budget] figures,' the second time immediately following Stafford's revelation, and only three days prior to the presentation of the Budget.[59] The Budget, in turn, was subjected to a four-night debate, and to ultimate defeat. With it collapsed the Ministry. Disraeli's first experience of office had ended, and the Navy Estimates contributed much to the debacle.

While Disraeli was frantically calculating and recalculating his Budget figures, Stafford's earlier machinations in the Dockyards first surfaced in public, courtesy of none other that than Admiral Sir Maurice Berkeley, MP, who on 23 November 1852 rose to ask the Parliamentary Secretary

> Whether the present Board of Admiralty ... gave directions that
> the names of the workmen and artificers, recommended for
> promotion, were to be sent direct to the Secretary of the
> Admiralty instead of being first submitted to the Surveyor ... as
> had previously been the rule? Whether any correspondence took
> place with the Surveyor in consequence of such order ... Whether
> a Commission of officers was appointed to inquire into and
> report on steam ships [and] steam engines ... as applied to naval
> purposes; and the reason for such Commission separating
> without coming to any conclusion or making any report.[60]

Stafford's response was an elaborate prevarication; he deliberately
misunderstood the first question, and alluded to an unrelated Minute
promulgated in 1847 which, he assured his listeners, 'had not been disturbed
by the present Board of Admiralty.' There had been 'no correspondence
with the Surveyor on the subject.' And no, the Committee on Steam Engines
had not separated; rather, it had been discovered that the inquiry would
cost 'a greater sum ... than was desirable' and 'for that reason the
Committee' had ceased its labors, although 'it was in contemplation for
them to resume their functions.'[61]

   This effrontery did not go unchallenged. Baldwin Walker, unsurprisingly,
immediately took issue with Stafford's claim, and demanded that he 'call the
attention of the Lords Commissioners of the Admiralty to Letters from me'
of 21 April and 10 May.[62] Although this matter was technically resolved
when Walker learned that Hyde Parker had destroyed the first letter without
ever having shown it to Stafford (although the latter was undoubtedly aware
of Walker's threat), and that the second had been addressed to Northumberland
personally rather than the Board, the dockyard appointments situation burst
forth as a full-fledged scandal following an election petition by the defeated
candidate for Chatham. The House of Commons Committee on the disputed
election quickly discovered that there had been overt manipulation of the
dockyard patronage on behalf of Tory candidate Smith. So notorious was the
matter that Stafford himself rose in Parliament on 10 March 1852 and drew
its notice to 'a matter in which he was personally concerned.' The previous
day 'an influential morning paper' had charged that although 'In 1850 the
Admiralty had resigned the dangerous patronage of the dockyard at Chatham
into the hands of Baldwin Walker ... who had exercised it without regard to
politics, the Duke of Northumberland and Mr. Stafford last year took it from
him, burked his remonstrances addressed to the Board, and threw the patronage
back into the old corrupt channel, so far as actually to degrade the efficient
men selected by Sir Baldwin Walker, and put partisans into their places.'[63]
Stafford gave 'the most unqualified contradiction' to the charge, and begged

the Commons to 'postpone its judgment on the conduct of the late Board of Admiralty' until the Committee's report was issued.

He had not long to wait. The Chatham Election Committee concluded that Smith was 'not duly elected Burgess,' and that the contest at Chatham was 'a void election.'[64] There quickly followed Benjamin Hall's motion 'That a Select Committee be appointed to inquire into the circumstances under which a 'Circular sent to the Superintendent [sic] of Her Majesty's Dockyards, dated September 26th, 1849,' was cancelled on the 19th day of April, 1852, without any Order or Minute of the Board.' [65] In addition, Hall called for the Committee to investigate why Baldwin Walker's letter of resignation had never reached the Board, the circumstances surrounding one of Stafford's appointments in Portsmouth Dockyard, 'and generally into the exercise of the influence and patronage of the Admiralty in the Dockyards' after 19 April 1852. Hall's motion, after debate and minor amendment, was passed, and thus was created the Select Committee which brought about Stafford's downfall and caused Derby and Disraeli such embarrassment.

Several problems associated with Disraeli's relationship with the Admiralty in 1852 resurfaced in 1858–59, 1866–68, and 1874–80. First, mid-Victorian Conservative First Lords generally lacked the will or desire to rein in their Naval Lords, although neither John Pakington (1858–59, 1866–67) nor Henry Corry (1867–68) nor George Ward Hunt (1874–77) were as out of touch with the activities of their subordinates as Northumberland seems to have been.[66] To be sure, neither Derby nor, especially, Disraeli appointed men to the First Lordship with the intention of having them become mouthpieces for the Naval Lords, and in this respect Northumberland's tenure was indicative of a larger problem for the party: the lack of qualified leaders. This lack was glaringly obvious in 1852. It certainly diminished over time, but remained significant through to the end of Disraeli's second Ministry. True, the Admiralty was hardly a choice enough plum to go to a first-echelon politician, but so desperate were the Conservatives for suitable candidates that, despite the experience of 1852, Derby offered the First Lordship to Northumberland again in 1858, only to have the Duke refuse.[67] Pakington, Derby's second choice, was certainly a more competent administrator than Northumberland, but he was no less dominated by the Naval Lords than his predecessor had been. Indeed, the historic decision to build Britain's first sea-going ironclad, H.M.S. *Warrior*, was taken by the Board (at the insistence of Baldwin Walker) and presented to Pakington as a *fait accompli*. Additionally, both Disraeli and Derby 'distrusted Pakington, their own selection for the Admiralty, and behind his back claimed that he was urging large estimates to curry favour with the Navy,' a view shared by at least one other cabinet member.[68] Corry was, if anything, an even greater thorn in Disraeli's side than Northumberland and Pakington, for he was undoubtedly the most ardent navalist to serve as First Lord between 1852 and 1885. Ward Hunt may well have been the greatest disappointment (not to say frustration) for Disraeli. When at the Treasury (1866–68) he had been a staunch proponent of economy: when appointed to the Admiralty, he immediately became an even stronger advocate of naval efficiency.[69]

Related to lack of political control, naval funding, so contentious an issue between the Admiralty and Downing Street in the waning days of 1852, continued to be a source of acrimony during the three subsequent Tory administrations. Northumberland, Pakington, Corry, and Ward Hunt were all enthusiasts for naval 'efficiency' rather than its obverse, 'economy.' Disraeli, as Chancellor of the Exchequer in 1852, 1858–59, and for all but the final months of the 1866–68 Ministry, and then as Prime Minister thereafter, was a strong proponent of the latter. In his frequent struggles with the Admiralty over naval spending, therefore, the First Lords were opponents, siding with their professional advisors, rather than with the Government. If anything, in fact, the level of acrimony increased in 1858–59 and reached its peak in 1867 and 1868. Pakington's Board won an increase of half a million pounds in 1867 through the expedient of two of its members' threatened resignations were its demands not met. In an effort to forestall a similar occurrence the following year, Disraeli dictated the total figure for the Navy to Corry, only to have the Board prepare draft Estimates calling for another substantial jump in funding.[70] Ward Hunt also pushed for and won three straight years of significant increases in the Estimates during his tenure. Not for nothing did the fifteenth Earl of Derby warn newly-appointed Tory Chancellor of the Exchequer Sir Stafford Northcote in 1874 about 'the military and naval departments, which have destroyed every Conservative budget in my recollection ... .'[71]

The Liberals had no such shortage of zealous economizers, most notably Gladstone's trusted lieutenant, Hugh Childers (First Lord, 1868–71), but also Sir James Graham (1853–55), Sir Charles Wood (1855–58), Lord Northbrook (1880–85) and, to a lesser extent, George Joachim Goschen (1871–74). Among Conservative First Lords, only W. H. Smith (1877–80) exhibited enthusiasm for economy comparable to that of Childers, and among Liberals, only the Duke of Somerset (1859–66) rivalled his Conservative counterparts as an advocate of efficiency. Tory First Lords' inability to dominate their Boards extended beyond the Disraeli era, for that matter; the 1889 Naval Defence Act passed by Salisbury's Government was a result of professional zeal triumphing over the civilian head of the Board, although in this case the Naval Lords were much assisted by public sentiment whipped up by one of their erstwhile colleagues, Lord Charles Beresford.

Ironically, Disraeli was as committed to the Liberal principle of retrenchment as was his great rival Gladstone; the crucial difference between the two men was that the latter could depend on many subordinates who shared his conviction: Disraeli could not. No Conservative First Lord was comparable to Childers with regard to his control over the Naval Lords, nor was any, Smith excepted, capable of keeping a tight rein on spending.

There was additionally a fundamental divergence between Disraeli and Derby which persisted through all three of the latter's Governments. Derby lent more credence to popular fear of Louis Napoleon in 1852 than did Disraeli. This split surfaced again in 1858, when Derby created a Parliamentary Commission to investigate the strength and sufficiency of the Navy, and informed Disraeli '[w]e must have a naval preponderance over the French, however inconvenient the outlay may be, and however unreasonable the system on her part which forces on us corresponding efforts.'[72] In this instance, Disraeli's experience with Derby paralleled that of Gladstone when Chancellor of the Exchequer during Palmerston's final administration. Only in 1868 did Disraeli, then Chancellor of the Exchequer, manage to enlist Derby's support in quashing the Board's attempt to secure a second straight substantial jump in naval funding.

A third circumstance of the 1852 experience was paralleled again in a subsequent administration: that being Disraeli's reliance on a close associate at the Admiralty as a 'mole,' to keep him apprised of the machinations of the Naval Lords. In 1852 this role was of course Stafford's; in 1866–68 it went to Lord Henry Lennox, who continually provided his friend with detailed descriptions of the Board's intentions and with ways of thwarting or circumventing them.[73] As for the motives for planting a spy at the Admiralty–presumably not the original reason for selecting Stafford–the presence of Lennox there in 1866–68 suggests one further result of Disraeli's first encounter with naval administration: a deep distrust of professionals and their assessments of national security requirements.

In this respect most of Disraeli's wrath in 1852 was directed at Baldwin Walker. His opinion of the Surveyor was by 1858 even more hostile: 'The Admiralty is governed by Sir B. Walker,' he wrote Derby, 'who has neither talents, nor science–& as I believe–nor honor–but the last is suspicion, the first are facts.' Certainly the Surveyor's central role in bringing to light the dockyard appointments scandal–not to mention implicating Disraeli and Derby in it through his testimony–generated much of this animus, but Disraeli's critique of Walker went beyond personal pique: '[h]e has frightened the country and has lowered its tone & his only remedy is building colossal ships wh[ich] have neither speed nor power & wh[ich] are immensely expensive from their enormous crews ... .'[74]

Nor was the rest of the professional element at the Admiralty absolved from guilt: Disraeli lashed out at Pakington's first Board, calling the Naval Lords 'the most inefficient men that could be selected.' Eight years later the epithets were even more pointed: 'A First Lord is surrounded by the criminals [i.e., the Naval Lords] ... .'[75] Hence, Disraeli complained of '[t]he maladministration, not to say malversation, of the Admiralty ... .' Even 'if the H[ouse] of Commons wished to increase its naval expenditures,' he claimed early in 1868, 'it would not entrust the office to a department constituted as a present,' and in February 1867, in the midst of yet another dispute over the Estimates, he bluntly asserted that 'it is useless to attempt to reason with them [i.e., the Naval Lords] ... the whole system of administration is palsied by their mutinous spirit.'[76]

Much of Disraeli's vitriol in 1858–59 and 1866–68 was doubtless owing to the specific circumstances of the moment, but through it it is easy to perceive views which had been set in 1852: an apparently dishonorable and untrustworthy Surveyor, Naval Lords ignorant of the exigencies of party politics and unwilling to match their funding demands to available revenue, and a First Lord under the sway of 'the criminals.' In these respects Disraeli's first experience with the Admiralty set the mold and probably did much to shape his attitude for subsequent relations with that department.

On the other hand, a factor which troubled the Conservatives less in subsequent administrations was that of party. It is clear that both Disraeli and Derby (to say nothing of Stafford) were obsessed with combatting a sinister Whig network which had infiltrated the entire naval administration. With the available evidence it is difficult to disagree with Blake's assessment that after five years in office, 'there was scarcely a job which was not filled by a Whig supporter,' merit promotions notwithstanding, since merit did not determine initial entry to the dockyards.[77] Moreover, Whig MP Berkeley's contacts with the First Naval Lord kept him as well informed of the Tory Board's doings as they were themselves; his questions in the House of Commons could only have been obtained through 'unofficial channels,' presumably either Parker or Walker, and, even more remarkably, he was present at the Admiralty when the Surveyor was checking his recollections of Stafford's words and actions against Parker's.[78]

If Stafford is to be believed, the Whigs were no less averse to manipulating political patronage in the dockyards than their opponents. In defending himself against Hall's accusation in the House of Commons the former Secretary quoted an anonymous source who charged that

When the Whigs, in 1848, began to feel their power declining, they thought it necessary to fall on some plan for continuing an system which would even if they retired from office, still leave the dockyard patronage in their grasp .... It became necessary to vest all recommendations with dockyard authorities, the channel for which was the Surveyor of the Navy–and thus erect a formidable *chevaux de frise* round their position. This order, framed with an apparent design of securing the avenue to employment, and promotion to ability, merit, and service, was notwithstanding all its pretense and flummery, in reality a document enabling the parties to carry on a system which had long grown up into a crying evil and public scandal.[79]

Whatever the truth of the main charges, in one notable respect this accusation was wide of the mark, although the error tends to lend credence to the remainder of the indictment. Although the Whigs had held office from 1830 to 1841 with only one brief interruption, and again from 1846 to 1852, Peel's 1841–46 administration formed a notable break in the Whigs' dominance of the government. And what had happened with reference to dockyard appointments in 1841? A table among Baldwin Walker's papers provides some enticing clues (see Table 7.1).

Table 7.1 Promotions, Vacancies, &c in the Dock Yards[80]

Year	Letters from Superintendents &c to Surveyor direct	Letters sent to Admiralty and referred to Surveyor	Admiralty Orders sent to Surveyor
1840	160	76	188
1841	189	56	269
1842	30	16	166
1843	17	5	164
1844	7	14	125
1845	2	8	147
1846	20	9	100
1847	18	17	89
1848	11	16	67
1849	55	58	134
1850	93	79	99
1851	97	91	89
1852	51	66	262

Although the circumstances of individual appointments cannot be divined, and while it is possible that many of the 1841 appointments took place before the Whigs' fall from power, the Admiralty appointed even more men to positions in the dockyards in 1841 than it did in 1852, and Peel's Board was generally much more willing to dispense patronage than was that of the subsequent Russell administration, perhaps a consequence of the Whigs' dominance of government in the 1830s. One other point is equally evident. Neither party completely renounced its power to make dockyard appointments, 1849 Minute or no, and even following that directive the Whigs continued to send virtually as many appointments to the Surveyor as he made on the basis of recommendations from the dockyard superintendents.

One final, if slightly less important, question remains to be considered: to what extent were Derby and Disraeli aware of what Stafford was doing with the dockyard appointments, and to what extent did they encourage him? Certainly both had a thorough knowledge of his general activities from his own descriptions of the struggles with Northumberland and Parker. Were there any doubt on the matter, it was explicitly corroborated by the First Lord's letter to Derby complaining of Stafford's attempt to make a patronage appointment in Chatham Dockyard. Did his actions stem from either Disraeli's or Derby's instructions? Here the evidence is more ambiguous. Baldwin Walker recounted that in his first interview with Stafford the latter bluntly stated 'there is no use blinking the question[,] the fact is I am so pressed by Lord Derby & the Chancellor of the Exchequer I cannot help myself.'[81] Both Disraeli and Derby explicitly denied this charge in their testimony to the Select Committee on Dockyard Appointments.[82] In the latter's case some corroboration of Stafford's complaint exists, for in pressuring Northumberland to turn the patronage at his disposal over to Stafford, the Prime Minister distinctly excluded 'professional appointments,' instead referring to the 'multitude of small civil offices, Clerkships, &c which former Governments have invariably used as a means of supporting their political influence ... .'[83] Unless Derby explicitly contradicted his stated views to Northumberland in private conversation with Stafford, it would appear that he told the truth to the Select Committee. Disraeli's words and deeds are unknown; unlike Derby he kept no copies of his outgoing correspondence, and again unlike Derby he was a long acquaintance and friend of Stafford, and much of their business was conducted face-to-face. In the end, therefore, Blake's judgment that the written evidence 'hardly bear[s] out' Stafford's 'claim that they pressed him against his will' is, for want of evidence to the contrary, as far as we can go without recourse to speculation.

NOTES

1 Robert, Lord Blake, *Disraeli* (New York: St Martin's Press, 1967), p. 346.
2 *Dictionary of National Biography*, (reprint edn, London: Oxford University Press, 1967–68), 15: pp. 835–6.
3 Derby to Northumberland, 27 March 1852 (Copy), Derby Papers, Liverpool Record Office, 920 DER (14), 179/2.
4 Milne, 'Abstract of measures introduced by Sir Alexander Milne while at the Admiralty,' (Printed), Milne Papers. National Maritime Museum, MLN/145/5 [2].
5 'Private and Confidential Memorandum on the politics of the Board of Admiralty,' probably by Augustus Stafford, nd., Hughenden (Disraeli) Papers, Bodleian Library, Oxford, B/V/H/2.
6 Ibid.
7 Michael Stenton ed., *Who's Who in Parliament, 1832–1885* (Hassocks, Sussex: The Harvester Press, 1978), 31–2; *DNB*, 2: pp. 343–4, 345–6, 356–8. See also Donald Southgate, *The Passing of the Whigs, 1832–1886* (London: Macmillan, 1965), appendix 2.

8   *DNB*, 15: 835; Southgate, Appendix 2, Table B.

9   See Berkeley to Stafford (Copy), 13 May 1852, and Walker to Baring (Copy), 28 April 1853, Walker Papers (Photocopy) National Maritime Museum, WWL/2; *Hansard*, 3rd ser., 125 (1853), col. 55.

10 'Private and Confidential Memorandum on the politics of the Board of Admiralty,' probably by Augustus Stafford, n.d., Hughenden (Disraeli) Papers, Bodleian Library, Oxford, B/V/H/2.

11 Derby to Northumberland (Copy), 27 March [1852], Derby Papers, Liverpool Record Office, DER 920 (14), fols 69–73.

12 Derby to Northumberland, 29 March 1852, Ibid.

13 Walker Memorandum [holograph], nd., NMM: WWL/2.

14 'Report of the Select Committee on Dockyard Appointments together with the Proceedings of the Committee, Minutes of Evidence, Appendix, and Index,' *Parliamentary Papers* 1852–53, 25: p. v.

15 Ibid., pp. iv, vii. The Minute of 1849 had been issued on the authority of First Lord Sir Francis Baring alone, without having been submitted to the Board. Stafford, upon consulting the Board Minute Book, found no record of it, and no indication in the Admiralty's General Minute Book that it had received Baring's imprimatur. He then, according to the Committee Report, 'without enquiring for the original document, concluded that the minute of September 1849 had been issued on the sole authority of the previous Secretary of the Admiralty,' 'made this erroneous statement to' Northumberland, and persuaded the Duke–who had repeatedly refused to cancel it–that the power to abrogate it belonged to the Secretary.

16 Walker Memorandum [Holograph], nd, NMM: WWL/2; *Dockyard Appointments Committee Report,* ix–x.

17 *Dockyard Appointments Committee Report,* pp. vi–vii.

18 *Hansard's Parliamentary Debates*, 3rd ser., 125 (1853), cols. 42–3.

19 Walker to Northumberland [Copy], 10 May 1852, Walker Papers, NMM: WW/2. A printed copy may be found in *Hansard*, 3rd ser., 125 (1853), cols 43–4.

20 Stafford to Derby, 3 May [1852], Derby Papers, 920 DER (14), 150/5. A copy can also be found in the Hughenden (Disraeli) Papers, Bodleian Library, Oxford University, B/XXI/S/475a.

21 Derby to Northumberland (Copy), 3 May 1852, Derby Papers, 920 DER (14), 180/2.

22 Northumberland to Derby, 4 May 1852, Derby Papers, 920 DER (14), 154/8.

23 Ibid.

24 *Hansard*, 3rd ser., 125 (1853), cols 42–3.

25 Stafford to Derby, 2 July [1852], Derby Papers, 920 DER (14), 150/5. Lushington had in fact a distinguished service career, interrupted by a lengthy bout of illness, and gained subsequent renown in the Crimean War. He reached the rank of full Admiral. See *DNB*, 12: pp. 293–94.

26 Stafford to Disraeli, 2 July [1852], Hughenden (Disraeli) Papers, B/XXI/S/473.

27 Disraeli to Derby, 2 July 1852, Derby Papers, 920 DER (14), 145/2.

28 Northumberland to Derby (Copy), 2 July 1852, Hughenden (Disraeli) Papers, B/XX/S/61a.

29 Derby to Disraeli, [2 July 1852], ibid., B/XX/S/61. Stafford stuck to his version. See Disraeli to Derby, 3 July 1852, Derby Papers, 920 DER (14), 145/2.

30 Stafford to Disraeli, 6 July [1852], Hughenden (Disraeli) Papers, B/XXI/S/

380.

31   Stafford to Disraeli 24 July [1852], Hughenden (Disraeli) Papers, B/XXI/S/480.

32   Derby to Disraeli, nd [July 1852], Hughenden (Disraeli) Papers, B/XX/S/93.

33   Stafford to Disraeli, Confidential, 27 September [1852], Hughenden (Disraeli) Papers, B/XXI/S/464.

34   Stafford to Northumberland (Copy), 28 September [1852], Hughenden (Disraeli) Papers, B/XXI/S/465a.

35   Stafford to Disraeli, 28 September [1852], ibid., p. 465.

36   Disraeli to Derby, 6 October 1852, Derby Papers, DER 920 (14), 145/2.

37   Derby to Disraeli, 7 October 1852, Hughenden (Disraeli) Papers, B/XX/S/77.

38   Stafford to Derby, 9 October [1852], Derby Papers, 920 DER (14), 150/5.

39   The General Election took place following the dissolution of Parliament on 1 July. The new Parliament opened on 4 November.

40   *DNB*, 192–3. Dundas's second wife's sister was married to one of the Berkeleys.

41   Stafford to Disraeli, 27 September [1852], Hughenden (Disraeli) Papers, B/XXI/S/464.

42   Stafford to Derby and Disraeli, 23 October [1852], Derby Papers, DER 920 (14), 150/5, Hughenden (Disraeli) Papers, B/XXI/S/474a.

43   Northumberland to Derby, 23 August 1852, Derby Papers, DER 920 (14), 154/8.

44   Stafford to Disraeli, 27 September [1852], Hughenden (Disraeli) Papers, B/XXI/S/464.

45   Stafford to Derby, Confidential, 29 September 1852, Derby Papers, 920 DER (14), 150/5.

46   Victoria to Derby, 23 October 1852, printed in Christopher Benson and Reginald, Viscount Esher, (eds), *The Letters of Queen Victoria: A Selection from Her Majesty's Correspondence between the years 1837 and 1861* (New York: Longmans, Green, and Co., 1907), 2: 481. Victoria's letter of 23 October refers to the earlier Memorandum.

47   Victoria to Derby, 13 November 1852, ibid., pp. 483–4.

48   Disraeli to Victoria, 14 November 1852, ibid., p. 484.

49   Derby to Disraeli, nd. [20 November 1852?], Hughenden [Disraeli] Papers, B/XX/S/102.

50   Disraeli to Derby, nd. [23 November 1852?], printed in William Flavelle Monypenny and George Earle Buckle, *The Life of Benjamin Disraeli, Earl of Beaconsfield* (New York: Macmillan Co., 1914), 3: 407.

51   See Derby to Disraeli, 30 November 1852, Hughenden [Disraeli] Papers, B/XX/S/81.

52   Stafford to Northumberland (Copy), 28 September 1852, Hughenden [Disraeli] Papers, B/XXI/S/465a.

53   Northumberland to Disraeli, 20 November 1852, Hughenden [Disraeli] Papers, B/XXI/N/177; Stafford to Disraeli, nd. [20 November 1852?], Ibid., B/XXI/S/479. Stafford's letter makes sense in no other context than this one.

54   Disraeli to Derby, Private, 30 November 1852, printed in Monypenny and Buckle, *Life of Disraeli*, 3: 425–26.

55   B.R. Mitchell and Phyllis Deane, *Abstract of British Historical Statistics* (Cambridge: Cambridge University Press, 1962), p. 397.

56   Disraeli to Derby, Private, 30 November 1852, printed in Monypenny and Buckle, *Life of Disraeli*, 3: 425–26.

57   Derby to Disraeli, 30 November 1852, Hughenden [Disraeli] Papers, B/XXI/
      S/81.
58   Stafford to Derby, Confidential, 3 December 1852, Derby Papers, 920 DER
      (14), 150/5.
59   Blake, *Disraeli*, p. 330. The Budget was unveiled on 2 December 1852.
60   *Hansard*, 3rd ser., 123 (1852), col. 350. Another MP, Admiral Sir George
      Pechell (who represented Brighton 'in the Whig interest' from 1835 to his
      death in 1860), complained later in the same debate 'of the mode in which
      the patronage of the Admiralty had been exercised ...'(col. 368). On Pechell's
      politics, see *DNB*, 15: 626–27.
61   *Hansard*, 3rd ser., 123 (1852), col. 350.
62   Walker to Stafford (Copy), 25 November 1852, Walker Papers, NMM: WWL/
      2.
63   *Hansard*, 3rd ser., 124 (1853), col. 1359.
64   Ibid., 3rd ser., 124 (1853), col. 1286.
65   *Hansard*, 3rd ser., 125 (1853), cols. 56–7. The motion was seconded by
      Pechell.
66   *Dockyard Appointments Committee Report*, vii. The Report quoted the Duke,
      who claimed that 'he never knew, from the day he entered the office until he
      left the office, whether the patronage was in the hands of the Surveyor, or
      whether it was in the hands of the Secretary: he never knew anything about
      it.'
67   Andrew Lambert, *Battleships in Transition: The Creation of the Steam
      Battlefleet 1815–1860* (London: Conway Maritime Press, 1984), p. 69.
68   Andrew Lambert, *Warrior* (London: Conway Maritime Press, 1987), p. 16;
      ibid., p. 75. The other cabinet member was Lord Stanley, later the 15th Earl of
      Derby.
69   John Beeler, *British Naval Policy in the Gladstone Disraeli Era, 1866–1880*
      (Stanford, CA: Stanford University Press, 1997). On Pakington, see pp. 69–
      73, on pp. Corry, 75–82, on Ward Hunt, pp. 150–63.
70   Ibid., pp. 67–74.
71   Derby to Northcote, 5 April 1874, Iddesleigh (Northcote) Papers, British
      Library ADD MSS 50022, fol. 99.
72   Derby to Disraeli, 12 October 1858, Hughenden (Disraeli) Papers, B/XX/S/
      182.
73   Beeler, *British Naval Policy in the Gladstone–Disraeli Era*, pp. 74–9.
74   Disraeli to Derby, 12 October 1858, Derby Papers, 920 DER (14), 145/5
75   Disraeli to Derby, 20 October 1866, Derby Papers, 920 DER (14), 146/2.
76   Disraeli to Derby, Confidential, 28 January 1868, Derby Papers, 920 DER
      (14), 146/4 and Disraeli to Derby, 2 February 1867, ibid., 146/3. For another
      instance, see Disraeli to Derby, 14 September 1866, Ibid., 146/2.
77   Blake, *Disraeli*, p. 321.
78   *Dockyard Appointments Committee Report*, vi. Evidence of this remarkable
      occurrence surfaced in the course of Parker's testimony to the Dockyard
      Appointments Committee.
79   *Hansard*, 3rd ser., 125 (1853), col. 65.
80   Walker Memorandum, nd., Walker Papers, NMM: WWL/2.
81   Ibid.
82   *Dockyard Appointments Committee Report*, p. vi.
83   Derby to Northumberland (Copy), 3 May 1852, Derby Papers, 920 DER (14),
      180/2.

CHAPTER 8

'Debtor to the Greeks and the Barbarians': Religious Periodicals and their Influence in the Victorian Prelude

Marsh Wilkinson Jones

Historians generally agree that Methodism was highly influential in Britain in the late eighteenth and early nineteenth centuries. Indeed, the historiographic debate on its influence in British society is so well known that it need only be briefly described here. The modern historiographical debate over the influence of religion in general and Methodism in particular in the pre-Victorian era was begun by Francois Guizot and W.E.H. Lecky in the 1870s and continued more earnestly in the early twentieth century by Elie Halevy.[1] The heart of Halevy's thesis was that the influence of John Wesley and Methodism reduced the probability that a French-style revolution would take place in England. The debate over Methodism's influence was reinvigorated by Maurice Quinlan in 1941 with his *Victorian Prelude: A History of English Manners 1700–1830*. Quinlan accepted Halevy's thesis, and in addition claimed that the conservative trends of the Victorian era were present decades before Victoria became Queen.[2] Halevy's argument was accepted by many scholars, including Bernard Semmel, who argued that the revolution was averted by the democratic impulse that Methodism peacefully introduced into English society.[3] Other scholars, notably E.P. Thompson and the Hammonds, accepted the Halevy thesis but with a pejorative twist: they claimed that Methodist and Evangelical influence created a brow-beaten, subservient class of workers who were either afraid or unwilling to attack the upper classes which Methodism had taught them to revere.[4] Recently David Hempton and Ian Christie have provided a new assessment of the Halevy thesis. Instead of allowing that Methodism was the primary restraint on revolution, they have argued that it was but one of many potentially calming influences during the stressful years between 1789 and the end of the Napoleonic Wars.[5]

SPLENDIDLY VICTORIAN

What all of these scholars agree on is that Methodism influenced British society, especially the working classes, and that that influence was a conservative one. What these scholars have failed to explain completely is how that influence operated and what that conservatism entailed. This oversight can be remedied by an examination of the *Methodist Magazine*, the official newspaper of the Methodist conference and the most widely read religious periodical of its day. That Methodism was an essentially conservative influence, and an often overt one at that, can be seen clearly in the pages of the *Methodist Magazine*.

The early nineteenth-century proliferation of periodicals in England may rightly be called a printing revolution. Led by the *Methodist Magazine* and other prominent religious monthlies, the output of the periodical press quickly escalated.[6] Circulating among a diverse slice of English society, these works became a model for later publications of the same type. In order to reach as many readers as possible–especially working-class readers– these publications often presented stories designed both to shock and enthrall. Their goal, however, was not merely commercial; it was also ideological. They sought to inculcate a particular brand of religious and political conservatism, a conservatism reflected in many of their articles and stories which, while shocking and enthralling, were also full of conservative Tory politics, sabbatarianism, fundamentalist teachings, and praise for John Bull.

Concurrent with the growing popularity of religious periodicals came changes in English society, changes which would be attributed to Queen Victoria in the decades to come, but which were actually in place long before she ascended the throne in 1837. Indeed, the *Methodist Magazine* and other religious periodicals did much more than provide a source of entertainment for the weary, browbeaten masses of industrial England. In both obvious and subtle ways, England's late eighteenth- and early nineteenth-century religious press influenced the political, social, and ethical views of an entire generation. The wide reach of this newly unleashed and powerful conservative force largely explains the early pervasiveness of what would later be called 'Victorian' values.[7]

The *Methodist Magazine* was not an entirely new phenomenon in British literary culture. It was, in fact, part of a long trend. Beginning in the seventeenth century, the periodical press became a powerful means for publishers both to inform and to influence public opinion.[8] The first major periodicals were primarily secular and contained a variety of news and information. The name 'magazine,' first used by the *Gentleman's Magazine* in 1731, was borrowed from the term used to describe a military warehouse. The warehouse model represented a significant difference between eighteenth- and seventeenth-century periodicals: eighteenth-century periodicals were departmentalized and featured information and entertainment in a variety of forms while seventeenth-century works had generally focused on a single subject.[9]

The first religious periodical was the *Post-Angel*, published in 1701. It included stories detailing 'the providence of God,' deaths of eminent persons, recent news, questions and answers, essays, and poetry. This format was atypical of the early religious periodicals, since religious periodicals of the first half of the century generally followed the style of periodicals such as the *Tatler* and the *Spectator* in that each issue focused on a single topic. Another religious periodical produced in the first half of the century that did not fall into the essay-periodical category was the *Weekly Miscellany*, which began publication in 1732 and continued for almost nine years. It featured weekly accounts of the 'religion, morality, and learning of the present times, with occurrences both foreign and domestic.'[10] This work and others like it became the standard for monthly publications after 1750.[11]

The first religious periodical to call itself a magazine was the *Christian Magazine*, published between 1760 and 1767 by William Dodd, chaplain to the King, who had the dubious distinction of being hanged for forgery.[12] The departments of Dodd's magazine would be reflected in the format used by later religious periodicals. These included 'Reflections on Death,' 'Systematical Divinity,' 'Historical Divinity,' biographies of religious leaders, and 'Occasional or Miscellaneous Divinity.'[13]

Other religious periodicals of the mid-eighteenth century included the *Spiritual Magazine*, first published by Ann Dutton in 1761, and the *Gospel Magazine*, begun in 1766. Methodists complained that the latter's editors 'viciously scourged' their organization at every opportunity. John Wesley, in fact, was moved to begin his own periodical in response to challenges issued in the *Gospel Magazine*. Less traditional in doctrine was Joseph Priestley's *Theological Repository*, begun in 1769 and published intermittently until 1788.

After 1790, the number of religious and secular periodicals kept pace with England's unprecedented population growth.[14] Between 1790 and 1825 over one hundred new religious periodicals were launched. The largest and most widely read before 1807 was the *Evangelical Magazine*, published first in 1793.[15] Other widely read miscellanies included the *Christian Observer* (1802), and the *Eclectic Review* (1805).

The religious periodical boasting the highest circulation for several decades after the turn of the century was the *Methodist Magazine,* a monthly journal founded in 1778 as *The Arminian* by John Wesley.[16] Although his Methodist organization was large and growing,[17] Wesley used contemporary publishing innovations to reach beyond the scope of his immediate organization and influence society's lower and middle elements.

Wesley did not begin publishing his magazine until he was seventy-six years old because there was already 'a multitude of magazines' in print, including the *Christian Magazine,* which Wesley felt was theologically sound and 'did honour to the publishers.'[18] The discontinuation of this work, which coincided with the ignominious end of its publisher at the end of a rope, left Wesley sorely disappointed. The success and growing influence of the *Christian Magazine* and other monthlies was not lost on Wesley and was one of the most important factors in his decision to launch his periodical. Wesley saw in this medium a potential for reaching those of his followers who were unlikely to read an entire book, but could possibly be induced to read short articles and anecdotes (or listen to them being read).[19] Another factor in Wesley's decision to start a periodical was the growing influence of Calvinistic Nonconformists; Wesley made it clear in the first edition that his periodical would attack false doctrines, especially Calvinism which was diametrically opposed to his Arminian theology of free will. Wesley declared that his publication, which was called the *Arminian* until 1798, would respond to 'those pestilent declamations the *Gospel* and the *Spiritual Magazine.*' 'I fight them at their own weapons … .' Wesley declared, 'I oppose them magazine to magazine.'[20] Though some thought the magazine would die with its founder in 1791, it continued to be the most important medium of communication of all Methodist Conference publications.

Because of its longevity, its wide circulation, its leadership at the beginning of the nineteenth century, and the fact that its contents are representative of similar publications, one can rightly focus on the *Methodist Magazine* as a model for early nineteenth-century periodicals. It, more than any other such magazine, led the way in innovations and adaptations that led to sizeable increases in circulation and, concurrently, in influence on society.

The circulation of the *Methodist Magazine* experienced a slight dip shortly after Wesley died in 1791, but by the early 1800s readership was again on the rise.[21] General circulation figures, obtained from committee minutes and gleaned from correspondence indicate that this was true for other religious periodicals as well. Precise yearly figures remain difficult to obtain since most subscription lists have been lost and in any case do not account for those who were not regular subscribers. Data in the *Book Room Committee Minutes of the Methodist Connexion* for 1806 disclose that the press was printing 21,500 magazines per month. Other figures from the same source indicate this was half again as many as in 1804.[22] For the next fifteen years this figure did not fluctuate much, though by the middle of the 1820s the number had increased by around 5000.[23]

Given the population of Britain in 1810, around 9.8 million, a circulation of 21,500 does not sound particularly influential. But the number of copies printed does not represent the number of readers. In 1813, for example, the *Evangelical Magazine,* with a circulation of not more than around 20,000, claimed a readership of 100,000.[24] Such multipliers were applied because most magazines fell into the hands of more than one reader and were generally perused by up to five or six. Often, one or more families would pool their resources so they could purchase one magazine and share it.[25] This was true of other periodicals and publications during the same period. In Ireland for example, where late eighteenth century stamp taxes on newspapers were inordinately high, several individuals would join together to buy the *Belfast Newsletter* or the *Commercial Chronicle* or, through the kindness of some rich neighbor, would obtain the expensive newspapers, take them to work, and read them aloud to others. In addition, country employers would often read newspapers to their laborers after the day's work was finished, and in Belfast in the 1820s, newspapers were carried around and left at houses for a penny an hour. Poor readers might also peruse magazines and newspapers in coffee houses or libraries, which usually charged a nominal yearly fee.[26] Methodist families would often participate in similar schemes, with one family purchasing a copy and then sharing it, a day or two at a time, with their neighbors. For many people, the magazine was their only source of outside information and entertainment, and demand for these publications rose quickly in the early nineteenth century. Thus, as literacy rates rose, so did schemes for getting the printed word out. By these means, and by word of mouth beyond the immediate circle of readers–for even more than today the printed culture and the oral culture were far from distinct–newspapers and periodicals had a profound effect.[27]

A profile of the typical magazine reader may be created from the make-up of Methodism in general, from letters, and from comments made in the magazine itself. The content of the magazine also reveals, to a certain extent, the type of reader addressed. A number of studies have been conducted in an effort to recreate the social composition of early nineteenth-century Methodism.[28] During the first four decades of the century, artisans and colliers were the largest group within the Methodist movement and among Nonconformists in general. These were followed by merchants, manufacturers and tradesmen. Laborers and farmers, because they were not centered in the cities where Methodism had focused, were under-represented in the movement, while the number of aristocrats was barely noticeable. This is not to say that the last group was not vocal or influential. On the whole, it appears that Methodism drew mainly from the middle or upper working class. This conclusion is borne out by evidence regarding magazine readership. Based on the content of the magazine, the stated goal of attracting as wide an audience as possible, and letters to magazine editors from readers who indicated that they did not read newspapers or similar publications, we can conclude that most readers were of the classes noted. A most revealing comment regarding magazine readership came in a letter from James Macdonald, an assistant editor to Joseph Benson, the editor of the *Methodist*

Magazine from 1805 to 1821. In the letter, Macdonald warns Benson to ignore complaints about magazine content made by preachers and others: 'They blame what they have neither taste nor learning to discern the value of. Were you to be guided by them, the magazine would soon fall into contempt. They seem to forget, that you are a debtor to the Greeks as well as to the Barbarians and that though the latter are by far the more numerous of your readers, a little in each number is due to the former.'[29] Another individual wrote Benson to compliment the magazine and noted that in its pages 'readers of different tastes find themselves gratified and pleasure leads to profit.'[30] On a more modern note, Edward Shils, in an essay entitled 'Mass Society and its Culture' argued that for a magazine 'to speak to the largest possible audience, it has been necessary to make the content of what is transmitted in a single issue as heterogeneous as the audience sought.'[31]

The *Methodist Magazine* in the early nineteenth century was clearly seeking to make its pages interesting and alluring to a wide range of English society. Hooks, continuations, and elaborations, as well as stories about sex, violence, and the supernatural were all popular with the lower elements of society and the magazine's editors did not hesitate to print them. A story in the November 1816 edition titled 'Divine Preservation During Sleep' told of two hunters sleeping in the same room after a day of shooting. One had a dream about killing a stag and when he came to the place where he plunged his stiletto into the animal, he actually picked up a knife and prepared to plunge it into his partner; the man was saved when the would-be-killer talked in his sleep and awakened his friend.[32] A more macabre dream account came in July 1816. Here the story is told of a man who dreamed that a witch-like woman came to kill him. Awakening in a sweat, the man soon forgot the incident. Twelve years later while in Germany, he encountered a woman at an inn who looked exactly like the woman in his dream. With his dream to guide him, the man spent the night awake and watchful. As expected, the woman came into his room in the middle of the night, ready to take his life; he was miraculously saved.[33] Also in the bizarre and strange category were stories such as the one about a girl who subsisted for four years on water alone,[34] a story about a one-hundred-foot long sea serpent, seen off the coast of North America and reported several times in the magazine between 1816 and 1818,[35] and the story of a soldier who died on the Island of Minorca during the Napoleonic Wars and whose spirit, accompanied by a bright light, was simultaneously seen by his family in England.[36]

The *Methodist Magazine* and other religious periodicals took full advantage of their readers' prurient interests to increase circulation. These tantalizing sentences were taken from the story of one William Andrew Horne, published in an 1808 edition of the *Methodist Magazine:*

He was the favourite of his father, and was indulged by him with a horse and money in early life, and permitted to ramble from one place of diversion to another. In this course of dissipation he gave loose to his passion for women. Not content with seducing his mother's maid-servants, he acknowledged that he had been the cause of the murder of a servant girl who was with child by him, and that he had criminal intercourse with his own sisters.[37]

Other articles designed to draw and hold the greatest number of readers included a story about Welsh-speaking native Americans, a crime story about how a murderer in Constantinople was discovered, the story of Androcles and the lion,[38] and stories about unusual animals such as the famous 'Methodist Dog' that came to church each Sunday in an effort to draw his supposedly sinful master after him; when his master died in a drunken stupor, the dog was never seen again.[39] Examples of more violent stories include the agonizing deaths of burn victims and the scenes after rampaging crowds in burning factories and even chapels had trampled many to death.

Reports of violence and gore also had their place as morality tales. Take, for instance, the story about the two butchers who had the temerity to make deliveries on the Sabbath: one of them died when his head was crushed flat with a great pop under a carriage wheel, the other was killed when his head was cracked against the wheel and his brains were dashed out and scattered on the spot.[40] Less gruesomely, a boy who chose to play football on Sunday was reported to have seriously injured his ankle.[41] These stories were designed to entertain; they were also designed to instruct and influence.

Of course, not all instruction was so titillating. A fictional account of a Christian family's Sunday described the proper demeanor for celebrating the sabbath: the children were seated obediently around their father (appropriately named 'Mr. Christian') while he read the Bible to them and quietly answered their questions about God.[42] Four years later the *Magazine* instructed its readers that on their way to church 'you will not be talking about the weather, the markets or the trade, or traducing the character of your neighbors ... your afternoon will be employed in searching the Scriptures, reading good books, visiting some poor persons, and relieving their wants.'[43]

The effect of the magazine on its readers can be discerned in the glowing reports sent to the editor and in personal diaries or journals. An 1808 letter to the editor, for example, called the *Methodist Magazine* 'a most excellent publication ... eminently conspicuous in the conversion of sinners.'[44] An oft-cited example of the magazine's extended readership and influence may be found in the case of the Brontë sisters. These popular Victorian authors were raised in part by an evangelical aunt who kept copies of the *Methodist Magazine* on her shelves. In her novel *Shirley*, Charlotte Brontë alludes to those childhood days when she and her siblings had nothing better to do than sit and look at 'mad Methodist magazines, full of miracles and apparitions, of preternatural warnings, ominous dreams, and frenzied fanaticism.'[45] George Eliot's mid-nineteenth-century-novel, *Adam Bede*, cites the *Methodist Magazine* as a tool used by turn-of-the-century Methodist leaders to influence social attitudes and opinions. When a character is considering how he should deal with Methodist preachers, he first asks himself what impact his actions might have and then decides not to act for fear it will be reported in the magazine. 'If I chose to interfere in this business now,' stated Eliot's cautious character, 'I might get up as pretty a story of hatred and persecution as the Methodists need desire to publish in the next number of their magazine.'[46]

With more readers and a more diversified readership than any other pre-Victorian periodical, the *Methodist Magazine* was in a position of great influence at the beginning of the nineteenth century. Not every article was a swashbuckler or an inspirational account: some had the obvious design of inculcating conservative social, moral, and political ideologies. And even those that seemed on the surface to have only entertainment value were supporting and encouraging a conservative Methodist agenda. Articles encouraged and praised the Church of England, which Methodism still claimed as its church. Support for crown and country was both implicit and explicit. Methodists had been accused of not upholding the state or the wars against Napoleon because they would not practice with the militia on Sunday and because they opposed government bills that would impinge upon their right to preach. To counter this, the magazine enjoined that military duty was a responsibility, incidents such as the assault by local militia on the tens of thousands of protesters who had gathered in Manchester in 1819 were applauded, and loyalty to the king was proclaimed.[47] The editor had a difficult time when Lord Sidmouth presented a bill to Parliament in 1812 which would have made it troublesome for Methodists and dissenters to obtain licenses to preach. The magazine, which had always made a point of supporting the government, was careful never to denounce the king or parliament, while at the same time publicizing the problem and encouraging Methodists to oppose Sidmouth's legislation; articles declaring the Church of England to be 'the most orthodox and best constituted national church in the world,' also noted the need for religious toleration and supported government acts allowing greater freedom for dissenters.[48]

Methodism had always had a strong interest in ending what it saw as social ills, and the magazine was a vehicle whereby a particularly conservative social agenda could be promoted. It came down strongly against slavery in 1806, encouraging the efforts of William Wilberforce and expressing the hope that this 'crying offense against humanity ... shall cease forever.'[49] An area of special concern was the failure of many people to keep the Christian Sabbath. Profaners were condemned and stories were often related how such evildoers could meet untimely deaths or injuries. In addition, the theater, the ballroom, the card table, the race course, the cockpit, and Sunday parties were all denounced. In one article, the author not only inveighed against cards and dancing, but also against Punchinello, blind fiddlers, and Madame Catalani, a famous Italian singer.[50] Other amusements that were continually attacked in the magazine in the early years of the nineteenth century were bull- and bear-baiting, snuff and smoking, recreational shooting, and immodest clothing.

These examples from the *Methodist Magazine* reveal that, in an age of machine breakers and riots, the Methodists were encouraging moral conservatism and support for the government. The *Magazine* praised the king, supported the efforts against Napoleon, and declared the willingness of Methodists to serve in the armed forces.[51] Lord Nelson's final words– 'England expects every man to do his duty'–were held up as a motto for Methodists and were declared in the magazine to mean nothing less than loyalty to the king and obedience to God.[52] The Duke of Wellington, as representative of English authority and power, was highly praised after Waterloo.[53] In relating the history of the mutiny on H.M.S. *Bounty*, the magazine took Captain Bligh's part and published the story under the title, 'An Account of the Voyages and Sufferings of Captain Bligh.'[54] Meanwhile, Thomas Paine, though long removed from the British scene, continued to be maligned in the magazine as a representative of anarchy and republicanism.[55] Thus, established governments, persons in positions of authority, and conservative political ideology were praised and recommended in the pre-Victorian *Methodist Magazine*.

The *Methodist Magazine* was not alone in expressing such conservative, Victorianesque sentiments. Many other religious periodicals, circulating in the same period, took very similar political, philosophical, and social stands. 'The first quarter of the nineteenth century was a time of unyielding partisanship,' wrote Quinlan, 'and most periodicals were on the side of the conservative powers.'[56] The only point of disagreement among the major religious periodicals was in the matter of theology, where remarks about rivals might be rather caustic.[57] The *Gospel Magazine*, for example, while leading the attack on Methodist theology, was at the same time supporting and encouraging a similar social agenda and for all intents and purposes, publishing a periodical mirroring the content and focus of the Methodists.[58] The *Evangelical Magazine*, meanwhile, often exchanged articles with the Methodists based on their understanding that both had widely varied readerships. Religious invectives as well as political stance were very similar in both. The *Eclectic Review* was yet another important religious periodical which was publishing ideas very similar to those which the *Methodist Magazine* encouraged. It openly affirmed its support for the British Constitution, 'which happily combines the advantages of Monarchy,

Aristocracy, and Democracy.'[59] The *Christian Observer* was perhaps more interested in politics than any of the evangelical magazines. When first published in 1802, its editors boldly stated that their purpose was to act as a friend of revealed religion and civil government, and to oppose impiety, skepticism, and sedition.[60] The *Observer's* regular attacks on political liberals and their attempts to equate liberal opinions with skepticism led the secular *Edinburgh Review* to declare that the *Christian Observer* 'appears to have no other method of discussing a question ... than that of accusing their antagonists of infidelity.'[61]

A conservative estimate of the combined circulation of these politically and socially conservative periodicals would be approximately 70,000, although they may have topped 100,000 by 1820. The *Methodist Magazine* and the *Evangelical Magazine* together were selling over 40,000 copies by the middle of the 1810s. The combined efforts of these very similar publications may have served to reach a minimum of 500,000 people each month, and probably even more.[62]

Evidence indicates both that a significant percentage of the population was being reached with conservative religious teaching on a monthly basis and that society was undergoing a transformation which Quinlan has called the 'Victorian Prelude.'[63] Elie Halevy also recognized that England was conservative especially when compared to its continental neighbors, but he offered little in the way of explanation for this phenomenon. The conservative religious periodical press in pre-Victorian Britain may offer a viable, if partial, explanation. The most difficult aspect of this argument is to verify the influence of the written word on the masses.

When we set out to demonstrate the influence of the written word in history we open a Pandora's box. The problem with influence is its esoteric nature. A number of scholars, primarily sociologists, have boldly assailed the impenetrable fortress of influence and have come away scathed and bruised. But the failures of others should not discourage still another assault. Indeed, a number of scholars, pollsters, and advertising agents have shown through controlled studies that what a person reads as well as sees can have a strong and lasting influence.[64] Modern psychologists express concern with the influence of those aspects of culture that are viewed by most to be negative: sex and violence in the media are prime examples. Oddly enough, it was through the reporting of sex and violence (admittedly in a controlled way) that the early nineteenth-century periodical increased readership and effected a social and political change.

We can elicit other historical examples that verify the power of the press to influence. In 1774 Goethe's *Sorrows of the Young Werther* was first published in Germany. Shortly thereafter, a wave of suicides led the governments of Denmark and Norway to ban sales of the work.[65] It is important to note that Goethe's work only implicitly, not explicitly, encouraged suicide and yet the response was so great that governments felt compelled to take legislative action against it. In the United States in the early 1900s, President Theodore Roosevelt spoke indignantly of muckrakers, magazines that managed to increase their circulations greatly by publishing true facts about criminals and their crimes.[66] Roosevelt's epithet not withstanding, these periodicals had an important effect on public policy in the United States. One scholar argues that 'by documenting dishonesty and blight, muckrakers helped to arouse public indignation. Most likely,' he concludes, 'no broad reform movement of American institutions would have taken place without them.'[67] Other examples of the press's potential influence may be found in pre-Revolutionary America and Napoleonic Era England; in both nations stamp taxes were required not simply to raise more money for the government, but also to reduce the circulation of revolutionary and inflammatory ideas. Interestingly enough, during these periods, the government of Britain did not place a stamp tax on periodicals, but as publications like the *Methodist Magazine* became more popular, a number of individuals began to push for some sort of restraint. The Rev. Sydney Smith, writing in the *Edinburgh Review* for 1808, issued a stern warning concerning the *Methodist* and *Evangelical Magazines*: 'Their circulation is enormous,' he declared, 'and so increasing they contain the opinions, and display the habits of so many human beings, that they cannot but be objects of curiosity and importance. The common and middling classes of people are the purchasers; and the subject is religion, though not that religion certainly which is established by law ... . This may lead to unpleasant consequence, or it may not; but it carries with it a sort of aspect, which ought to insure to it a serious attention and reflection.'[68]

The periodical press and the press in general have clearly had a much earlier and more important influence on English culture than previously assumed. The mass culture of our media-rich society was already visible in the early 1800s. Just as the modern media may generate praise and adoration for a sports figure or movie star, or raise world wide curiosity about the private lives of presidents, so the pre-Victorian media was able to rally the masses against a particular government bill, in favor of anti-slavery legislation and in favor of a more civilized stance toward cruelty to animals. In general, it promoted an attitude favorable towards individual moral improvement that either had not been present previously, or at least had been generally subdued. Mass culture, which may be said to have had its beginnings in the printing houses of England's sectarian and political press, was born of industrialization, encouraged by a plethora of new readers, and disseminated in a world that was hungry for information as it had never been before. Sometimes unwittingly, often with a clear sense of purpose, this new and dynamic information mill influenced attitudes, beliefs, and perceptions. In this way, the *Methodist Magazine* and periodicals like it

serve as a key to explaining another one of history's ironies: the presence
of a Victorian ethos long before Victoria ever came to the throne.

NOTES

1   F. Guizot, *A Popular History of England*, 4 vols. (Boston, 1876); W.E.H.
Lecky, *A History of England in the Eighteenth Century*, 8 vols. (London:
Longmans, Green, 1878); Elie Halevy, 'La Naissance du Methodisme en
Angleterre,' *Revue de Paris* (1 and 15 August 1906).

2   Maurice Quinlan, *Victorian Prelude: a History of English Manners, 1700–
1830* (Hamden, Connecticut: Archon Books, 1965). Similar ideas have been
presented by Harold Perkin and Ford Brown, the latter tending to discount
the influence of the Methodists in favor of the Evangelical Anglicans. Harold
Perkin, *The Origins of Modern English Society* (London: Ark, 1985); Ford
K. Brown, *Fathers of the Victorians, the Age of Wilberforce* (Cambridge:
Cambridge University Press, 1961). Though well written and extensively
researched, Brown's work does not appreciate the impact of the continued
expansion of Methodism after Wesley's demise, nor does it acknowledge the
influence that Methodist institutions such as its press had in a rapidly changing
world.

3   Bernard Semmel, *The Methodist Revolution* (New York: Basic Books, 1973).

4   E.P. Thompson, *The Making of the English Working Class* (New York:
Vintage, 1966); J. L. and B. Hammond, *The Town Labourer, 1760–1832*
(London, 1917).

5   David Hempton, *Methodism and Politics in British Society, 1750–1850*
(London, 1984); Idem, 'Evangelical Revival and Society: a Historiographical
Review of Methodism and British Society, c. 1750–1850' *Themelios*, n.s., 8
(April 1983): pp. 19–25; Ian R. Christie, *Stress and Stability in Late
Eighteenth-Century Britain* (London: Macmillan, 1980); Idem, *Wars and
Revolutions: Britain, 1760–1815* (Cambridge: Harvard University Press,
1982).

6   See Josef L. Altholz, *The Religious Press in Britain, 1760–1900* (New York:
Greenwood, 1989), p. 10, and Richard D. Altick, *The English Common
Reader* (Chicago: University of Chicago Press, 1957), p. 318.

7   In the context of this essay, 'Victorian values' means sexual prudery,
controlled interaction between the sexes, a general dislike for frivolity, a
strong interest in religion, and that moral and political conservatism that
was, and is, often associated–whether rightly or wrongly–with Queen Victoria.

8   For works that detail early periodical history see Altick, *English Common
Reader;* Altholz, *The Religious Press in Britain,* Altholz, 'The First Religious
Magazines,' *Notes and Queries* 32 (June 1985): 223–4; Francis Mineka, *The
Dissidence of Dissent* (Chapel Hill: University of North Carolina Press, 1944);
and Michael Harris and Alan Lee, eds, *The Press in English Society From
the Seventeenth to the Nineteenth Centuries* (London, 1986), pp. 113–32.

9   The *Gentleman's Magazine* was followed by the *London Magazine* in 1732
and the *Scots Magazine* in 1739. By 1800, when religious periodicals began
to increase in circulation at a rapid rate, there were many secular rivals. The
two heavyweights were the *Edinburgh Review*, first published in 1802 and
favoring Whig politics, and the *Quarterly Review*, created in 1809 by Tories
to answer their critical Whig counterpart. Both magazines regularly drew

swords against Nonconformist religion, a disaffection that was aggravated by the fact that *The Methodist Magazine* and *The Evangelical Magazine* both had higher circulations than their secular counterparts. See Altick, *Common Reader*, Appendix C, 392.

10 Altholz, *The Religious Press in Britain*, p. 8.
11 Ibid.
12 Dodd, a well-connected person with a penchant for living above his means, was hanged in 1777 for forging Lord Chesterfield's signature on a bond and using the false bond as security for a loan. Great efforts were made by Samuel Johnson and others to save Dodd from the noose, but they were to no avail. Dodd himself asked the hangman to prevent 'fatal effects' and after the hanging his body was rushed to a surgeon in hopes that he could be revived. See Percy Fitzgerald, *A Famous Forgery, being the Story of the unfortunate Mr. Dodd*, 1865.
13 Mineka, *The Dissidence of Dissent*, p. 27.
14 E. A. Wrigley and R. S. Schofield, *Population History of England, 1541–1871* (Cambridge: Harvard University Press, 1981) and David Coleman and John Salt, *The British Population* (Oxford: Oxford University Press, 1992).
15 Ibid., p. 64.
16 In 1798 the name was changed to the *Methodist Magazine ... Being a Continuation of the Arminian Magazine*. The magazine's name was changed again in early 1821, to *The Wesleyan Methodist Magazine ... a continuation of the Arminian or Methodist Magazine*.
17 His Methodist organization, formed in 1739, included over 100,000 followers by the time of his death, and continued to grow for another thirty or forty years at a pace faster than that of industrial England's rapidly increasing population.
18 *The Works of John Wesley*, 3rd edn., vol. VI (Grand Rapids, MI: Baker Book House, 1978, reprint of 1872 edn.), p. 108.
19 For a discussion of increasing literacy and the ability of the periodical to capture public attention see Altick, *English Common Reader*, chs 1 and 2 as well as chapters 14 and 15.
20 *The Letters of the Rev. John Wesley, A.M.*, ed. by John Telford, vol. VI (London: Epworth Press, 1931), p. 295.
21 Circulation figures previous to 1800 are difficult to obtain on a yearly basis; some data are available in a manuscript copy of *The Book Room Committee Minutes*, The John Rylands Library, University of Manchester. For a brief discussion regarding the difficulty of ascertaining circulation figures for early periodicals, see Altick, *Common Reader*, Appendix C, pp. 391–2.
22 *Book Room Committee Minutes*, May 1804, manuscript, Manchester, Rylands Library.
23 Ibid., 1825, manuscript, Manchester, Rylands Library.
24 Mineka, *The Dissidence of Dissent*, p. 64.
25 Horace Frederick Mathews, *Methodism and the Education of the People, 1791–1851* (London: Epworth Press, 1949), p. 170.
26 See Altick, *English Common Reader*, p. 323.
27 J. R. R. Adams, *The Printed Word and the Common Man: Popular Culture in Ulster, 1700–1900* (Belfast: The Institute for Irish Studies, 1987), p. 131.
28 See, for example, Thompson, *Making of the English Working Class*; R. Wearmouth, *Methodism and Working Class Movements, 1800–1850*, 2nd ed. (London, 1947); Elie Halevy, *A History of the English People in 1815* (London: E. Benn, 1949); and Robert Currie, *Methodism Divided: A Study*

in the Sociology of Ecumenicalism (London: Faber and Faber, 1968).

29 Macdonald to Benson, 21 October 1809, 72.4.11, Rylands.

30 *Methodist Magazine,* XXIX (1806): p. 560.

31 Edward Shils, 'Mass Society and its Culture,' in Norman Jacobs, ed., *Culture for the Millions?* (Princeton: D. Van Nostrand Company, Inc., 1959), p. 9.

32 *Methodist Magazine,* XXXIX (November 1816).

33 Ibid. (July 1816).

34 Ibid., XXXVII (1814), p. 629.

35 Ibid., XLI (1818), p. 205.

36 Ibid., XLII (1819), p. 209.

37 Ibid., XXXI (1808), p. 29.

38 The story concerning Welsh-speaking native Americans was found in ibid., vol. XL (April 1817), pp. 298–9. The murder case was in ibid., XXXIX (July 1816): pp. 603–4. Androcles and the lion was retold in ibid., XXXIII (December 1812).

39 'The people who frequented the meetings at [Birstal] had repeatedly observed a dog that came from a distance; and as at the house to which he belonged, the Methodists were not respected, he always came alone. His regular attendance had often been the subject of public debate: and merely to prove the sagacity of the animal; the meeting, for one evening, was removed to another house. Whatever were the thoughts entertained concerning him; surprising as it may seem, at the proper and exact time, he made his appearance! A few weeks after this, his owner returning intoxicated from the market at Leeds, was in a narrow, shallow stream, unfortunately drowned: and, astonishing to relate, the faithful dog no longer attended the preaching! … The frequent attendance of this dog, at the meeting, was designed to attract his master's curiosity, and engage him thereby to visit the place; where hearing the Gospel, he might have been … saved. But … the end to be answered, being frustrated by his death, the means to secure it were no longer needful. Thus, God speaketh once, yea twice, but man perceiveth it not.' Ibid., XXXII (January 1809): p. 39.

40 Ibid., XXXIV (1811): 69.

41 Ibid., XXIX (April 1806): 282.

42 Ibid., XXXIX (December 1816): 803.

43 Ibid., XLIII (August1820): 612–613.

44 Ibid., XXXI (June 1808): 265.

45 Charlotte Brontë, *Shirley* (London: Allan Wingate, 1949), p. 379.

46 George Eliot, *Adam Bede* (New York: Frank F. Lovell & Co., n.d.), p. 63.

47 *Methodist Magazine,* XXXI (July 1808), p. 319.

48 Ibid., XXXV (September 1812), p. 664.

49 Ibid., XXIX (1806), p. 184.

50 Ibid., XXXI (November 1808), p. 500.

51 For an example of the conservative patriotism that was a regular feature in the magazine, see a sermon, which ran over several editions, beginning with vol. XXXIV (December 1811): p. 448. The sermon was entitled 'Christian Patriotism.'

52 Ibid., XXXI (July 1808), p. 319.

53 Ibid., XXXIX (1816), p. 299.

54 Ibid., XXXIX (1816), p. 846.

55 Ibid., XLI (1818), p. 287.

56 Quinlan, *Victorian Prelude, a History of English Manners, 1700–1830,* p. 191.

57 Joseph Benson, editor of the *Methodist Magazine* during the first two decades of the nineteenth century, attacked works like the *Catholic Magazine* both in his Methodist publications and in letters to associates. Writing to Rev. S. W. Tracy in February 1813, Benson called the *Catholic Magazine* a 'most false, bigoted, and abusive publication.' Benson to Mr Rev. S.W. Tracy, 8 February 1813, PLP 7.11.16, Rylands. Another example of the caustic rivalry is that which existed between the *Evangelical Magazine* and the *Gospel Magazine*. The *Gospel* described the *Evangelical* (both were Calvinistic in doctrine) as being 'daubed over with the honeyed varnish of Arminian ingredients, for the purpose of catching flies.' *Gospel*, II (1797), p. 479.

58 For a discussion of the vicious verbal assaults see Mineka, *The Dissidence of Dissent*, pp. 61–2.

59 *Eclectic Review*, I (1805), preface, pp. ii–iii.

60 *Christian Observer*, IV (April 1805): 234ff.

61 *Edinburgh Review*, XII (April 1808): 181.

62 Altick, *English Common Reader*, Appendix C.

63 Quinlan explains his use of the phrase in ch. 1 of *Victorian Prelude, a History of English Manners, 1700–1830*.

64 It is very difficult to prove satisfactorily the connection between the media and behavior, though many have tried. See, for example Edward Shils, 'Mass Society and its Culture,' in Jacobs, Adams, *The Printed Word and the Common Man*. For more recent assessments of influence and the media see *Impact of the Mass Media*, ed. by Ray Eldon (White Plains, NY: Longman Group, 1995), and Kathleen Hall Jamieson and Karlyn K. Campbell, *The Interplay of Influence* (Belmont, CA: Wadsworth Publishing, 1988). Focusing more on film and television, but nevertheless related is Neil Postman, *Amusing Ourselves to Death* (New York: Viking, 1985).

65 Jostein Gaarder, *Sophie's World* (New York: Berkley Books, 1996), p. 349.

66 See Arthur Weinberg, and Lila Weinberg, *The Muckrakers* (New York: Simon and Schuster, 1961), especially the introduction.

67 James West Davidson et al., *Nation of Nations*, vol. 2, (New York: McGraw-Hill, 1990), p. 828.

68 *Edinburgh Review* (January 1808), p. 342.

CHAPTER 9

Pyrrhic Victory? The Bismarck Myth and the Congress of Berlin in the British Review Press, 1878–79

Todd E. A. Larson

British Anti-German Sentiment and the Shadow of the Great War[1]

The question of why Germany and Great Britain, two nations with strong traditions of political, cultural, religious, and economic cooperation, went to war with each other in 1914 has preoccupied historians of the twentieth century arguably as much as any other single issue.[2] Perhaps it is because of the horrific nature of the Great War that many historians writing after the conflict took it for granted that the two countries were fated to be the most bitter of enemies. This assertion is untenable for many reasons, not the least of which is that it ignores any shift in British opinion towards Germany in the pre-war period. As late as 1884, it can be argued that Germany occupied a position of esteem in Britain exceeded only by the United States and rivaled by no other Great Power in Europe. This fact makes the Anglo-German falling out seem even more confusing, for virtually every historian who broaches the subject finds that the decade of the 1880s is central to the formation of mutual antagonism. Added to this is the belief of some scholars that Germany was the least of the threats facing the British during the very same decade that it became Britain's greatest enemy. This apparent conundrum is too often left unexplained.

The most common answer to the problem of the growth of Anglo-German antagonism is imperialism. There are a number of books purporting to explain the causes, effects, and implications of German colonialism, and though scholars still differ on the origins of German imperialism, it is important to remember that all the major interpretations concentrate on affairs in Germany as being the critical ingredient in explaining imperial antagonism and conflict, and not on the reactions these events gave rise to in Britain.[3] While German colonialism should never be ignored, and the motives behind it are historically important, they offer little insight into changing perceptions in Britain. Many studies argue conclusively that a fundamental shift occurred between Germany and Britain; few bother to try to explain the changing mentality behind this shift, especially as it concerns the British point of view. Fewer still try to delineate the key events that together can be seen as the origins of their mutual antagonism. This paper will look at one of the fundamental bases upon which later enmity between the two nations was built: the myth of German Chancellor Otto von Bismarck as an 'honest broker' created during the Congress of Berlin in 1878, and the backlash which arose when the British later discovered that, at least in their eyes, he was neither a broker of peace nor particularly honest.

A number of good works on the subject of Anglo-German rivalry have been published, but even the best full-scale studies of the Anglo-German rift, such as Paul Kennedy's *The Rise of Anglo-German Antagonism 1860–1914*, repeat a common mistake. By concentrating so heavily on Bismarck's motives, they forget that for Britain it was not his motives that mattered the most–they remained unclear even to the Chancellor's advisors–rather, it was the *perception* created by his actions that was the critical point. They spend little time explaining the way that British mentalities were fundamentally altered by contemporary perceptions of German action and reactions to those perceptions.

It is, of course, true that understanding changing mentalities and perceptions is a difficult task for any historian. Because of the intangible nature of a nation's collective mentality, explaining it and the forces that shape it can be a frustrating task, the more so when what one is attempting to explain appears incongruous. The bitter racial rhetoric invoked on both sides during the years 1914–19 was unparalleled in history. Examples of this sort of attitude are touched on in Paul Fussell's work *The Great War and Modern Memory*, where he argues that powerful myths created in the pre-war period on both sides helped form an atmosphere of hatred in both countries.[4] In most cases, it appears, this kind of atmosphere grows from, or perhaps is the creation of, long-held stereotypes.[5] Stereotypes–perceptions of a group–are also created, wittingly or not. British perceptions of Germany in the First World War were certainly constructed, but they were built upon earlier stereotypes and myths, most of which had their origins decades before the outbreak of war in 1914. A cornerstone of the anti-German sentiment that so strongly imbued negative German stereotypes in Britain was the creation of a damaging and dangerous myth surrounding Otto von Bismarck. It is to the construction of this myth, and the process of modern myth-making, that this paper now turns.

Bismarck, the Congress, and the Process of Modern Myth Making

The British press never quite knew what to do with Bismarck before the Congress of Berlin. Was he, as some Liberals asserted, the war-mongering leader of a war-mongering people? Or was he, as many Conservatives claimed, the master diplomat who alternated between subterfuge and veiled threats to achieve his ominous goals?[6] For some he was both; for most he was an enigma. One thing is certain, however. There was nothing approaching a general agreement on Bismarck's character before 1878. Yet, within the span of eighteen months, he became–in the eyes of both the Liberal and Conservative British review press–the champion of peace in Europe. How and why this shift occurred, and its ramifications for the future of Anglo-German relations, are the concerns of this paper.

Understanding both the how and the why becomes easier when one has some background information about the Congress itself. The Congress of Berlin is one of the seminal events of nineteenth-century diplomatic history. Following their convincing triumph over the Ottoman empire in the war of 1877–78, the Russians imposed the harsh Treaty of San Stefano, which left Constantinople in Turkish hands but took away most of the Ottoman Balkan territories. This completely upset the balance of power in Europe, which had for many years been built upon propping up the Ottoman empire as a buffer zone for the Great Powers. Britain, which had gone to war in the Crimea in 1854–56 to prevent Russian influence in the Mediterranean, refused to accept this settlement, and a crisis erupted that threatened to engulf Europe in a war over 'The Eastern Question.' It was at this time that Bismarck, who felt the preservation of Continental peace at this time was vital to the best interests of his country, offered himself up as a mediator and Berlin as a neutral meeting site, informing the Reichstag that he would be an 'honest broker' between the other Great Powers. After some debate, all the sides agreed and the Congress was convened on 13 June 1878.

The Congress itself, which lasted precisely one month, saw Bismarck revel in the international attention. Britain was represented by Prime Minister Benjamin Disraeli, ably assisted by the Foreign Secretary the Marquis of Salisbury; Russia was led by Prince Alexander Gorchakov, seconded by Count Peter Shuvalov; and Austria by Count Julius Andrássy. With such an all-star cast, the Congress was bound to be a font of spectacular news, much of which centered on Bismarck.[7] As the historian Erich Eyck commented, 'The German Chancellor was certainly a most energetic President, whose authority was fully acknowledged by every statesman of every country.'[8] As Otto Pflanze further noted, Bismarck 'established the agenda and directed the flow of the deliberations ... [his] procedure was to raise one issue at a time, beginning with the most critical (Bulgaria), invite the delegates to state their general positions ... then adjourn for private conferences between the conflicting parties at which differences were hammered out.'[9] The Congress ended far more quickly than anyone other than Bismarck anticipated, after only twenty sessions, leaving the participants to thrash out the details and evaluate the gains and losses.[10] For Britain the Congress was a success. More importantly, Bismarck's actions, as Pflanze put it, 'finally succeeded in dispelling the British government's perennial suspicion that the new German Reich and its chancellor were a continuing threat to European peace and stability.'[11] Bismarck, once depicted as the war-mongerer, was now presented as the champion of peace–at least in Britain–and was even granted the highest honor the British press could bestow: being named Mr Punch's 'Man of the Year.'

The transformation in the British perception of Bismarck coincided with a shift in his foreign policy. The period 1878–79 was as much a turning point in his career as 1866 or 1871, yet historians have come to no clear consensus on either the causes of his dramatic reversal of foreign policy or its ramifications for future European history. Many scholars believe that the Congress marked the apex of both Bismarck's diplomatic career and his esteem in Britain. As Bruce Waller argues, 'at the Congress of Berlin Bismarck seemed to have climbed a new pinnacle of prestige and power ... he received at the Congress, or so it seemed, the due recognition of Europe for his accomplishment in the service of peace.' Indeed, had there been such a thing at the time, he would have undoubtedly received a Nobel Peace Prize for his actions, but like many past prize winners, whether he actually furthered the peace process is highly questionable. Following the Congress, Bismarck chose to undertake a risky new foreign policy that saw him embrace an Austrian alliance when just eighteen months earlier he had emphatically argued against just such a union.

One of the least studied aspects of the Congress and the foreign policy reversal that followed is its effect on Anglo-German relations. If 1878 marked the high point of Bismarck's prestige in Britain, then by 1885 Bismarck and Germany had become the great villains of the British press, and, in the eyes of Liberal and Conservative British politicians, the force in Europe to be most feared. Such hostility was in sharp contrast with the history of Anglo-German relations, which had been, if not always warm, then at least rarely hostile and most often amicable.

The important point of the Congress and its aftermath is that although 1878 marked the height of Bismarck's popularity in Britain, that popularity was due to a misapprehension of his motives and actions and came at a heavy price. Most studies agree that a fundamental shift occurred in Anglo-German relations long before the onset of the twentieth century; few bother to try to explain the changing mentality behind this shift, especially as it concerns the British point of view. This fact will become apparent: the later backlash against Bismarck's actions at the Congress helped construct and amplify a 'myth' of Bismarck in Britain that had serious implications for and deleterious effects on later Anglo-German relations.[12] Myth is a difficult concept to deal with, but according to one historian, it 'exist[s] for us as a set of keywords which refer us to traditions, and ... transmit coded messages from the culture as a whole to its individual members.'[13] Thus myths become narratives whose broad dissemination and wide acceptance come through their embeddedness in linguistic and symbolic forms, in particular through organs of the mass media.[14] In short, they are often commonly held fictions and mistruths, with the potential for serious disillusionment when they are debunked. This is indeed what happened in Britain following the Congress.[15]

Bismarck in the Review Press, 1878–79

Bismarck excelled at using the semi-official German press as an instrument for both internal and external politicking, and he was a master at the modern art of spin doctoring.[16] Thus it comes as no surprise that this subject has been touched on by works dealing with his domestic policy and foreign affairs. There have even been several studies on perceptions of Bismarck in the European press, but these works spend very little time talking about the Congress of Berlin and afford no space to a discussion of modern myth-making.[17]

British historians are mostly silent about perceptions of Bismarck in the British review press. Stephen Koss's two-volume study of the British press in fact fails to mention Bismarck; it is concerned mainly with an analysis of the press as an organ of public manipulation. Koss argues that journals and newspapers at this time increasingly reflected British public opinion and were more susceptible to sensationalist tactics of manipulation. This was as true about Bismarck as it was about anything, for as the press accurately reflected the mood of the country in extolling Bismarck's role at the Congress, it also worked diligently to construct and further myths that would harm Anglo-German relations just a few years later.

To illustrate this argument, I will use as a case study the British review press, specifically four of the major review journals: *The Fortnightly Review*, *The Contemporary Review*, *The Spectator*, and *The Saturday Review*. These journals were among the most popular and important of their day, and although it is difficult to say exactly where they stood on the political spectrum at any given time, in general *The Contemporary* was moderate, *The Fortnightly* liberal, *The Spectator* whiggish–liberal in nature, and *The Saturday Review* staunchly conservative. Review journals digested the latest news and offered editorials, original commentary and articles, as well as fiction, essays, and poetry from most of the leading writers of the day. Their prestige was great. As R.C.K. Ensor once noted:

> A great influence was wielded by the monthly and quarterly reviews, which everybody in the government read, and to which all the best writers of the day contributed. Their vogue was more nation-wide than that of the London dailies, since they were not, like the latter, ousted in the provinces by provincial organs ... The articles were few and long; they amounted to small treatises; and the components of many of the more famous Victorian books first appeared in this form. Besides the monthly, two weekly reviews had in the period great importance–the *Spectator* ... and the *Saturday Review*.[18]

A close analysis of those articles dealing with Germany, the Congress and Bismarck should reveal much about how the Bismarck myth was constructed and furthered through use of the popular press.

The Saturday Review was one of the most widely-read and influential of all British periodicals, Ensor calling it during this period 'the brilliant organ of an intellectual conservatism [that] numbered among its writers Lord Salisbury and Sir Henry Maine.'[19] Overall, its depiction of Bismarck shifted significantly during 1878–79, changing from an attitude of skeptical admiration to one of active praise. In so doing it helped form several strongly held Conservative convictions about Bismarck, including the belief that Bismarck embodied the German state to such a degree that the two became difficult to separate. Several months before the Congress, in a commentary on German affairs, it set forth an argument that would only be strengthened throughout the Congress period. 'When Bismarck is ill,' it contended, 'the whole German Ministry is ill; when he is at Varzin, it is at Varzin; when he is sulking or weary, its temper is soured and its energies affected.'[20] It argued that no other modern state was as indistinguishable from the character of its leader as Germany.[21] As for Bismarck's attitude towards the Eastern crisis, it predicted that Bismarck would keep a relatively low profile in order that 'Russia shall do no harm to Austria, and through Austria to Germany.'[22] As for Anglo-German relations, it argued that Germany would make no decisions either way as to England's actions: 'Prince Bismarck knows perfectly well that no one dreams of despising Germany, and he therefore does not allow his tranquillity to be easily ruffled.'[23] One week later, it commented with a hint of alarm on a recent Bismarck speech to the Reichstag where he had noted that although he had no quarrel with England, he nonetheless would offer no aid except in the form of mediation.[24]

The news that Bismarck would preside over the upcoming Berlin Conference caused *The Saturday Review* to publish a feature article on his character. The first of many such articles during the time period, it is perhaps the best depiction of British sentiment on the subject published before the

Congress. It stated the British fears that Bismarck would be swayed by German sentiment favoring Austria, and noted that his recent ailments could play a factor in such important negotiations. It argued that 'The real call on his imaginative mind is that, when once the path of new combinations is open, there are endless complications to be encountered, conflicting interests to be considered, a distant future to be regarded. [He] has to calculate what arrangements can endure ...'[25] More importantly, however, it touched on another important theme that the Congress strongly reinforced:

> The country could not hope to find any one to replace Prince Bismarck ... [He] is entirely alone in Germany, not only from intellectual superiority and the eminence of an exceptional position, but from the habits of his life. He never works with any one, never knows any one, never trusts any one ... He only feels truly himself when he can bully his vassals and mock at honest, plodding subordinates. For Germany this is a misfortune. The day must come when Germany will exist and Prince Bismarck will be no more; and unfortunately Germany and Prince Bismarck seem at present to be equally unwilling and unable to face and prepare for the situation which that dark day will bring with it.[26]

This is an important (and prescient) observation. The Congress reinforced this belief, and helped it become an integral part of the overall Bismarck myth. In addition, this illustrates that British opinion–at least as one of the leading Conservative organs presented it–did not always praise Bismarck before the Congress, but could be decidedly wary and pessimistic.

With the Congress looming ever nearer, *The Saturday Review* subtly began to alter its view of Bismarck. While still wary, it none the less hoped that Bismarck would give fair treatment to England. 'The prospects of the Congress are, on the whole, encouraging,' it noted. 'Prince Bismarck, who has from the beginning of the Eastern troubles and throughout the war seemed to incline to the Russian cause, has, since he ascertained that the resolution of the English Government was immovable, urged upon Russia, with final success, the expediency of conceding a demand that was obviously just.'[27] It noted in another article that his health had improved so that he could press forward with preparations for the Congress 'which he has done so much to render possible.'[28]

However, the coming of the Congress was a time of great anxiety in Britain, not the least over Bismarck's role in it. *The Saturday Review* noted that Germans seemed less preoccupied by the events than the other European peoples, for the 'Germans get their foreign affairs done for them by Prince Bismarck. What he thinks they think, and what he does they approve.'[29] Still, it noted that overall the Germans and Bismarck were genuinely interested in peace. 'Prince Bismarck is pleased to exhibit himself as the champion of peace,' it stated, although later it somewhat sarcastically called attention to his earlier inclination to resort to military force. It further argued that his press organs were working to convince the world of his genuine interest in the peace process, and that 'it is through his labours that peace is now almost ensured.'[30] The Saturday Review made no definitive comment on this, pointing out only that most Germans felt that 'if Bismarck had willed otherwise, the policy of their nation would have been totally different.'[31]

Bismarck's actions at the Congress itself were, in the eyes of The Saturday Review, if not always pro-British then at least not pro-Russian, and this perception went a long way towards raising his esteem in their eyes, as did his personal involvement in smoothing over rocky spots. Bismarck's role as a bulwark against Russian expansion cannot be underestimated at this juncture, and goes a long way towards explaining why so many Britons were so willing to support him, despite his dubious track record. For example, when a controversy erupted between Russia and England, The Saturday Review asserted that 'Prince Bismarck exerted himself to procure the assent of the Russian Government to the original English demand.'[32] Indeed, it declared by 6 July that the success of the Congress was all but assured, and its main goals met. It noted that, although 'it is not necessary to accept literally Prince Bismarck's assurance that the English Government has obtained great advantages by the action of the Congress,' the benefits for Beaconsfield and Salisbury should not be denigrated.[33] Still, as the Congress drew to a close, praise for Bismarck became more frequent. His 'vigorous adroitness,' The Saturday Review gushed, 'is not less willingly acknowledged.'[34] As the Congress closed, it claimed that, although not every side got what it wanted, for the British the settlement was sound, and for that it owed a debt to Bismarck's diplomacy.[35]

The Saturday Review further argued that Germany would remain a power to be reckoned with, its influence greatly increased with Bismarck at the helm. It was even able to find some humor in his interactions with the assembled plenipotentiaries:

> [Bismarck's] methods for dealing with the Congress appear to be three. When there are any signs of loitering his chronic illness reappears, and he threatens to go to a bath or die unless a more ardent desire for dispatch is shown. When discussions seem likely to become warm, he gets up and goes away, so that the sitting is brought to a convenient close. Lastly, he establishes good humour by dilating to the English representatives on the enormous success they have gained, and explaining to them alternately how monstrous it would be, and how painful to him personally as an impartial critic, if such very successful people

tried to push their success too far.[36]

Looking beyond the tongue-in-cheek tone shows an appreciation for the way Bismarck got the Congress to concentrate on the business at hand instead of sputtering off on to useless tangents.

Following the Congress, *The Saturday Review* outlined a different view of Bismarck in light of his success in preventing war. Beginning not long after the closing of the Congress, *The Saturday Review* published several feature articles outlining its new view of Bismarck's character. A lead article on 14 September 1878, although critical of his internal policy, none the less argued that Bismarck 'has for many years, as far as Parliaments are concerned, had the exclusive control' of foreign affairs, and, since that was what was important to the British in the end, they had no reason to quarrel.[37] Another, dated 9 November 1878, highlighted a recent biography by Moritz Busch that would cause quite a stir in Britain and commented with some mirth that 'it has apparently been his lot in life to have principally to deal with two classes of men—cowards and fools; and he delights in thinking that he has bullied the former and gauged the capacity of the latter.'[38] After delineating a number of his escapades, it concluded that 'Prince Bismarck was much abler and much bolder, and it may be added, much more unscrupulous, than those with whom he had to deal. The work he had to do was rough as it was great, and probably a less dictatorial man could not have done it. Success has glorified a character which failure would have exposed to much merited reproach.'[39]

The Spectator was the other influential weekly review during this time period, and its view of Bismarck also altered significantly during 1878. Early in that year it declared that Bismarck's object was 'to mystify the public of Europe, to conceal the ultimate policy of Germany, and to leave her as free as possible to act, either in Conference or after its dispersion,' but although he took pains to hide his true feelings, nonetheless 'the drift of his speech ... is more important than his words.'[40] It declared that Bismarck was likely to be favorable to Russia, unfavorable to Austria, and an obstacle for Britain.[41] Bismarck was depicted as authoritarian, opportunistic and skillful as a leader in all fields, but also as someone whose style of rule was alienating many Germans.[42]

One notable difference between *The Spectator* and *The Saturday Review* was the former's decision mainly to eschew the title 'Prince' in favor of 'Chancellor' when referring to Bismarck. It is possible that the title 'Prince' carried more respect than *The Spectator* desired to give when speaking of Bismarck, something in tune with Liberal thought of the day; more likely it had to do with differing styles of editing and the different readership of the two weeklies. There are obvious differences in the depiction of Bismarck's character, too. *The Spectator*, for example, always presented Bismarck as being 'prepared for the measure of physical repression with which it is the defect of his temperament to fancy that intellectual errors can be crushed.'[43] It argued that his main weapon in internal policy was the same as in external: force.

As the Congress opened, *The Spectator* was still skeptical of Bismarck's leadership and pessimistic about the outcome of the Congress.[44] 'It is true that Bismarck is known to have a plan,' it stated, 'and it is vaguely understood that the plan is large; but has he appeased the deep-seated jealousies of Russia, Austria, Italy, and England?' The answer was an emphatic no; in fact, it predicted that not even Lord Beaconsfield would find a solution.[45] But as the Congress progressed, *The Spectator* slowly softened its stance on Bismarck.[46] Previously distrustful of Bismarck's intentions and actions, by the end of the year it had at least as much good to say about him as bad, quite a leap for a journal that avowed sympathy for the German socialists who were Bismarck's sworn domestic enemies. It recognized Bismarck's importance as a great historical figure at an historically important conference:

> The members of Congress are most of them among the foremost statesmen of Europe, and two of them, at least, will live in future history. There will, in no long time, be a Bismarck literature in Germany, possibly in Europe, and centuries hence historians will make reputations by their pictures of the great Reiter-diplomatist, the dragoon-statesman, the Goetz-Richelieu, the man who in himself sums up so well the characteristics of the old and the new of Germany.[47]

This perhaps more than anything else captures *The Spectator*'s attitude towards Bismarck. In him were the old and the new, for good and bad. For example, describing Beaconsfield's theatrics at the Congress, it noted 'it is very improbable that Lord Beaconsfield, fond as he is of display, has made himself ridiculous by pompous acting ... as it is also improbable that Prince Bismarck, a German *Junker*, 'dyed in the wool,' is immensely impressed with the heroic greatness of the English representative.'[48] But as the war scare receded it was ultimately able to reconcile the two sides of Bismarck.

As the Congress progressed and it appeared that Britain's major goals would be achieved, *The Spectator* slowly softened its stance on Bismarck, whom it had consistently condemned in the previous six months for his repressive internal policies.[49] In a series of news digests, it outlined Bismarck's key role in keeping the Congress moving steadily ahead. For example, on 6 July it noted that 'there remain the Grecian and Armenian questions, but Prince Bismarck presses on negotiations with decisions.'[50] When it ended, the paper reported that 'Count Andrássy, whose master has acquired two provinces without paying for them, rose and proposed a vote of thanks for Prince Bismarck, "the eminent statesman who has directed our labours.'"[51] *The Spectator* saw little reason to challenge the Austrian ambassador's praise.

One interesting sidenote was *The Spectator's* short commentaries about Bismarck's life that accompanied the main body of news about the Congress. On 22 June, for example, it reported that one of Bismarck's great hounds was credited by the German press with discovering that the Russian ambassador Gorchakov was the true enemy of Germany. It reported that:

> [Gorchakov], who is in a very weak state of health, began to totter before he reached a chair, when Bismarck ran hastily forward to assist him and prevent him from falling–an action which the dog mistook for a hostile onset, whereon he joined his master in the fancied attack, knocking down Gortschakoff with his great paws and holding him there. Bismarck, in spite of his great muscular strength, had much ado to pull off this 'dog of empire.'[52]

For *The Spectator*, even such innocuous events could carry menacing overtones where the German Chancellor was concerned.

The Congress altered *The Spectator's* view of Bismarck in some important ways. The journal continued attacking his repressive internal policies, especially his anti-Socialism, which it was at a loss to explain. But it qualified its criticism in light of his recent actions. 'With all his high qualities and amazing powers,' it stated, 'the great Chancellor has never been able to see that no sword will kill a ghost, that you cannot fight thoughts with material means.' But it held out hope for the future, for Bismarck was 'a diplomatist before all, and a diplomatist who cannot recede does not know the first conditions of the warfare in which he is so consummate an expert.'[53] Finally, it noted that Bismarck's foreign policy took precedence over his internal politicking, arguing that the present was 'an hour when the great Chancellor, ruling the strongest army in Europe, has much to think about and to do in departments which his Parliament leaves entirely in his hands.'[54]

The best overview of *The Spectator's* view of Bismarck comes, as in *The Saturday Review*, from a review of Dr. Busch's 1878 biography of the Chancellor. It roundly rebuked the book because 'we do not believe that this description is a true portrait of the greatest living German. It is not the impression which he has made upon contemporaries.'[55] It explained away the invective so apparent within its pages as a side of Bismarck that came out in after-dinner conversations as a kind of bawdy entertainment. Regardless of the veracity of the volume, however, the paper argued that it would help propel the Bismarck myth to new heights:

> All men shall think of him for the next twelve months as Jules Favre thought of him for forty-eight hours–as the resistless, high-handed, full-blooded, drinking, menacing German giant, against

whom contest was impossible, except by those who were prepared to endure all that a remorseless mind wielding irresistible power was prepared to inflict. They shall see him in his frankest mood, denouncing nations, damning agents, jeering at royalties ... lamenting only that he had not been harder on France, and trusting in Providence principally because Providence had raised him up.[56]

Yet *The Spectator* increasingly participated in the mythologizing of Bismarck that it deplored in the Busch article. By the end of the year it argued that Bismarck 'values the German unity wrung by blood and iron from its opponents much more than he values the unity produced naturally by the assimilation of national genius and of national instincts.'[57] It never realized that the 'blood and iron' characteristic was as much a part of the Bismarck myth as anything else, and that by invoking it, it was perpetuating it. By 1884–85, even for *The Spectator*, this kind of characterization became commonplace.

Unlike the weeklies, the monthly reviews concentrated on more detailed analyses of the major events of the time. *The Contemporary Review* is a good example of this practice. Despite a general anti-German attitude its view of Bismarck altered significantly in the course of 1878 as well. It moved from a critical stance towards Bismarck to one of admiration, awe, and fear. Every three months it published a long article entitled 'Contemporary Life and Thought in Germany.'[58] These articles provide a unique glimpse at the way Germany's day-to-day events were depicted in the British press and offer a good overview of its changing characterization of Bismarck. For example, a December 1878 article noted that his reconciliation with the National Liberals should not have been a surprise to anyone. 'How was it possible that Bismarck, ignoring the past, should take this course? The question is easily answered. Bismarck is the most practical of politicians.'[59]

A good example of the growing importance of Bismarck in British eyes was the proliferation of books on the subject of Germany and Bismarck beginning soon after the Congress. *The Contemporary Review* reviewed four of the most important works on Bismarck in a feature article in January 1879.[60] Drawing on these sources, it gave its own analysis of his character. For example, it argued that 'his strength lay in the depth of his convictions, which he expressed or blurted out in vehement unmeasured language, devoid of rhetorical grace or polish, but occasionally warmed and animated by burning words, condensed thoughts, and striking images, which came flashing through his tangled periods like lightning through clouds.'[61] It argued that Bismarck utilized the truth as a diplomatic tactic: '[Bismarck] made no secret of his ultimate designs, acting throughout on the theory that, even when it is an object to keep things doubtful or dark, there is no blind like the truth, nothing so sure to throw dust in the eyes of professional diplomatists, most of whom are too clever by half.'[62]

The article praised Bismarck for his 'blood and iron, fire and sword' policies. The portrait of Bismarck painted by *The Contemporary Review* is of a pious man, very superstitious, audacious, diplomatically acute, and ruthless to the point of cruelty. It was startled to find a man who made truth and justice subservient to expediency and led his sovereign through blood and slaughter to an imperial throne all the while contending that it was as a strict Christian that he did so. Beyond this, though, it likened him to Oliver Cromwell:

> It would be a satire on our common nature ... to suppose that his system, a system based on force, on never-ceasing war and absolutism, could last; but it may endure his time: he may go on throwing sixes with the iron dice of destiny; and the dazzling brilliancy of his career may continue to cast its blots into the shade until, haply and happily, mankind shall be agreed upon some sounder and less demoralizing criterion of greatness than success.[63]

Although they found much to admire in his character, there was more than a hint of fear in the descriptions of Bismarck. Like most other journals, *The Contemporary Review* praised and feared him at the same time.

The Fortnightly Review was edited at this time by John Morley, a future Liberal MP who had already gained fame as the editor of the *Pall Mall Gazette*. It had a more measured view of Bismarck and Germany during this time period than any of the other review journals surveyed. It saw Germany as playing a key role in European peace, and it did not depict Bismarck as an enemy of Britain. But it asked 'Who can tell what the state of Europe may be ten years hence ... when Bismarck may be gone?'[64] Since no one could be certain of what policy a Germany without Bismarck might follow, the importance of finding a lasting solution to the Eastern Question became critical.

The Fortnightly Review recalled happier days when 'Germany ha[d] been always regarded as England's natural ally. But the popular English feeling has been eager to detect the contrarieties, much more than the resemblances, between the English and German manner of looking at the Eastern question.'[65] Indeed, there had nearly always been good relations between the two countries, and generally there was optimism that Bismarck would not prefer the Russians, for 'in Germany no favor has been displayed at Russian successes.'[66] But, it warned, others in Europe were fearful of Bismarck's leadership of the Congress. 'France has displayed a mistrust,' it noted, 'that such an assembly might be used by Prince Bismarck not to reform Eastern Europe, but to obtain a European ratification of the advantages obtained in Western Europe by Germany.'[67] *The Fortnightly Review* disregarded French fears; it did note, however, that Bismarck inspired in his admirers the belief that, no matter what happened, he would foresee it, and Germany would gain in some manner or another.[68]

On the eve of the Congress, *The Fortnightly Review* expressed significant reservations over the German role. 'England has waited,' it lamented, 'and sees Austria apparently engaged in trying to strike a favourable bargain with Russia, [and] Germany treating Russia and Great Britain as alike in the wrong.'[69] Still, it credited Bismarck for his zealous attempts to mediate the Anglo-Russian dispute, as he had earlier mediated the disputes between Russia and Austria.[70] While not referring nearly as often to internal affairs as did some of the other journals, it still noted that he 'has manifested clearly enough his intention to make Conservatism and reactionary capital out of the assumed affinity of Liberalism with Socialism.'[71]

The Congress itself was received with guarded optimism, and Bismarck was singled out for his efforts to further European peace because he 'accepted the task of avoiding a vast European convulsion by discovering a common term for Russian ambition and British fears.'[72] One thing becomes clear in looking at the pre-Congress literature and those articles that followed. Increasingly, *The Fortnightly Review* saw Germany as a benevolent European power. It argued that Bismarck's Germany 'enabled us to feel absolutely secure ... That Germany should place a limit to the Russian advance is essential ... As long as Germany sees no danger to herself ... and until her empire show signs of decay, we may dismiss apprehension and trust our safety to the guardianship of the manifest, the inevitable, the destined antagonist of Slav domination.'[73]

As 1878 came to a close, *The Fortnightly Review*–like the other review journals discussed in the paper–chose to publish a retrospective on the character of the 'new' Prince Bismarck. 'It is too soon to declare a definite opinion upon Prince Bismarck,' it began, 'on the man and on his work.'[74] Predictably, it then launched into a 20,000 word treatise on just that subject. It postulated that Busch's new biography could not have been published without the Chancellor's approval; it thus was more inclined to believe its contents: 'Opinion, as all the world knows, is in our days the great and supreme power, which in the long run directs events. Bismarck understands this, he has organized this new force on system, and he has insisted on getting it into his own hand.'[75] Thus, it hypothesized, the work was a calculated attempt by Bismarck to reinforce his own myth. What emerges is that the driving force behind the man was simple and had a single aim: the greatness of Germany. *The Fortnightly Review* depicted a man of strongly marked character:

> His force is evident ... . He has perceived clearly what are the
> forces now active in Europe, and now effective in working the

various transformations of Europe–the principle of nationalities,
democratic aspirations, the press–and he has found out the secret
of using them all in turn, and making them his instruments ... .
But he is hard, and pays little heed to the lives of men. War has
no horror to him. The German of the primitive time survives in
him; or rather, he appears among us like the god Thor of the
Scandinavian Olympus, bearing in his hand his iron hammer,
and unchaining the tempests.[76]

Thus emerged a 'new' Bismarck, a force for peace in Europe, but one with
a potential for aggression that appeared ominous and omnipresent to the
British. This curious mix of admiration and fear exemplifies the
transformation in the way Bismarck was perceived, and mythologized, by
the British review press.

Conclusion

When the review journals are assessed together, a clear pattern emerges.
Regardless of political bias, all, for various reasons and to varying degrees,
were critical of Bismarck before the Congress. But because he brokered a
peaceful settlement that was hailed by many as a victory, a significant change
in the British perception of his character occurred. While this might seem
an obvious point, it was not the fact that he was rehabilitated by the press
that was important. What was significant was the way in which it was done.
Building on existing myths, Bismarck was recast as a new man for a new
age, a peace-loving leader of the most peaceful nation in Europe and, along
with Disraeli, the leading statesmen of the era. He was still the Iron
Chancellor, but instead of using his considerable skills to undermine
European equilibrium, he now worked for continental peace, and therefore
worked for British interests seemingly without asking for anything in return.
Thus British Liberals hailed him and nourished a naive belief in his
newfound non-aggressiveness, while Conservatives lauded him for doing
what no other European leader could do: directly promote British interests
by working as a bulwark against Russian expansion. Many British leaders,
on both sides of the political spectrum, felt they had found a steadfast and
indefatigable ally in Bismarck. It only took a few short years to shatter
their faith.

     This is because both the Liberal and Conservative characterizations were
constructed myths, myth being defined here as attributed characteristics
that reach larger-than-life proportions and thus substitute for objective
reality. The reality was that Bismarck acted with two purposes in mind:
German security and intra-European peace. With these overarching goals
as his reality, the Bismarck myth created and fostered by the review press

was bound to disappoint the naive view of the British Liberals, for he was simply never the man they believed him to be at the time. Likewise, the Conservative expectation that Germany would serve British interests was refuted in the early 1880s when Bismarck saw Gladstone constructing an anti-Austrian policy that he deemed dangerous to European peace, and so he worked to foil Gladstone's version of the Concert of Europe.[77] It was inevitable that Bismarck would disappoint both parties because he believed that Britain should contribute something, when in reality both Liberals and Conservatives wanted Bismarck and Germany to do their continental dirty work for them.

An analysis of the review press shows that part of the Bismarck myth resulted from Britain's genuine fear of the prospects of war with Russia and its corresponding relief when European stability was preserved. This is clearly evident in the articles published before the Congress convened, when Britain still did not know the direction Bismarck would lean. Unsure of the prospects, they badly wanted to believe Bismarck's own claims of being an 'honest broker' with nothing to gain from the proceedings and pinned their hopes for success on his ability to mediate an Anglo-Russian rift. Thus they characterized him as honest in his actions and believed what he told them. This had the residual effect of impairing their ability to see that, soon after the Congress, Bismarck was moving in a new direction and that as early as 1880 he seemed to be working behind the scenes to undermine British interests. The fact that Bismarck did not see or intend things this way is of less consequence; the British perception of German policy was what mattered in the end.

In fact, the results of the Congress were of dubious value to Britain in particular, and to European peace in general. A.J.P. Taylor noted that the Congress was significant 'so far as Bismarck was concerned, with what it left out, not for what it discussed or settled. Statesmen of the earlier nineteenth century ... would have been astonished at a European Congress where the questions of Poland, Germany, and Italy were not mentioned. All of these questions had received an answer in previous years, largely according to Bismarck's wishes.' Bismarck's contempt for the Balkans was legendary–all of the region, he had noted earlier, was not worth the bones of a single Pomeranian grenadier–and he felt his purpose was not 'to consider the happiness of the Bulgarians but to secure the peace of Europe.'[78] The British did not realize until too late that the Congress ultimately accomplished neither. Erich Eyck summed it up best when he noted that

> [many] questions raised at the Congress ... were decided only
> in principle, and a number of details were left to be worked out
> later. But there was no time for this, nor had Bismarck the
> necessary patience ... the consequence was that ... real
> friendship and harmony were impossible while so many

problems of the practical application of the treaty kept the
chanceries of Europe a-buzz with discussions ... It is even less
true to claim that the congress brought peace to the Balkans.
The occupation of Bosnia and Herzegovina ... was a very bloody
and costly business. And other peoples of the Near East struggled
for years to cast off the shackles of the Berlin Treaty. This brings
us to its cardinal fault ... the Congress treated the Balkan peoples
like mere pawns on a chessboard.[79]

More ominous than this, even, was a telling snippet penned in November,
1878–four months after the Congress ended–that gives a valuable insight
into Bismarckian diplomacy. Writing to the Crown Prince, the Chancellor
wrote 'It would be a triumph for our statesmanship if we succeeded in
keeping the Eastern ulcer open and thus jarred the harmony of the other
Great Powers in order to secure our own peace.' Here, in plain view, is
Bismarck's true goal. As Eyck rightly noted, 'A policy dictated by this
Machiavellian maxim was, indeed, unfitted to bring lasting peace either to
the Balkans or to Europe.'[80] Or, it might be added, to Britain.

When Bismarck's true colors became known to the British, there was a
justifiable if belated backlash against him. The effects of this alteration in
British opinion were significant. Bismarck alienated his new Liberal
admirers in Britain, who returned to power in 1880, when he actively
opposed Gladstone;[81] as W.N. Medlicott has noted, the post-Congress period
must be seen in terms of 'conflicting German and English programmes, and
in a personal sense in terms of a Bismarck–Gladstone rivalry ... . During
the short period from 1879 to 1882 Bismarck's new course gave Germany
the mechanism of security while imposing in Europe a deadlock which was
a preventative of war rather than a guarantee of peace.'[82] This alienation,
however, did not extend to many British Conservatives, who saw in Bismarck
not a rival of Britain but an opponent of Gladstonian principles, and saw
Bismarck's policies as being essentially in step with those of Disraeli.

Medlicott further argues that 'it is right to speak of this conflict in terms
of Anglo-German rivalry ... but as the rivalry was unacknowledged on
Bismarck's side and, as far as we can see, only dimly perceived by Gladstone,
it is easy to underrate its importance in the context of Anglo-German
relations.'[83] Yet it was an important step towards the creation of anti-German
sentiment in Britain. At the Congress, Germany appeared as a strong but
amicable neighbor to whom it was wise to give a wide berth; but Bismarck's
reorientation of policy helped to create an anti-Bismarck and an anti-German
antagonism that eventually became an important factor in British politics
and that produced a distrust of him that caused even greater skepticism
towards German intentions. The failure of the Concert due to Bismarck's
actions changed all that. Medlicott concluded that 'Bismarck's support of
British policy in Egypt in 1882 and 1883 concealed the extent of Anglo-

German antagonism a little longer, but its existence became clear enough in the colonial crisis of 1884–85, and by this stage the country had become conscious for the first time of Germany as a serious ... rival.'[84]

Despite having alienated the Gladstonians by blocking the Concert, Bismarck still had supporters among the Conservative party in Britain. Disraeli's and Salisbury's most loyal followers formed a 'Cult of Bismarck' that held Bismarck up as a shining example of Conservative principles in Europe and was responsible for muting some of the criticism of anti-Bismarck British Liberals. These same Conservatives, however, reexamined their position when Bismarck seemed to stab them in the back by creating an overseas empire. They had chosen to believe that Bismarck ruled Germany absolutely when he in fact did not; thus when he turned to imperialism, they saw it as a deliberate choice on his part and never imagined he was responding to internal pressure. This is due to the fact that during the Congress, while Kaiser William was recovering from an assassination attempt, 'from 2 June until December 1878 ... Bismarck enjoyed an authority in government as unimpaired as any autocrat in Germany's history.'[85] Thus, what else could German imperialism be, they asked, other than a conscious decision by Bismarck to challenge Britain? Believing the 'honest broker' myth they helped create in 1878, it took a crisis like 1884–85 for them to wake up. When they did, many Conservatives became more anti-German than anyone else in Britain.

The Bismarck myth created at the Congress and debunked soon after had other lasting ramifications. The myth saw Bismarck as the arbiter of Britain and Europe's destiny and as the only individual who could control the German state. The British feared that when he was gone things would fall apart. In fact, for many Britons Bismarck *was* Germany. Despite the sense of personal betrayal they came to feel towards him, most maintained a love–hate relationship with him during the last years of his life, which helps explain several periods of *détente*, like those surrounding the Mediterranean Agreements of 1887 and the Heligoland Treaty of 1890. Indeed, by the time he left office in 1890, some British politicians believed the prospects of amicable Anglo-German relations went with him. His state, a product of his own creation, had broken free of its Bismarckian constraints and was unleashed on Europe, demanding more colonies, European dominance, more economic control, and a larger navy. The myth the British constructed was simple yet damaging in its implications: Bismarck raised a monster, and it devoured him in the end. Now it threatened Britain, and Europe, and the world.

Bismarck in part believed his own myths, and strove to further them through such works as Moritz Busch's semi-official biography. But the British review press played a key role helping construct the Bismarck myth, and when this myth fell apart, as it was almost bound to do, the backlash to it became an important column upon which later Anglo-German antagonism was built. This myth helped discredit Gladstone and worked to bring down his government, earning the eternal enmity of Gladstonian Liberals; in so doing, Bismarck alienated half the British electorate. This in itself did not herald the decline of Anglo-German relations, as many Conservatives in Britain used Bismarck as a foil to Gladstone. Herein, however, lies the problem. Bismarck simply never would play the role they wanted him to, and when he sponsored German colonization, he alienated even the staunchest supporters, the British 'Cult of Bismarck.' In so doing he unknowingly united Britain in opposition to him and to Germany. The full story of that is told in the events of the Colonial Crisis of 1884–85; indeed the years 1878–85 form one of the pillars of Anglo-German antagonism. Bismarck played the 'honest broker' only when he saw the role as a means to meet German aims, and for that he should not be faulted. He was interested only in Germany and furthering its (and his own) interests. The myth of the 'honest broker,' however, was something he actively fostered and indeed reveled in, and in the end he was rewarded for his actions with increasing British antagonism. That such reactions at times seemed to baffle him shows just how great of a gap existed between his intentions and the perception his actions created.

That being said, the commonly held belief that the Congress of Berlin marked the high point of Bismarck's diplomatic career becomes a bit more difficult to support. Instead, it must be seen as a short-term success, but in the long run something of a failure. Not only did it fail to create a lasting solution to the Eastern Question, but it also produced a complex diplomatic situation where German and British interests were increasingly likely to collide. Seeking security for Germany by a new method of balanced antagonism, as Medlicott argued, Bismarck did 'nothing to remove, and was indeed doing much to perpetuate, the sense of irrevocable antagonism which after a certain point seemed to paralyze all capacity for constructive negotiations. He had made a deadlock and called it peace.'[86] The British press helped to create expectations about Bismarck he was never willing or able to meet. Thus, although he achieved his immediate goals, in the long run the cost outweighed the purchase, for it came at a price that imperiled future Anglo-German relations and unwittingly helped push Europe down the twisted path towards the First World War. That Bismarck never realized what he had wrought, or what others had wrought with his image, is one of the great ironies of his long and storied career.

NOTES

1 The author is indebted to Professors Walter L. Arnstein, Paul W. Schroeder, Josef Altholz, and Michael H. Shirley for comments on various drafts of this

paper. An earlier version of this work was presented at the Midwest Conference on British Studies in Lawrence, Kansas in October 1998.

2   Germany, of course, only became a united entity following the Franco-Prussian War of 1870–1871. But Britain traditionally had strong ties with a number of Germanic countries (e.g. Prussia), and indeed it must be remembered that the Four Georges were all of German heritage. Whether this hurt or helped the image of Germany within Britain, however, still remains a point of debate.

3   See for example Hans Ulrich-Wehler's works on the subject, and Erich Eyck's *Bismarck and German Imperialism* (London: G. Allen & Unwin, 1950).

4   For example, when the British poet Edmund Blunden noted that German corpses looked 'pig nosed ... and still seemingly hostile,' Siegfried Sassoon commented on their 'look of butchered hostility,' and John Easton called them 'wraiths in spiked helmets', they were invoking images and stereotypes created over a period of years. Paul Fussell, *The Great War and Modern Memory* (New York, 1975), p. 78. Fussell's work gives a lucid explication on the submerged meaning of such descriptive writings. A similar theme is echoed in John Dower's *War Without Mercy*, which outlines the integral role racism played in the Pacific theatre of the Second World War. John Dower, *War Without Mercy: Race and Power in the Pacific War* (New York, 1986). Dower points out that the Americans and Japanese viewed each other in distinctly racist ways, and this was a culmination of years of negative stereotypical beliefs. He argues: 'The greatest challenge has not been to recall the raw emotions of the war, but rather to identify dynamic [historical] patterns in the torrent of war words and graphic images.' Ibid., p. x. This approach is, of course, more easily seen when combatants differ racially, but the same kind of rhetoric and behavior was evident in Anglo-German interaction during the Great War.

5   This is the main reason it has always been a difficult proposition for governments to mobilize support for sudden, unexpected war or peace. A historical example of this is Tsar Alexander I's turnabout concerning Napoleon, which created a massive negative response following the Tilsit peace. A more modern example is the increasingly angry campaign against Saddam Hussein leading up to the Persian Gulf War that culminated with the depiction of Hussein as a 'modern Hitler.'

6   The Marquis of Salisbury, the Foreign Secretary at the Congress of Berlin and the Conservative successor to Lord Beaconsfield, might have agreed more with the Liberal depiction of Bismarck. According to Eyck, 'Bismarck was suspected by foreign statesmen of fomenting war between other countries. Salisbury compared him to Sir Lucius O'Trigger in Sheridan's comedy *The Rivals*, who does his best to bring about a duel between two men who are by no means anxious to fight.' Eyck, *Bismarck and German Imperialism*, p. 247.

7   For example, a constant topic of discussion was Bismarck's ever-increasing girth. Disraeli, among others, was quick to note Bismarck's enormous and eclectic appetite. As A.J.P. Taylor noted of the Congress, 'Protocol was ignored; everything subordinated to punctual and enormous meals. Bismarck was to be seen, stuffing shrimps into his mouth with one hand, cherries with the other, and insisting–not surprisingly–that he must leave soon for a cure at Kissingen.' Taylor, *Bismarck*, p. 138.

8   Eyck, *Bismarck and the German Empire*, p. 248.

9   Otto Pflanze, *Bismarck and the Development of Germany*, Vol. II (Princeton,

NJ: Princeton University Press, 1990): p. 437. Bismarck's role as President of the Congress was greatly aided by the secret meetings held before the Congress was convened between Salisbury and Shuvalov in which the general structure of the agreement over Bulgaria was agreed upon. For good overviews of the Congress and the Eastern Question, see W.N. Medlicott's *The Congress of Berlin and After*, 2nd edn. (London: Athlone, 1963) and Richard Millman's *Britain and the Eastern Question, 1875–1878* (New York: Oxford University Press, 1979).

10   Alan Palmer, *Bismarck* (New York: Scribner's, 1976), p. 201. The particulars settled upon at the Congress and confirmed in the Treaty of Berlin included the creation of an autonomous Bulgaria; the formation of the province of Eastern Rumelia; territorial gains for Serbia and Montenegro; the confirmation of Romania's independence; and, in an ominous decision that would greatly effect the outbreak of the First World War, the granting to Austria-Hungary the right to occupy and administer Bosnia-Herzegovina.

11 · Pflanze, *Bismarck and the Development of Germany*, Vol. II, p. 441.

12   There has been some work on the concept of modern myth and German statesmen, and a recent article analyzes the Bismarck myth in the cinema; Lothar Machtan's 'Der inszenierte Mythos: Bismarck im Film' in J. Dülffer, Hans Hüber et al., *Otto von Bismarck: Person–Politik–Mythos* (Berlin: Academie Verlag, 1993).

13   Richard Slotkin, *The Fatal Environment: The Myth of the Frontier in the Age of Industrialization, 1800–1890* (New York: Athenaeum, 1985), p. 16.

14   Slotkin argues further that 'the language of myth … renders ideology in the form of symbol, exemplum, and fable, and poetically evokes fantasy, memory, and sentiment.' Ibid., p. 22.

15   Some common British myths about Bismarck included a belief that he and the German state were one and indivisible and that he could not be defeated in battle. The biography of Bismarck by Dr Moritz Busch mentioned later outlines these and many other commonly held myths and misconceptions about its subject.

16   According to A.J.P. Taylor, 'Bismarck used one weapon to influence public opinion which brought down on him much high-minded disapproval. He issued directives to the press and employed his own men, [Moritz] Busch and [Lothar] Bucher, to write leading articles which were then widely distributed. More than this, he drew on the sequestered funds of the ex-King of Hanover to bribe the press directly.' Taylor, *Bismarck*, p. 136. For his part, Bismarck was acutely aware of what was written about him in the foreign press, and could change the course of his foreign policy accordingly. Writing about the Congress of Berlin in his memoirs, he recalled: 'The passionate and bitter language of all the Russian organs, the instigation of Russian popular opinion against us which was authorized by the censorship of the press, seemed to make it advisable that we should not alienate from us the sympathies we might still possess among the non-Russian powers.' Otto von Bismarck, *The Man and the Statesman, Being Reflections and Remembrances of Otto Prince von Bismarck*, Vol. II (London: Smith, 1898), p. 239.

17   Hans Ulrich Rentsch's *Bismarck im Urteil der schweizerischen Press 1862–1890* (Basel: Helbing & Lichtenhahn, 1945) is mainly concerned with how such things as German unification and the *Kulturkampf* were depicted in a variety of Swiss newspapers.

18   R.C.K. Ensor, *England 1870–1914* (Oxford: Clarendon Press, 1949), p. 146.

19   Ibid., p. 145.

20 'Germany,' *The Saturday Review of Politics, Literature, Science and Art*, No. 1164, Vol. 46 (16 February 1878): 195.
21 It summed this up as 'the oddest arrangements for dealing with the affairs of a great country which have ever found a place in real history.' Ibid., p. 195.
22 Ibid., p. 196.
23 Ibid.
24 'The Eastern Crisis,' *The Saturday Review*, No. 1165, Vol. 46 (23 February 1878), pp. 223–4. See also 'Russia and Europe,' *The Saturday Review*, No. 1168, Vol. 46 (16 March 1878), pp. 321–2 and 'Russia and Europe,' ibid., for further elucidation of early British fears on the eve of the Congress.
25 'Germany and Prince Bismarck,' *The Saturday Review*, No. 1167, Vol. 46 (9 March 1878), p. 288.
26 Ibid., p. 289.
27 'The Congress,' *The Saturday Review*, No. 1180, Vol. 46 (8 June 1878), p. 707.
28 'German Assassins,' *The Saturday Review*, No. 1180, Vol. 46 (8 June 1878), p. 708.
29 'Germany,' *The Saturday Review*, No. 1181, Vol. 46 (15 June 1878), p. 740.
30 Ibid.
31 Ibid.
32 'The Congress,' *The Saturday Review*, No. 1183, Vol. 46 (29 June 1879), p. 807.
33 Lord Beaconsfield was the Conservative Prime Minister Benjamin Disraeli and the Marquis of Salisbury was his Foreign Minister. They were joined in negotiations by the Ambassador to Berlin Odo Russell.
34 'The Congress,' *The Saturday Review*, No. 1185, Vol. 46 (13 July 1878), p. 35.
35 Lengthy descriptions of British gains/losses at the Congress can be found in 'The Treaty of Berlin,' *The Saturday Review*, No. 1186, Vol. 46 (20 July 1878), 66–7. The basic analysis was as follows: 'It is possible that Lord Beaconsfield and Lord Salisbury may have made mistakes; but, on the whole, they have done their best; nor is there reason to suppose that any other English diplomatists would have obtained better results.' 'The Berlin Protocols,' *The Saturday Review*, No. 1187, Vol. 46 (27 July 1878), p. 97.
36 'Germany,' *The Saturday Review*, No. 1184, Vol. 46 (6 July 1878), p. 4.
37 'Prince Bismarck,' *The Saturday Review*, No. 11194, Vol. 46 (14 September 1878), p. 323.
38 'Prince Bismarck,' *The Saturday Review*, No. 1202, Vol. 46 (9 November 1878), p. 576. Note: the biography in question is D. Moritz Busch's *Graf Bismarck und seine Leute während des Kriegs mit Frankreich* (Leipzig, 1878). Moritz Busch was one of Bismarck's 'semi-official' journalists and a government official. One of Bismarck's biographers, Emil Ludwig, noted of Busch and his close cohort Lothar Bucher that 'Interesting men are Busch and Bucher. A little younger than Bismarck, both had been revolutionists of note, and were taken into the public service. Busch is clever and unscrupulous, pliable and shallow. After travelling widely, he became editor of the 'Grenzboten,' and attracted Bismarck's attention. He rose to favour before the Franco-German war, but was after it sent away in disgrace. Then, by underhand ways verging on blackmail, he made himself indispensable once more, and was again employed by Bismarck, who had more to fear from him than Busch had to fear from the chancellor. As a reporter he was a past master, seeing, hearing, and noting all that happened. His diary provides invaluable

material for an understanding of Bismarck, who himself had to admit its unwelcome truth.' Emil Ludwig, *Bismarck: The Story of a Fighter* (Boston: Little, Brown, 1928), p. 467. An example of the kind of descriptions that caused so much controversy includes Bismarck's description of the occupation of Paris: 'If at first the Parisians get a supply of provisions, then are again put upon half rations, and have to starve a little, that will work, I think. It is just the same with flogging. If a man gets too many lashes one after the other, it is very disagreeable.' Moritz Busch, *Bismarck in the Franco-Prussian War*, Vol. II (New York: Howard Fertig, 1973), p. 252.

39   Ibid., p. 577. See also 'Germany,' *The Saturday Review*, No. 1212, Vol. 47 (18 January 1879), pp. 66–67.

40   'Prince Bismarck's Speeches,' *The Spectator*, No. 2591 (23 February 1878), p. 238.

41   Ibid., pp. 238–9. For a description of the three British aims at the Congress, see 'The Three British Questions in Congress,' *The Spectator*, No. 2591 (23 February 1878), p. 236.

42   'Prince Bismarck's Home Troubles,' *The Spectator*, No. 2593 (9 March 1878), pp. 302–3.

43   'Prince Bismarck and the Socialists,' *The Spectator*, No. 2604 (25 May 1878), p. 658.

44   See 'Russia in June, 1877 and in February 1878,' *The Spectator*, No. 2591 (23 February 1878): pp. 237–8; 'The Congress,' *The Spectator*, No. 2594 (16 March 1878), pp. 332–3; 'The Debates on the Eastern Question,' *The Spectator*, No. 2598 (13 April, 1878), pp. 461–2; and 'Topics of the Day: Prince Gortschakoff's Memorandum,' *The Spectator*, No. 2598 (13 April 1878), p. 460.

45   'Topics of the Day: The Situation,' *The Spectator*, No. 2606 (8 June 1878), p. 720. It stated of Disraeli: 'Beaconsfield is a genius, but to frame a plan which shall settle the Eastern Question, yet satisfy Europe, yet content both English parties, yet not excite the Turks to resistance, may overtask even the capacities for which his adulators claim the admiration of the world.' p. 720.

46   See for example, 'The Internal Policy of Prince Bismarck,' *The Spectator*, No. 2587 (26 January 1878), pp. 112–13; 'Prince Bismarck's Home Troubles,' *The Spectator*, No. 2593 (09 March 1878), pp. 302–3; and 'Prince Bismarck and the Socialists,' *The Spectator*, No. 2604 (25 May 1878), Ibid.

47   'Topics of the Day: The Congress of Berlin,' *The Spectator*, No. 2607 (15 June 1878), p. 752.

48   'Topics of the Day: Progress in Berlin,' *The Spectator*, No. 2609 (29 June 1878), p. 816.

49   See for example 'The Internal Policy of Prince Bismarck,' *The Spectator*, No. 2587 (26 January 1878): pp. 112–113; 'Prince Bismarck's Home Troubles,' *The Spectator*, No. 2593 (9 March 1878), pp. 302–3; and 'Prince Bismarck and the Socialists,' *The Spectator*, No. 2604 (25 May 1878), p. 658.

50   'News of the Week,' *The Spectator*, No. 2610 (6 July 1878). See also the news digests for the months of June and July.

51   'News of the Week,' *The Spectator*, No. 2612 (20 July 1878).

52   'News of the Week,' *The Spectator*, No. 2608 (22 June 1878). Perhaps in an unintentional nod to Shakespeare, the British seemed to be fixated on Bismarck's 'dogs of empire.' In 1889 during the great naval reform debates, Lord Charles Beresford traveled to Germany and paid a call on Bismarck, who 'said that he could not understand why my own people did not listen to

me (nor could I!); for (said he) the British Fleet was the greatest factor for peace in Europe ... I stayed with him for two hours; and we drank much beer, and all the time his gigantic boar-hound, lying beside him, stared fixedly at me with a red and lurid eye.' Lord Charles Beresford, *Memories of Admiral Lord Charles Beresford* (Boston, 1919), p. 360.

53   'Prince Bismarck and the Socialists,' *The Spectator*, No. 2620 (14 September 1878), pp. 1145–6.

54   Ibid. Note: On his stance towards the Socialists, it argued 'we believe Prince Bismarck hates the socialists with all his heart, and intends to put them down; while as his methods, he has but one – the steady, unrelenting, scientific application of force.' p. 1145.

55   'The Newest Portrait of Prince Bismarck,' *The Spectator*, No. 2630 (23 November 1878), pp. 1462–3. Note: the kind of description given in this book is exemplified in his description of the typical Frenchman–'You may lay twenty-five lashes on a Frenchman's back with impunity, if you only deliver meanwhile a speech on the liberty and dignity of mankind. The imaginative victim will scarcely realize that you are flogging him.' Ibid., p. 1462.

56   Ibid.

57   'The Relapse Towards Protection,' *The Spectator*, No. 2635 (28 December 1878): p. 1627.

58   Similar articles were published for Russia, Italy, and France.

59   'Contemporary Life and Thought in Germany,' *The Contemporary Review*, Vol. XXXIV (December 1878): p. 168. To a greater degree than the other journals reviewed, *The Contemporary Review* was anti-German. It depicted the German people thus: 'combined with the good qualities and aims, always to be found among the German people, [the Germans] have a satiety, gloom, ill-humour, discouragement, discontent, disappointment, self-interest, egotism, particularist tendencies ... [they] are not of the opinion that things will soon mend.' It did not blame Bismarck for these tendencies, rather it hinted that he was one of the forces keeping them in check. Ibid., p. 173.

60   The four books reviewed were the aforementioned biography by Busch; J.E.L. Hesekiel's *The Life of Bismarck, Private and Political: With Descriptive Notices of his Ancestry* (London, 1870); Fitzhugh Maxse, ed., *Prince Bismarck's Letters to his Wife, Sister, and Others, from 1844 to 1870* (London, 1878); and M. Julian Klaczko's *Deux Chanceliers, le Prince Gortchakoff et le Prince de Bismarck* (Paris, 1876).

61   'Prince Bismarck,' *The Contemporary Review*, Vol. CXLVII (January 1879), p. 63.

62   Ibid., p. 67.

63   'Prince Bismarck,' *The Contemporary Review*, Vol. CXLVII (January 1879), p. 75.

64   S. Laing, 'A Plain View of British Interests,' *The Fortnightly Review*, Vol. CXXXIII (February 1878), p. 346.

65   'Home and Foreign Affairs,' *The Fortnightly Review* Vol. CXXXIII (April 1878), p. 642.

66   Ibid., p. 644.

67   Ibid.

68   Ibid., p. 646.

69   'Home and Foreign Affairs,' *The Fortnightly Review*, Vol. CXXXIII (May 1878), p. 797.

70   Ibid., p. 801.

71 'Home and Foreign Affairs,' *The Fortnightly Review,* Vol. CXXXIV (July 1878), p. 158.
72 'Home and Foreign Affairs,' *The Fortnightly Review,* Vol. CXXXIV (August 1878), p. 303.
73 Ralph A. Earle, 'Mr. Gladstone's Policy and the New Equilibrium,' *The Fortnightly Review,* Vol. CXXXIV (October 1878): p. 575. Note: See also Emile de Laveleye, 'Two Foreign Opinions on the Treaty of Berlin,' *The Fortnightly Review,* Vol. CXXXIV (October 1878), pp. 616–27, for further arguments on Germany as a bulwark against Slav encroachment.
74 Emile de Laveleye, 'Prince Bismarck,' *The Fortnightly Review,* Vol. CXXXIV (November 1878): p. 765.
75 Ibid., p. 766.
76 Ibid., p. 786.
77 See W.N. Medlicott, *Bismarck, Gladstone, and the Concert of Europe,* (London: Athlone, 1956) for an excellent discussion of this subject.
78 Taylor, *Bismarck,* p. 137.
79 Eyck, *Bismarck and German Imperialism,* pp. 250–51.
80 Ibid., p. 251. The italics are Eyck's.
81 Eyck noted that Bismarck's unwillingness to thrash out any details at the Congress was the root of their problems. 'When Gladstone returned to power in 1880, he found some of the questions (from the Congress) still unsolved and began to tackle them in his own way, which was not at all appreciated by Bismarck.' Eyck, p. 250.
82 Medlicott, *Bismarck, Gladstone, and the Concert of Europe,* p. vii.
83 Ibid., p. 4.
84 Ibid., p. 15.
85 Palmer, *Bismarck,* p. 199.
86 Medlicott, *Bismarck, Gladstone, and the Concert of Europe,* p. 337.

CHAPTER 10

The London Missionary Society's Mongolian Missions: British Insight into the 'Great Game' in Asia

Helen S. Hundley

Dr Walter Arnstein's great contribution to nineteenth-century British history lies in his works which remind us today of the multiple roles, both conscious and unconscious, played by religious organizations. As his Roman Catholic nuns in *Protestant vs. Catholic in Mid-Victorian England: Mr Newdegate and the Nuns* sought to mold religion, class, and gender roles to serve their needs, even the seemingly single-minded London Missionary Society presents the scholar with unexpected insight into British attitudes about the Russian Empire and Asia.

Between 1813 and 1890, missionaries from the London Missionary Society formed part of what the Society called the first and second Mongolian Missions.[1] The first mission, to the Buriat-Mongols in the Transbaikal of Russian Siberia, was followed three decades later by a mission to the Mongols in Khalka Mongolia in the Chinese Empire. While the great effort of the missions resulted in very few official converts, the 'idea' of these missions evoked a powerful mystique back home was used to call for financial support and as a recruiting tool.

This article will demonstrate that, in addition to this expected religious use of the missions, the missionaries discussed their views of the international political aspect of their locations and the actions of the great powers, which provides us today with an interesting inside view of the 'Great Game.' As on-site observers, their statements of the perceived impact of Russian and Chinese rule over the Mongols are of interest to us today. In addition, the role of the comparative value of Russian and Chinese culture as seen by the missionaries reflects British Victorian views of the 'less civilized' foreign cultures, even European ones.

The First Mongolian Mission

The institution behind the missions to the Mongols played an increasingly active role in the nineteenth century. Founded in 1794, the London Missionary Society encompassed a wide range of Protestant Nonconformist groups and became known for its drive to reach peoples in far corners of the earth.[2] To aid in conversions, the Society created alphabets for non-literate populations and regularized grammar in the process of translating and publishing the gospels. Not surprisingly, given their far-reaching interests, the London Missionary Society became involved with not one but two missions to the center of Asia. The initial mission to the Mongols arose in unique circumstances, because the mission was invited in by the sovereign head of an Orthodox Christian state. The idea of sending a Christian mission to the Buriats came together sometime around 1813. The first mission to a branch of the Mongols, the Buriat-Mongols, occurred in the Russian Empire when the London Missionary Society, in conjunction with the Russian Bible Society, sponsored a mission to the Buriats in Siberia from 1817 to 1841.[3]

Officially, the Russian Bible Society played host to the mission. Established in 1812 at the initiative of the British and Foreign Bible Society and with the blessing of Tsar Alexander I, the Russian Bible Society sought to disseminate the scriptures without comment, thus making an inter-denominational movement possible. The Society also specifically sought to provide the gospel in the native tongues of the numerous peoples of the Russian Empire.[4] The main goal of this mission, like the goals of other Russian Bible-Society-related activities, was to translate the Bible into the native languages of the various peoples, and then make these translations widely available to them.

The First Mongolian Mission actually began in St Petersburg. There the missionaries learned Russian and became acquainted with the London Missionary Society leadership in Russia. Edward Stallybrass (1793–1884), his first wife, Sarah Robinson Stallybrass (d. 1833), both English, and Cornelius Rahmn, a Swede, and his Scottish wife, were the first missionaries sent to Irkutsk, the largest city in the midst of the Buriats. The Stallybrasses and Rahmns began their trek to Siberia in December of 1817. En route to Irkutsk, the capital of Siberia, they stopped off for an audience with Tsar Alexander I in Moscow, where they received both his blessing and promise of aid for the mission.[5] Prince A.N. Golitsyn, the head of the Russian Bible Society and Minister of Ecclesiastical Affairs and Public Instruction, had already promised all of the aid that he could provide.[6]

Thus armed, the group arrived in Irkutsk on 30 March 1818,[7] only to decide within two months that Irkutsk was not the right place for them.[8] Edward Stallybrass's reasoning for the move to Selenginsk in the Transbaikal is found in Sarah Stallybrass's *Memoirs*. In his view, the Irkutsk Buriats would make poor subjects for conversion, as they spoke an 'impure' Mongolian dialect and were not accustomed to the use of books, as he believed the Selenginsk Buriats were.[9] Moreover, as the majority of the nomadic Buriats did not live in towns, the mission needed to go to them.[10] John Paterson, a London Missionary Society representative in St Petersburg and an officer of the Russian Bible Society, agreed heartily to the move and suggested that a mission at Selenginsk would be a good idea as the two Buriat converts who had been working in St Petersburg translating the Bible were about to return home to Selenginsk. They could provide invaluable assistance to the mission.[11] Although all foreign missionaries required permission to reside in the Russian Empire, as well as specific permission for their location, the mission moved with political ease to the Transbaikal.

From the beginning, great physical hardship played an important role in missionary activity in Asia. Because of Mrs Rahmn's poor health, the Rahmns left the mission in May of 1819 before it could actually begin work.[12] No mission could accomplish anything with only one couple, and by October the Stallybrasses learned that they would have help in the persons of Robert Yuille (1786–1861) and his wife (d. 1827), and William Swan (1791–1866), all Scots.[13] They left St Petersburg on 27 November 1819, having also received the Tsar's blessing, and arrived in Selenginsk in July of 1820.[14] Thus, only in 1820 had the entire complement of the mission been assembled and moved to what they regarded as an appropriate location to begin their work in earnest. Both the London Missionary Society and the Russian government continued their support, which was essential if the mission were to succeed.

In addition to their work translating the Bible, the various missionaries traveled a great deal throughout their tenure, in order to reach larger numbers of nomadic Buriats. At first, all three and their families lived in Selenginsk, going out to follow or meet the Buriats. As the years passed, the missionaries sought to achieve their goals by simultaneously approaching their mission on a variety of levels. These approaches included their original mission of translating the Bible, preaching in Buriat by 1823, teaching not only adults, but also boys and girls, and printing not only the Bible, but religious tracts as well. Finally, they provided medical service to the Buriats. The effort involved in carrying out these activities, in addition to the problems inherent in working thousands of miles from 'civilization,' take up a great deal of space in the letters from the missionaries to the directors of the London Missionary Society.

In 1828, the missionaries made their final moves; Swan and the Stallybrasses moved even closer to the nomadic Buriats at the Ona and Khodon stations respectively, while Yuille remained in Selenginsk. Every move of the mission, from St Petersburg, to Irkutsk, to Selenginsk, to the

Ona and Khodon stations, reflected a desire to reach more people and a growing understanding of nomadic culture. Until the end of their mission in 1841, continued official Russian support from the center, no matter how difficult to obtain, remained a necessary ingredient in their actions.

The Second Mongolian Mission

In 1870, thirty years after the first mission left Asia, James Gilmour (1843–91), a Scot, hoped to establish a mission to the Mongols. While the location and even the people to be proselytized shifted somewhat, Gilmour personally saw his mission as an extension of the earlier effort, a mission he idolized. By this time, however, the Russian Empire no longer needed, nor would it tolerate, the aid of the London Missionary Society in the Transbaikal.[15] If Gilmour wished to work with Mongols, it would have to be in the Chinese Empire. It was the Mongols with whom Gilmour chose to work, and there is evidence that he made this decision because of his fascination with the first mission. This fascination dated back at least to his 1869 interview in Edinburgh with a surviving member of the first mission, Mrs. Swan; throughout his life, he continued to refer to the original inspiration of his work.[16] His first act in China was to travel to Selenginsk, Siberia, in order to visit the graves of those missionaries and their families buried there.[17]

Gilmour had applied to the London Missionary Society while attending the Theological Seminary at the University of Glasgow. After his meeting with Hannah Swan, he interrupted his studies and seemed to be in a great hurry to get to China, the closest approach to the Mongols in the 1860s. Gilmour's path was clear to him, and the Directors of the London Missionary Society concurred by assigning him to China.[18]

If Gilmour saw his mission as being a continuation of the first mission to the Mongols, an official connection to the earlier mission clearly was seen as important by others as well. Official publications, such as C. Silvester Horne's *The Story of the London Missionary Society, 1795–1895*, presented Gilmour's mission as a technical continuation of the Stallybrass mission. The widely differing physical circumstances of the missions were explained as being made necessary by the shifting political reality in Russia.[19]

Unlike the first mission, Gilmour's mission joined an established one in Beijing in 1870, far from Mongol lands. The political realities of the 1870s and 1880s, added to the lack of supplemental missionaries, had precluded any independent approach. Despite his permanent assignment, he insisted on traveling into Mongolia by camel. Off and on for the next twenty years, Gilmour rode into Mongolia, and when that was not possible, he sought out Mongols in Beijing.

On these trips Gilmour was accompanied by his wife, a guide, a servant, and an occasional traveling missionary companion. Leaving for Mongolia in late spring, and returning to Beijing in late summer, he carried medicine, Bibles, and tracts. It was a nine-day trip of 270 English miles through Kalgan. Once in Mongolia, Gilmour spent much of his time on the road seeking out the nomadic Mongols. Despite the lack of necessary additional personnel to help in the establishment of a permanent mission in Mongolia, Gilmour remained steadfast in his drive to establish an ongoing mission among the Mongols.

Gilmour's work was aided through visits with his co-workers from the American and Foreign Missions Board, but he lacked any substantive support from London. This practical isolation, combined with the physical difficulties he faced, great distances he had to travel, and the loss of his wife from these hardships, resulted in the late 1880s in a physical and mental breakdown. The breakdown became fodder for public discussion of Gilmour's sacrifices. The *Chronicle of the London Missionary Society* even wrote on his mental strain.[20] After a too short stay in England, the missionary returned to China, only to die suddenly soon after his return in April of 1891.

In fact, despite his efforts at proselytization, Gilmour's reputation among the Mongols rested primarily on his activities as a doctor. Although he had no formal training, and was always short of medicines, his efforts here proved to be his most visible, and sought after, activity.[21]

Working in Asia

Successful foreign mission work is helped by full understanding of the political and social realities of the locality. The first mission required the permission, and even overt support, of the Russian government, in order to work in a society with the capacity to exclude them and to control their every move. The fact that Great Britain and the Russian Empire were allies also played a role in the need to 'get along' in Russia. Despite existing official support, even the move from Irkutsk to Selenginsk required permission from the Eastern Siberian government.[22]

The First Mongolian Mission began its work with the approval of both Tsar Alexander I and Prince Golitsyn, two all-important supporters. Upon arrival in Irkutsk, the Stallybrasses and Rahmns made friends with the Governor-General of Siberia, Michael Speransky, a deeply religious man known for his willingness to explore new ideas and develop innovative approaches to problems. Their mutual admiration proved most helpful to the mission's future. Even the day-to-day funding for the first mission was aided and facilitated through Russian governmental intervention, especially in the early years. After the mission had moved to Selenginsk, Speransky offered to set up a credit for them of 5000 rubles with the Russian-American Company in Irkutsk, in order that the mission not be financially 'embarrassed' should money from England not arrive on time.[23] Speransky demonstrated additional support for the mission by suggesting to Alexander I that he give the mission the land that it lived upon.[24] The Tsar did grant them land, tax-free status for thirty years, and even 7000 rubles to help pay for the construction of buildings.[25]

The mission to the Mongols was not alone in its presence in the Russian Empire, however. In addition to the special missions to specific peoples, the London Missionary Society representative in St Petersburg, Robert Pinkerton, was given virtual *carte blanche* to set up Bible Societies throughout European Russia, with the goal of circulation of the scriptures. In his travels south to the Black Sea and west to Polish Russia, Pinkerton was aided by a number of letters of introduction from power brokers such as Prince Golitsyn, the Minister of the Interior, and Orthodox and Catholic leaders, as well as the Moslem Commander General of all the Tatar Cossacks in the Crimea.[26]

Politically, Gilmour faced a completely different set of circumstances than had the First Mongolian Mission. By the 1870s, the Chinese Emperor's support was unnecessary for Gilmour to settle in the Chinese Empire. Unlike the first missions' letters, which are filled with dealings with the local Russian officials, Gilmour's letters make few references to that subject.[27] The presence of European missionaries was made possible 'legally' through agreements with European governments. Gilmour's attempts to expand into Mongolia in order to create more permanent stations faced their greatest opposition from London rather than Beijing. The failure of the Society to provide additional missionaries, especially missionaries with some medical training, constituted an insurmountable obstacle to any practical mission to the Mongols. Secondly, the political instability of Mongolia made it at times impossible for Gilmour to travel there.

The seemingly endless and time-absorbing in-fighting with London Missionary Society colleagues and conflicts with the local population did not preclude some useful actions on the part of both missions. The most notable accomplishment of the two Mongolian Missions was the translation of the Bible into Buriat. Not until the second half of the nineteenth century did the Russian Imperial Biblical Society begin to complete translations of the Bible. In this, the London Missionary Society provided a great service. The New Testament, completed in 1824, was reworked in 1846, while the Old Testament was printed in 1840.[28] The first mission's tracts and Bibles were used in Russia and China well into the twentieth century.

Conversion remained the main and ultimate goal of missionary work. A number of observers, albeit influential outsiders, threw doubt on this major activity of the first mission. English travelers in Siberia including Capt.

Cochrane, Mr Atkinson, Mrs Hill, and Henry Lansdell all told their wide reading public, through their travel books, that the first mission was a failure, as it had created very few converts.[29] However, given their almost complete lack of knowledge of Russia, Siberia, Russian or Buriat languages, and their swift excursions through Siberia, their opinions should not be given great weight by scholars.

While making converts was the missionaries' underlying goal, it was not legal for the Russian mission to do so. The First Mongolian Mission was officially constrained from baptizing converts by the Russian government; anyone who converted to Christianity had to be baptized in the Orthodox faith.[30] While it is impossible to know the exact number, the London Missionary Society estimated that perhaps twenty might have been converted. For their part, the Russians opposed baptism because of fear that those who were converted by the 'English missionaries would desert Russia.'[31] The first mission may not have received official credit for its work, but in the 1870s, Gilmour noted their continued moral legacy, not the least of which was the credit for spurring the Russian Orthodox Church to begin actual missionary work itself.[32] Certainly one convert, Shagdur, continued to attempt communication with the London Missionary Society throughout his life, writing at age seventy to obtain copies of the Gospels to use in his work with Chinese traders in the Transbaikal.[33]

In fact, the Russians themselves took the first missions' work seriously. Actually, the missionaries' supposed success was seen as betrayal by the local Orthodox Archbishops as well as by government leaders. All sides traded accusations in this matter. Swan complained that the Irkutsk Archbishops were always falsely accusing the mission of baptizing.[34] On occasion, these accusations became more specific. In 1835, the Ministry of Internal Affairs received a complaint that the mission had baptized more than 700 people in five years.[35] A Siberian scholar, S.S. Shashkov, believed that perhaps as many as 3000 Buriat-Mongols had been converted by the missionaries.[36]

Some Orthodox leaders may have been unhappy with the thought of the 'English' missionaries, but their work facilitated the efforts of later Orthodox missionaries. When a Russian Orthodox priest, Aleksei Malkov, went on a mission to the Transbaikal in 1868, he handed out books printed by the London Missionary Society mission and discovered twenty-six years after the fact that the mission still was remembered in the region.[37]

In contrast, Gilmour's Second Mongolian Mission may very well have inspired, let alone converted, far fewer Mongols than did the earlier mission. Despite his lack of success as a saver of souls in foreign places, Gilmour became a hero in his lifetime and was considered to be a 'Protestant Saint.' How did he achieve such a status, and why did that reputation endure for decades?

Unlike the first mission, the second one had no practical governmental constraints on conversion. Notwithstanding his relative freedom to act, Gilmour's actual conversions were probably fewer than twenty. Nevertheless, his apparent lack of success in no way limited his reputation in the missionary world. Gilmour became a hero in his own lifetime, and a super-hero after his death, appearing in print as a 'Robinson Crusoe,' a hero whose life should be a beacon for young Christians.[38] His obituary in the *Chronicle of the London Missionary Society* called him the 'second founder and apostle of the Mongolian Mission.'[39] Even in the twentieth century, a historian of the London Missionary Society described Gilmour as 'Robinson Crusoe.'[40]

Why was Gilmour so honored? By the second half of the nineteenth century, exotic locations, peoples, and cultures in far corners of the earth, held great appeal for a growing middle class and a broadening literate society. In Gilmour's writings, the locales in which he labored became especially exotic, while his powers of observation and description served the missionary cause very well. Gilmour became famous through his countless articles for the London Missionary Society's publication, *The Chronicle of the London Missionary Society*; in his own book, *Among the Mongols*; and in books based on entries from his journals and letters compiled by others. The London Missionary Society deliberately used Gilmour's story to inspire others, such as missionaries in various parts of the world, especially Africa.[41]

After all, Gilmour's life was rather romantic to Victorians. Not only did he repeatedly travel into Mongolia by camel, but his young, altruistic wife travelled with him, and even her death became an occasion to celebrate his work. In announcing her death, the journal noted that Gilmour's name was so well known, that everyone would want to wish him sympathy.[42]

Had conditions changed by the 1870s from those of the 1820s and 1830s to create this 'star' system? Some individuals were beginning to stand out even in the earlier era, but the degree of publicity did increase later in the century. A combination of elements, including a growing middle class that funded and peopled missionary activities, the development of a variety of publications, and a British imperial policy that suggested that Britons 'owned' the empire and had a role to play around the world, all aided in the promotion of the more public nature of missionary activity.

Spies Like Us

The missionaries may have become heroes back in England, but the local people and governments often doubted their sincerity. Damned both as outsiders and as possible favorites of powerful factions in the host country, the missionaries faced opposition on all fronts. The local population often sought to find an explanation for the missionaries' presence. Initially, missionaries were accused of attempting to subvert the local religions, including Russian Orthodoxy and Buddhism. An even more sinister explanation for the missionaries' presence surfaced occasionally: if missionaries were not there for religious reasons, then their presence must have a political reason. Despite the official support from St Petersburg, the Stallybrass Mission faced constant local opposition. Siberian Governor-General Lavinsky (1822–33), wrote to the Ministry of Internal Affairs in 1831 to say he thought that the missionaries were English spies, sent to monitor Russian trade with China.[43]

The complaint that the missionaries were spies for their national governments became a common accusation in the second half of the nineteenth century. Gilmour met this problem clearly in 1880, at a time when the Russian and Chinese empires were facing an impending war. He was warned by a Mongolian friend to stay away from Mongolia during this particular year. Gilmour especially blamed the antics of the Russian explorer and agent, Nicholas Przhevalskii, for this deteriorating state of affairs. Not long before this incident, Przhevalskii had unsuccessfully 'passed himself off' as a trader in Mongolia, resulting in his discovery, and the creation of an assumption that all travelers in Mongolia must be Russians, and that all Russians were spies.[44] Gilmour was furious at this state of affairs, and averred that he had 'no deep political or other purpose' for his wanderings.[45]

Russians, Russian Orthodoxy and Buriats v. Missionaries

In addition to the accusation of spying, the Russians had one constant, important complaint against the missionaries: that they were anti-Orthodox. Variations on this theme came from various quarters and at regular intervals throughout the first mission.

Opposition came repeatedly from expected sources. Both Bishop Mikhail (1814–30) and Archbishop Ireni (1830–31) of Irkutsk accused the missionaries of poisoning the minds of the Buriats against Orthodoxy.[46] Again in 1834, the Archbishop of Irkutsk, Meletii (1831–35), accused the missionaries of having made anti-Orthodox statements, and this time he sent out three priests to counter their work, one to Selenginsk to be near Yuille, one to the Ona River near Swan, and a third to Khodon near Stallybrass. The missionaries themselves realized from these actions that the religious community in Irkutsk was just beginning to react to their presence.[47] A further type of accusation centered on the issue of whether, against orders, the mission was baptizing the Buriats in the Protestant faith. The Ministry of Internal Affairs received several such allegations, one claiming that the mission had baptized 700 Buriats in five years.[48] By 1838 the complaints had increased, and one of them originated from 'men of influence.'[49]

From this point on, it was only a matter of time before these accusations would erode their good will in St Petersburg. Stallybrass quoted a letter from the Archbishop Nil of Irkutsk (1838–53) to the Holy Synod stating that the mission was 'propagating lying subtleties, disseminating the errors of infidelity, opposing the interest of the Greek Church, and contributing to keep the people in their present state of heathenism.'[50] By 1 October 1840, the missionaries sensed their impending removal.[51] Stallybrass quoted extensively from this removal order in a letter of 19 October 1840:

> The Ober-Procurator of the most Holy Synod communicated to me that the Archbishop of Irkutsk, in consequence of evident signs of opposition to the dominant faith observed by him on the part of the Boriats who dwell in the vicinity of the Baikal, near those places where the English Missionaries reside, who were permitted by his Imperial Majesty in 1817 to engage in the work of converting the heathen to Christianity in Siberia– expressed in his report to the most Holy Synod his fear that their teaching produces the effect of extending lying subtleties concerning the faith. He adds, moreover, that the Boriats [sic] who have received instruction in the schools of these missionaries remain in their former heathenism; while in places remove from the Missionaries, they of their own accord request baptism to which they are called by grace ... (list of misdemeanors). Having all these circumstances in view, in consequences of the above-mentioned   reasons,   that   the English Missionaries not only do not act to the advantage of the Orthodox faith, but even secretly propagate the errors of infidelity, the Holy Synod regard it as indispensably necessary to forbid the Missionaries any longer to act as, or *to call themselves by the name of Missionaries.*[52]

On 18 January 1841, the Swan and Stallybrass families left Siberia.

It was not only representatives of the Russian government and the Orthodox Church who expressed misgivings about the presence of the foreign missionaries; some of those complaints came from Buriat sources as well. In 1830, the Khambo-lama, the leader of the Buddhists in the Russian Empire, complained about the mission, but Stallybrass believed that the Russians had really been behind his action.[53] Stallybrass may or may not have been right, as their mission honestly could have interfered in Buddhist activities in the area.

For practical reasons, while serving in foreign countries, the missionaries attempted to keep their most negative feelings about the local religion to themselves. They were not always successful.[54] They felt free to give full vent to those feelings upon their return to England, even if the mission continued in the host country. Robert Pinkerton, D.D., served as the resident representative for the London Missionary Society to the Russian Bible Society in St Petersburg. He was also the brother-in-law of the great orientalist and supporter of the London Missionary Society, Isaac Jacob Schmidt. After he left Russia, Pinkerton wrote a history of Russia that focused on the religious history of that country and that gave full vent to his anti-Catholic and anti-Orthodox feelings throughout its 486 pages.[55]

Anti-Russian Orthodox sentiment, in fact, permeated the missionaries' beliefs. In 1823, Swan articulated deep disgust when he wrote, 'What forms a grievous stumbling block to these from heathen people is the exhibition of Christianity in the lives of its professors. Missionaries in various parts of the world have occasion to mourn the effects of an unworthy or corrupted form of the gospel in steeling the minds of the heathen against it.'[56] He continued the theme in 1832, when he lamented that proselytizing in Russia required that the London Missionary Society missionary first 'convince him [the Buriat] that *we* are not idolators … .'[57]

Here then is the strong evidence to show that the Bishop of Irkutsk's complaints were not altogether based on illusion. As early as 1821, in a letter to his friend, Paterson, Swan clarified one of the earliest problems he saw for the mission: 'Suffice it to say that every day shews us more clearly the necessity of our appearing to stand upon different ground from the Russians … .'[58] Further, Swan had actually acted on this feeling: two months earlier, while in Irkutsk, he had dissuaded some Buriats from being baptized into the Greek Orthodox faith. He felt that they really did not want to be Orthodox, as only the worst sort of Buriats converted to Orthodoxy.[59] In May of 1822, Swan warned,

> The memoir I shall immediately send you by post direct from this place. Were I to send it in the way you direct I am afraid it would never reach you. The old drunken lying, cheating … (meaning Bishop Mikhail) is not to be trusted with anything. You have little idea my friend how things are carried out in that quarter, the detention of our boxes, the abstraction of articles from them which are still obstinately withheld does not surprise us after we heard of the letter concerning them which he addressed to the Com. [Committee] in Petersburg for that letter was with the worst possible intentions both to you and us … .[60]

Perhaps Swan and company had real grievances against the Orthodox leadership in Irkutsk, but that does not explain away the anti-Orthodox statements. At least Swan's distrust of the Russians had not abated by the end of the decade. In a letter to the directors of the London Missionary Society in 1829, he obliquely referred to activities and problems there that could not be discussed in any of their letters as they 'may pass through we know not what hands, and [are] therefore written with reserve.'[61]

Although one Governor-General accused the mission of spying, persistent claims that the missionaries were denigrating the Orthodox religion served, in the final analysis, as the cause of their removal. In Stallybrass's letter, including the translation of the removal order, he complained that the missionaries had not received a chance to defend themselves against these charges and intimated thereby that they could have successfully defended themselves once again.[62]

The Russians, therefore, were not making unfounded complaints against the missionaries, especially Swan. Absolutely no evidence can be found, however, to support the accusation that the mission spied on the Russo-Chinese trade in the Transbaikal. Aside from the lack of physical evidence, Edward Stallybrass was temperamentally incapable of spying, Yuille would have done a poor job, and William Swan would have deemed any other responsibilities as interference with his work as a missionary.

The Stallybrass mission was not alone in its interest in Russia's religious and political role in Asia. Even from his vantage point in China, Gilmour had important pronouncements to make on the Russian role in Asia. One of Gilmour's first acts in Asia was to travel to Selenginsk. That visit convinced him of a number of facts, which included the view that Russia would soon annex Mongolia, an action he anticipated happily. A number of circumstances moved Mongols closer to Russia, including the lack of safety for Mongolians in Mongolia, and poor government. Frankly, the Russian currency was stronger than the Chinese currency and that provided a strong pull towards the Russian government. In the end, 'The inference is obvious, if the Chinese can't govern Mongolia the Russian both can and will. Now I am not sorry that the Russians should get Mongolia. They can civilize it and teach it a form of Christianity. While the Chinese can only plunder it and propagate the most pernicious superstitions.'[63]

While the Russian Empire in Siberia was lacking in Fortnum and Mason-style amenities, in comparison to China it did have advantages, including an extensive and cheap postal system and a good transportation infrastructure.[64] James Gilmour explicitly and repeatedly stated his belief that the Russians 'raised up, elevated and developed' the Buriats. In contrast, he asserted, the Chinese did not and could not raise up the Mongols, and even taught the 'superstition' of *Feng shui* for example.[65]

Even Russia's exile system in Siberia elicited support from Gilmour: '[Russia] neither crushes nor debases the criminal, and gives him facilities for returning to respectability that more civilized countries find it difficult to afford to such as transgresses its laws.'[66] Note that although he was stating his acceptance of the Siberian exile system, Gilmour did indicate his implied point that Russia was still less 'civilized' than Great Britain.

His home base in Beijing analogously gave Gilmour an excellent opportunity to know China, the Chinese, and the Mongols. His reports to the *Chronicle of the London Missionary Society* added to Western knowledge of daily life in the capital. His greater knowledge did not lead to greater understanding, however. He had two major areas of complaint concerning his hosts: that they were dirty and that their religion, Buddhism, was the worst form of paganism. These attitudes were not softened by greater knowledge or closeness to the local population. He returned to these themes throughout his twenty years in Asia.

As the first mission's emissaries decried the 'adulteration' of Christianity as practiced by the Russian Orthodox, Gilmour saw exposure to Buddhism as equally damaging to religious development in Asia. To him, 'the exaggerated marvels of their religion ruined their ability to discern reality.'[67] Gilmour especially disliked the Mongolian Buddhist Lamas, describing them as licentious.[68] He described Urga, the 'Rome of Buddhist Mongolia,' as a 'very seething sink of iniquity.'[69] Despite his general dislike of the lifestyle of the lamas, however, he was capable of cultivating a relationship with one individual lama, whom he called a 'great friend.'[70]

Gilmour openly held the Chinese and Mongols–among whom he lived and with whom he visited–in great disdain. He criticized their lack of cleanliness and the low level of their amenities in his 1883 book on his first twelve years in China, *Among the Mongols*. He said that Mongol women looked 'slovenly,' and that 'Bathing is not customary.'[71] Both in his private letters and in his publications, Gilmour repeatedly decried the evils in China and Mongolia. To Gilmour, the rampant use of tobacco, whisky, opium, and gambling by Mongolian society in general, and lamas specifically, resulted from a corrupt system. In 1887, he told the readers of the *Chronicle of the London Missionary Society* just that.[72] In contrast to his attitudes towards the Mongols of the Chinese Empire, in his first year in Asia Gilmour expressed a noticeably different attitude towards the Buriat-Mongols just over the border in the Russian Empire. His conviction of future Russian success in Mongolia, as well as his discussion of the disintegration of the Chinese polity, put his reports home above the usual missionary report. Gilmour could not have, and did not, miss the clear signs of internal disintegration in the Chinese Empire. From his arrival in the early 1870s during the Tientsin massacres, and his subsequent 'hiding out' in Siberia, to repeated problems facing his missionary travel due to uprisings in Mongolia, Gilmour noted the long term implications of these actions in his letters home. His letters are alive to the political realities around him. We can only guess at the insights he might have provided had he lived through the Boxer Rebellion.

Conclusions

A close analysis of these missions illuminates important aspects of the disparate nature of the British Missions in Asia in the nineteenth century. Not only thirty years, but also profound political differences separate the first and second missions. The circumstances of these missions and the observations of Imperial Russia and China evoked by the missionaries' conditions reflect the changing role played by Great Britain in Northeast Asia throughout the nineteenth century. The London Missionary Society missionary was not 'an innocent' living in a abstract world of theological discourse. Shifting geopolitical battles inundated the daily life of the missionary, a state of which they were acutely aware.

The basic role of the first mission is quite surprising in some aspects. While the individual missionaries sought the Mongols' religious salvation, if not their actual baptism, the London Missionary Society and the Russian Bible Society clearly understood the missions' political role. The British missionaries were to prepare the ground for conversion, thus bringing the local non-Russian population closer to Russia. In essence, the mission had the affect of shoring up the Russian Empire. The Russian government sought to bring a politically volatile and strategically important region closer to the Russian culture of Christianity. In so doing, it would separate the Buriats from their Buddhist cousins across the border in Mongolia. Eventually, after years of in-fighting in St Petersburg, the faction that wished the first Mongolian mission to stay either died or lost critical mass for support for the continuation of the mission, and the missionaries were told to leave, with no final recourse.

The basic administrative details of James Gilmour's Mongolian mission could not have been more different from those of the first mission. Although Gilmour wished to recreate the conditions of the first mission, by 1870 that was politically impossible. The first mission was invited in by a sovereign state, a political and equal ally of Great Britain's. This basic fact had a profound influence on the role and functioning of that mission. Alexander II certainly did not share Alexander I's religious fervor, and moreover, the era of good will in the post-Congress of Vienna era had certainly passed after the Crimean War. Finally, in the second half of the century, the 'Great Game' in Asia precluded the kind of ecumenical project as found in the first mission. No London Missionary Society representative would be welcome in the Baikal region in the second half of the nineteenth century.

Gilmour settled then for attachment to the Beijing mission. Although the Chinese Empire continued to exist and play an important role, it no longer could successfully oppose activities within its boundaries, such as the missions of the London Missionary Society. Thus, Gilmour's presence among the Mongols was limited by other forces, including the comparative absence of Chinese governmental power in the region, difficulties to access, failure to establish a permanent mission in Mongolia, and the failure to provide the requisite support staff to make such a mission possible. Some of these failures arose from the decisions of the Directors in London, others were beyond anyone's control.

The Gilmours' Northern Mission in China faced increasing threats from the growing anti-foreign sentiment and disintegrating Chinese government. The London Missionary Society mission would face closure in 1894 as a result of the Sino-Japanese War, and closure and physical destruction during the Boxer Rebellion. In the final analysis, Gilmour had been correct as to who would move into the political void in Mongolia.

NOTES

1   The author wishes to acknowledge the following, who made this article possible: The archivists at the University of London School of Oriental and African Studies, and the former Dean, Dr. Charles Bawden, the librarians of the University of Illinois Slavic Reference Service, the archivists of Ohio Wesleyan University, Delaware, Ohio, and Taylor Institute Library Annex, Oxford, England.

2   See Richard Lovett, *History of the London Missionary Society 1795–1895*, 2 vols (London: Oxford University Press, 1899); C. Silvester Horne, *The Story of the London Missionary Society 1795–1895*, 2nd rev. ed. (London: London Missionary Society, 1895), Cecil Northcott, *Glorious Company: One Hundred and Fifty Years Life and Work of the London Missionary Society 1795–1945* (London: The Livingston Press, 1945), and Jean Paquette, 'An Uncompromising Land: the London Missionary Society in China, 1807–1860' (Ph.D. diss., University of California, 1987).

3   A number of articles and one classic book have been written on the activities of the first mission. See D.S.M. Williams, 'The "Mongolians Mission" of the London Missionary Society: An Episode in the History of Religion in the Russian Empire,' *Slavonic and East European Journal* 56 #3 (July 1978), 329–45; and C.R. Bawden, *Shamans, Lamas and Evangelicals, The English Missionaries in Siberia* (London: Routledge and Kegan Paul, 1985).

4   See Judith Cohen Zacek's 'The Russian Bible Society, 1812–1826' (Ph.D. diss., Columbia University, 1964), for the most complete study of that group.

5   Stallybrass to Hankey, 3 Jan. 1818 o.s. Hankey was the Director of London Missionary Society in London. University of London, School of Oriental and African Studies Archives, London Missionary Society, Russia: Incoming Correspondence (subsequently SOAS-LMS) Box 1, Folder 2, File C.

6   Stallybrass to Hankey, 9/21 June 1817, SOAS-LMS Box 1, Folder 2, File A.

7   The Russian calendar was behind the British calendar twelve days in the nineteenth century. In the text, I am using only the dates used in the rest of Europe. The footnotes contain the dates used by the authors, with the date in Russia first, followed by a slash, and the date in England.

8   Stallybrass to Hankey, 18/30 March 1818, SOAS-LMS Box 1, Folder 2, File C.

9   Edward Stallybrass, ed, *Memoir of Mrs. Stallybrass*, intro. by Joseph Fletcher

(London: Fisher, Son & Co., 1836), p. 134; Swan to directors, 3/14 February 1819, quotes Stallybrass.

10 Ibid., 133, from journal entry 28 May 1819.

11 Paterson to Hankey, 15/27 May 1818, SOAS-LMS Box 1, Folder 2, File C.

12 Stallybrass, *Memoir*, p. 133. Journal entry, 28 May 1819.

13 Ibid., p. 135. Journal entry, 16 October 1819.

14 Paterson to Hankey, 29 November 1819 o.s., SOAS-LMS Box 1, Folder 3, File B.

15 Family letters in the 1830s and 1840s indicate that the younger generation of Stallybrasses was very interested in continuing the mission in Siberia. Ohio Wesleyan University Archives, Stallybrass Collection.

16 Richard Lovett, *James Gilmour of Mongolia* (London: Religious Tract Society, n.d.), p. 19.

17 James Gilmour, *Among the Mongols* (London: The Religious Tract Society, 1883), pp. 38–40. Upon his death, Gilmour left instructions and money to establish a fund to support further missions to the Mongols in the name of Hannah Swan.

18 Gilmour, J., SOAS-LMS Candidates Papers 1796–1899, Box 6/19.

19 Horne, *The Story of the London Missionary Society, 1795–1895*, p. 374.

20 *Chronicle of the London Missionary Society* (July 1889), pp. 236–40.

21 James Gilmour, *More About the Mongols*, Richard Lovetee, ed. (London: the Religious Tract Society, 1893).

22 V.I. Vagin, 'Angliiskie missionery v Sibiri,' *Izvestiia Sibirskogo otdela impertorskogo russkogo geograficheskogo obshchestvo* 1, No. 4–5 (March 1871), pp. 70–71.

23 Henderson to Burder, 8 August 1820. SOAS-LMS, Box 1, Folder 4, File A. Ebenezer Henderson was a founder of the Russian Bible Society.

24 Vagin, 'Angliiskie missionery v sibiri,' p. 70.

25 Knill to Hankey, 3 April 1822, SOAS-LMS, Box 1, Folder 5, File C.

26 Robert Pinkerton, *Extracts of Letters from the Rev. Robert Pinkerton on his Late tour in Russia, Poland, and Germany; to Promote the Object of the British and Foreign Bible Society* (London: Tilling & Hughes, 1817), pp. 1–2.

27 Other members of the mission did spend time dealing with the local governments, and opposition.

28 C.R. Bawden, 'The English Missionaries in Siberia and their Translation of the Bible into Mongolian,' *Mongolian Studies* VI (1980), pp. 5–39.

29 See Henry Lansdell, *Through Siberia on Horseback* 2 vols, 2nd edn. (London: Spamson Low, Arston, Searle and Rivinton, 1882); Thomas Witlan Atkinson, *Travels in the Regions of the Upper and Lower Amoor* (New York: Harper and Brothers, 1860); and Charles Herbert Cottrell, *Recollections of Siberia in the Years 1840 and 1841* (London: John W. Parker, 1842).

30 However, this fact does not seem to have become clear to the mission until 1822, and arose as an issue repeatedly. Rahmm to Directors 5 July 1822, SOAS-LMS Box 1, Folder 5, File C.

31 Gilmour, *Among the Mongols*, p. 51.

32 Ibid., p. 53. The Russians were paying attention. See V. Zhmakin, 'Angliiskaia missiia za Baikalom (1817–1840), *Khristiianskoe chtenie* 9–10 (Sept.–Oct. 1881), pp. 454–72.

33 J. Edkins to Whitehouse, July 23, 1880, pp. 8–9. Council of World Missions, University of London School of Asian and African Studies Archives (hereafter CWM-LMS) North China, Box 4, Folder 2, Jacket A. Earlier, in a 9 March,

1842 letter, Shagdur listed about fifteen Buriat Christians as published in John Crombie Brown, *First Fruits of a Mission to Siberia, Revs. Mssers Yuille, Stallybrass, and Swan* (Cape Town: Saul, Soloman and Co., 1847), pp. 115–117.

34   Swan to Bludoff, 21 July 1833, SOAS-LMS, Box 2, Folder 5, File A.

35   Vagin, Angliiskie missionery,' p. 73. 29 June 1835 #1579.

36   Shashkov, 'Sibirskie inorodtsy,' *Narodnoe Bogatstvo* 208 (1863), p. 238.

37   Aleksei Malkov, 'Iz zapisok Zabaikal'skogo missionera,' *Pravoslavnoe obozrenie* 25 # 11(November 1867), pp. 207–14.

38   Rev. Harlan P. Beach, 'James Gilmour "Brave" Missionary to the Mongols, 1843–1891,' *Modern Apostles of Missionary Byways* (New York: Student Volunteer Movement for Foreign Missions, 1899), pp. 46–69.

39   R. Lovett, 'James Gilmour,' *Chronicle of the London Missionary Society* (July 1891), p. 204.

40   Cecil Northcott, *Glorious Company: One hundred and Fifty Years of Life and Work of the London Missionary Society 1795–1945* (London: The Livingston Press, 1945), p. 50.

41   Lovett, 'James Gilmour,' p. 206.

42   'News From Abroad,' *Chronicle of the London Missionary Society* (Dec. 1885), pp. 370–71.

43   Vagin, 'Angliiskie Missionery,' p. 70, information from 20 July 1831, report #837, to the Ministry of Internal Affairs.

44   Gilmour to R.W. Thompson, 6 Sept. 1881, 1, CWM-LMS North China, Box 4, Folder 4, Jacket C.

45   Gilmour to Whitehouse, 2 July 1880, 4–5, CWM-LMS, North China, Box 4, Folder 2, Jacket A.

46   Swan to Bludoff, Re: Document No. 1429, 21 July 1833, SOAS-LMS, Box 2, Folder 5, File A.

47   Stallybrass to Ellis, 15 Jan. 1834, SOAS-LMS, Box 2, Folder 5, File C.

48   Vagin, 'Angliiskie missionery,' pp. 70–71.

49   Swan to Thomas Wilson, 12 October 1838, SOAS-LMS, Box 3, Folder 3, File A.

50   Stallybrass to J. Jackson, 16 November 1840, SOAS-LMS, Box 3, B&FBS, RIL.

51   Stallybrass & Swan to Ellis, 1 October 1840, SOAS-LMS, Box 3, Folder 3, File B.

52   Stallybrass to Thomas Wilson, 7/19 October 1840, SOAS-LMS, Box 3, Folder 3, File B.

53   Stallybrass to Hankey, 5/17 May 1830, SOAS-LMS, Box 2, Folder 3, File D.

54   Stallybrass wrote to his sister and her husband in the United States of his attacks on Buriat beliefs made directly to Buriats. He acknowledged that these attacks caused pain to the Buriats. OWU Archives. Stallybrass Collection, Stallybrass to Joseph and Anna Monds, 6/18 April 1821.

55   Robert Pinkerton, *Russia: or Miscellaneous Observations on the Past and Present State of that Country and its Inhabitants* (London: Leeky & Sons, 1833).

56   Swan to Hanky, 19 January 1823, SOAS-LMS, Box 1, Folder 6, File B.

57   William Swan, 'Notes respecting the Mission in Siberia,' 1832 Mss., SOAS-LMS, Box 2, Folder 4, File C.

58   Paterson MMS, Swan to Paterson, 5 December 1821, SOAS-LMS, B&FBS, Box 1.

59   Ibid.

60   Swan to Paterson, 27 May 1822, SOAS-LMS, B&FBS Paterson MSS, Box 1.

61   Swan to Wm. Orme, 18 May 1829, SOAS-LMS, Box 2, Folder 3, File B.

62   Stallybrass to Thomas Wilson, 7/ 19 October 1840, SOAS-LMS, Box 3, Folder 3, File B.

63   Gilmour to Mrs. Muller, 8 April 1871, CWM-LMS, North China Box 2, Folder 4, Jacket A.

64   Gilmour, *Among the Mongols*, pp. 42–3.

65   Ibid., pp. 371–2.

66   Gilmour, *More about the Mongols*, p. 178.

67   Gilmour to R.W. Thompson, 6 September 1881, CWM-LMS, North China Box 4, Folder 4, Jacket C.

68   Gilmour to Mullers, 18 August 1877, 8–9, CWM-LMS, North China Box 3, Folder 1, Jacket D.

69   Gilmour to Thompson, 16 Nov. 1888, CWM-LMS, North China, Box 5, Folder 5, Jacket B, 15.

70   Gilmour to Mullen, 30 May 1878, 1, CWM-LMS, North China Box 3, Folder 2, Jacket B.

71   Gilmour, *Among the Mongols*, pp.321–2.

72   Gilmour, 'Six Months work in Mongolia,' *Chronicle of the London Missionary Society* (Oct. 1887), pp. 419–22.

CHAPTER 11

The Nineteenth-Century British Townscape and the Return of the Market Place to Victorian History[1]

James Schmiechen

One of the most profound changes in nineteenth century urban life was a spatial reordering of society: bridges to carry railway cars, vast dock warehouses and 'pools' for steamships and their cargo, hotels and railway stations for travelers, city halls for municipal bureaucrats, public baths, hospitals, concert halls, museums, and so on, all an outgrowth of technological innovation, urbanization, and population growth, and all reflecting changes in spatial function.

These spatial inventions, or 'building types,' were largely regarded by contemporaries as salutary, but unfortunately they stood side by side with a number of careless and unwholesome spatial innovations, such as back-to-back houses and prison-like textile mills which were seen by nineteenth-century social commentators such as Charles Dickens, Mrs. Gaskell, Friedrich Engels, and Benjamin Disraeli as the confirmation of social deterioration.[2]

Be they commendable or depraved, these new spaces and places were, in effect, new venues for social action and interaction, or, as we might say, the physical outlines of nineteenth-century life. All in all, they demanded an ongoing retraining of the Victorian eye and called for new awareness of how the everyday world fit together: a new factory and school here, a new street or point of reference there, an entirely new town built to serve a new industry, a formerly open village space now filled-in with a factory or a drainage pool, and so on. They all point to a Victorian obsession with spatial specialization and spatial segregation according to function, social class, economy, and so-called 'Victorian morality,' and they all affected daily life in such fundamental ways that one could regard them as a sort of ongoing reinvention of urban life. For the Victorians the physical outline of town and village was so fluid that they read the urban environment with a mixture of fear, alienation, and applause.

The contemplation of all of this by twentieth-century historians is equally ambiguous. From the perspective of the British town the Victorian era is seen by some as an age of progress, particularly in the later decades; but relying on the assertions of Victorian architects, social commentators and urban reformers who complained about the chaos of urban space, most historians have generally concentrated on the darkest side of the picture: that of an urban housing picture of deterioration and class segregation for most people, and a picture of the British town which shows it 'beastly' as Dickens called Leeds, in terms of municipal services and public and private space. Indeed, the Parliamentary 'Blue Book' reports such as those of Chadwick in 1837-42, the Sanitary Commissioners Reports in the 1840s, and the Municipal Corporations Reports in the 1830s, can be regarded as verification of the corrupt administration, misuse of public funds, and gross neglect of municipal services on the part of most British towns.[3]

Putting the Market Place back into the History of the Nineteenth Century

How has the town's most important space, the market place, fared in this assessment? Generally, the picture of the town market sketched out by historians has been either one of food shortage, riot, and poor sanitation,[4] or is a picture hardly considered in urban, social, or economic history at all. One very influential (and controversial) inquiry into the British market place was Friedrich Engels's *The Condition of the English Working Class* of 1844. He argued that the public market place in the new industrial town was filthy and disease-ridden and worked so much against the interests of the working class that working people received nothing but leftover food largely unfit for human consumption.[5]

It is the intent of this essay to demonstrate that the history of the nineteenth-century market place presents a more complex scene: that a pattern of blind neglect of municipal services and willful physical segregation of the classes is certainly grounded in fact but at the same time these problems existed side by side with another pattern, one of a progressive reinvention of the market place that provided for a new definition of modern consumer behavior and a new understanding of the relationship between architecture, building, and everyday life.

This story of spatial change begins in the late eighteenth and early nineteenth centuries. It was then that the 'traditional' market place–an open space and contiguous series of streets within which most towns' food and other comestibles were sold–was in a state of crisis. Everything that was wrong with this age-old setting had become heightened because of unprecedented urban growth, improvement in wages which generated increased demand, and more and more food and other goods piling on each other in an already congested market. The market place became, more than ever before, the locus for fraud, crime, adulteration, street fighting, and, often enough, food riots. To make conditions even worse, most working-class entertainment, including bull-baiting, took place in the same space: in one town, for example, it was the market keeper's duty to provide a bull collar and rope for the baiting of the bull by dogs in the market place. In addition to being exposed to the wind and rain, the market place was subject to unpleasant sights and sounds, not the least of which was the butchering of animals and the filling of streets and footpaths with carts. Fighting over prices, market tolls, and selling space was common, and the market place was still the site for public punishment, usually reserved for the market day crowd to witness. The public market, in short, was seen as promoting bad habits, low morals, public disorder, and an interruption in the town's food supply.

To address this spatial crisis and with new ideas regarding the moral and physical arrangement of public space at hand, over 600 public market buildings, many of them in the form of a new building type called a 'market hall,' were constructed in Britain between 1750 and about 1950. The vast majority of these were built in nearly 400 English, Welsh and Scottish towns between 1820 and 1880. Earlier market structures go back to late medieval times as simply appendages to the open-air market, sometimes as the lower floor of a town hall (called 'market house' or even sometimes a 'butter market') which accommodated a portion of market activity. Then by the late eighteenth century a new 'enclosed' market form evolved: a walled but usually not roofed structure that concentrated most all of the formerly traditional open-air marketing in one manageable space. Then the market hall emerged in the early 1800s as the public market's most perfect form. By the 1850s British towns were outdoing and outspending one another with breakneck speed to bring the entire traditional market place indoors into the market hall. Often the largest public structure in the town, this entirely roofed market with amenities such as heat, running water, and even plate-glass shop fronts, not only ushered in a revolution in the buying and selling of food, but was the forerunner to the later nineteenth-century department store and the twentieth-century shopping mall. Most important, it gave the municipal government what turned out to be a surefire way of raising the quantity and quality of consumer goods entering the town. Indeed, it became admitted municipal wisdom that a progressive public market hall meant a better-fed population at a lower cost.

The kind of lethargy pointed to by critics like Engels was real, but it was not necessarily due to class interests and municipal sloth. The fact was that many towns had little or no jurisdiction over their own market places and in many such cases it was the manorial owner who chained the market to its past. Through over 300 (often costly) private acts of Parliament between 1801 and 1880, various health acts, and the 1858 Local Government Act, local governments were able to gain control or purchase the market place and market rights, or even acquire the power to finance new markets. The 1858 Act made the process much easier and less costly. Much of this reform was connected to urban population explosions, and thus the timing of market building varied from town to town, often with a sort of purchase lag period during which the town acquired market rights. Not surprisingly, most market hall building occurred in the industrial Midlands and northwest Manchester belt, although there were remarkable bursts of market reform activity in the towns of the southwest and Wales.[6]

In his condemnation of the public market, Engels makes specific references to Liverpool, Manchester, and the 'working-class' towns surrounding Manchester as examples of flagrant municipal neglect of the markets and the town's food supply.[7] While there is little doubt that the markets of most of these towns needed reform, what Engels fails to point out is that most of these towns (and other towns of the same sort) had undertaken or were undertaking such profound market rebuilding and reform that the experience of many working people of Lancashire (and, we may add, of nearby West Yorkshire and elsewhere) in Engels's time must have been that of improving rather than deteriorating marketing conditions. Liverpool's giant new market hall of 1820-23 was nothing if not revolutionary and was almost immediately the model for market place reform elsewhere, including a vast new market hall in Birmingham in 1835 which was 365 feet long and 108 feet wide. This market, which replaced the traditional open-air 'Bull Ring' market place, had a massive classically dressed entrance at both ends, allowing the structure to serve as a covered avenue for 600 separate market stalls. It is of particular interest in the history of the nineteenth-century urban diet because it pioneered in the promotion of fish as a part of the regular diet of urban dwellers. By the 1880s, and by way of twenty years of an organized system of fish imports, the fish market portion of Birmingham's market hall was making fish a part of the daily diet for a vast number of people in the Midlands of England.

Although Wigan, Preston, Stockport, and Heywood had to wait until after 1850 for new market buildings, in Lancashire Engels could have visited the new fish market and two new covered 'general markets' (Brown Street in 1822 and London Road in 1824) in Manchester in 1828, a market hall in Rochdale in 1823, with a larger one in 1844 (with 24 shops and 180 stalls), a large market hall in Ashton in 1828, a market hall in Stalybridge in 1831 and expanded in 1843, and in Bury a 32,000 square foot market hall built in 1839 to replace what was regarded as a dangerous street market and to serve 'the ladies of the town.'[8] Several other markets were in planning stage at the time, including a market hall in Oldham (1856) and a giant hall in Bolton in 1853. In addition, Engels missed market-building activity in nearby Burnley (a new market building in 1829), at Fleetwood (1840), and a 24,000 square foot market building at Salford (1825). Indeed, within Engels's lifetime, Lancashire boasted several of the largest market halls in Britain: Accrington (1869), Blackburn (1848), Preston (1875), and the gigantic Shudehill market hall at Manchester begun in 1854 (107,360 square feet).

Engels's misinterpretations aside, what is the significance of this building boom in markets? A closer look at several market halls of the industrial north allow us to assess more carefully the relationship between spatial innovation and the changing function of the town market.

Britain's pioneer market hall was the nearly two-acre St John's Market built by Liverpool municipal authorities in 1822 to replace the traditional open market, with 404 stalls and 58 shops arranged in five 'avenues' under an enormous wood and glass roof. It was said that on a Saturday night 25,000 people 'passed between the rows of brightly-lit stalls.'[9] Some of these stalls were reserved for regional farm people (called 'pannier' sellers because they sold from their baskets, or 'panniers') who brought food to the market to sell directly to the consumer. For the next century St John's market hall was acknowledged to be both a 'showpiece' of the town as well as its principal supplier of food–and at the lowest cost. Being illuminated by 144 gaslights, the market was opened from early morning (some days at 5 or 6 a.m.) until 8 o'clock every night, except on Saturday when the market-closing bell rang at 11 p.m. The discipline was stiff. The market even forbade market sellers to solicit business by standing above the level of the floor or to engage in 'hand-selling'–that is, the waving of one's hands to attract customers.[10]

In 1841 in the West Yorkshire wool-manufacturing town of Leeds, the Leeds Borough officials shut down privately owned markets, and in 1856 it prohibited outdoor stalls in the town's major streets. The next year it opened the Kirkgate Market Hall, about half the size of Liverpool's market hall, but as it was rebuilt and added to over the next half-century it came to cover nearly four and a half acres. The 1857 hall, built in the style of London's famous Crystal Palace of 1851, was recreated in 1904 in a grandiose 'Renaissance' manner fitting for a regional capital, complete with a splendid roof of glass and iron that provided the interior and exterior with the 'picturesque' look desired by its users. [see Plate 18].[11] Market activity was strictly regulated and food inspection was frequent. As in Liverpool, market inspectors sought to make market sellers respectable, prohibiting them, for example, from making 'a great noise or wearing an objectionable costume' in front of stall or shop. It was claimed in 1888 that the food in the market hall was 25 per cent cheaper than in the town's shops, and that, as the town's mayor reported, municipal government needed 'always to keep

Plate 18: 'Leeds Kirkgate Market Hall of 1872' Replacing the street-front portion of the town's first (1857) rather utilitarian looking market hall, this rather flamboyant municipal market hall (in what its architects called the 'Renaissance' style) included 84 stalls and 83 shops (20 of which were for butchers) in its interior, 23 shops facing the street. Still standing today, it perhaps best represents the spatial reordering of the public market which swept Britain in the nineteenth century.

... in view that it is their duty to develop the business of the market for the benefit of the public in supplying them with good and cheap provisions.'[12]

In the Lancashire town of Bolton, town officials had little control over the town's market place until a quasi-public 'Improvement' trust was formed to enable the town to purchase the market rights from the local lord of the manor in 1826. It was at this point that the unsanitary and crowded market was reorganized and improved, although it took the trustees and the town government twenty-five years to acquire a special act of Parliament (the Bolton Improvement Act of 1850) that enabled the town to go the next step and build the sort of vast covered market that many other towns had already put in place. The result of the 1850 Act was arguably the most ambitious of Bolton's municipal projects ever undertaken. The Bolton Market Hall project of 1856 resulted in a total reconstruction of a slum-ridden part of the town and the physical merger of the two towns, Little Bolton and Great Bolton, into one. The market was designed to improve the town's health, to bring the market closer to the population, and to furnish a statement in civic architecture that would place Bolton in the ranks of the great boroughs of the nation. A grand Corinthian portico fronted the market hall, and the interior boasted the most advanced glass and iron roof structure of its day, with two decorated central transepts, which reached 112 feet above the market floor. It originally had 600 stalls and shops and was enlarged in 1865, in 1871, and again in 1894, when the blank bays of the exterior were given over to shop fronts to give the market a department store look. It was modernized again in 1934 and then again in 1989 to become the centerpiece of a new shopping mall. Between 18,000 and 20,000 townspeople, including 3,000 women of Bolton seated in the galleries, crowded into the market on 19 December 1855 for a great civic meeting to commemorate the opening of the market[13] (see Plate 19).[14]

Two West Yorkshire towns, Huddersfield and Bradford, further illustrate how private ownership of the markets inhibited market place reform. It was not until the 1860s that Huddersfield was able to do anything about its market, described as being 'in very bad condition;' only then did it gain legal permission to acquire the market and satisfy the steep price for it demanded by its owner Sir John Ramsden. The new market hall opened in 1880, and it was in many ways the typical English market hall: multiple entrances but with a grand central entrance, an imposing market clock tower (106 feet high), modern shop fronts to the street, rows of butchers' shops extending along both sides of the market and opening to the street, and an imposing architectural presence ('domestic Gothic' with corner turrets and a roof of green slate–all fitting for a town 'rising in importance'[15]) (see Plate 20).[16]

In nearby Bradford, despite citizen attempts to carry out reform of the town's markets that were regarded a 'great nuisance,' the town government

PLAN OF BOLTON MARKET.

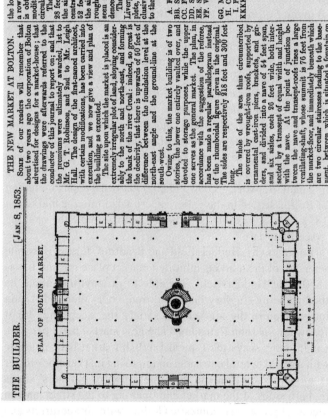

THE NEW MARKET AT BOLTON.

Some of our readers will remember that about two years ago the corporation of Bolton advertised for designs for a market-house; that the drawings were afterwards referred to the conductor of this journal to report on; and that the premiums were ultimately awarded, 1st to Mr. G. T. Robinson, and 2nd to Mr. Leigh Hall. The design of the first-named architect, with certain modifications, has been carried into execution, and we now give a view and plan of the building as executed.

The site upon which the market is placed is an extremely irregular plot of land, sloping considerably to the north and north-east, and forming the bank of the river Croal: indeed, so great is the declivity, that there is upwards of 50 feet of difference between the foundation level at the north-east angle and the ground-line at the south-west.

Owing to this, the market building is of two stories, the lower one entirely vaulted over, and devoted to storage purposes, while the upper one serves as the general market. The plan, in accordance with the suggestion of the referee, has been made a regular parallelogram instead of the rhomboidal figure given in the original. The sides are respectively 218 feet and 300 feet long.

The whole of the area thus circumscribed is covered by wrought-iron roofs, supported by ornamental cast-iron piers, brackets, and girders, and divided into a nave of 54 feet span, and six aisles, each 20 feet wide, both intersected by a transept of equal width and height with the nave. At the point of junction between the nave and transept-roofs rises a large ventilating-shaft, whose summit is 76 feet from the market-floor, and immediately beneath which are two circular staircases leading to the basement, between which is situated a fountain on

the lower level. To the exterior wall is affixed a row of shops, each 16 feet high, and over them is obtained a gallery for the sale of light commodities, and receiving additional light from the circular apertures surmounting the arcade.

The internal height of the exterior walls is 28 feet from the market-floor. The height of the aisles' roofs is 38 feet to the apex; and the central and transeptal roofs have an altitude of 52 feet, being raised above the narrow roofs of the aisles by a clerestory of cast-iron, filled with rough plate-glass louvres. The angle-buildings seen in the perspective contain offices and residences for the market inspectors and others.

The contractor is Mr. William Tomkinson, of Liverpool; and the probable cost, when complete, will be, we are told, about 20,000l. exclusive of the two viaducts and a retaining wall to the river Croal, which are now in hand.

REFERENCES TO PLAN.

A. Fountain in basement.
BB. Stairs to basement.
CC. Fountains in market.
DD. Stairs to gallery.
EE. Shops, with gallery over.
FF. Ventilating-shafts and flues from heating-apparatus.
GG. Market inspector's residence and offices.
H. Clerk of market's office.
I. Public weighing-machine.
KKKKK. Entrances.

SCALE OF FEET
100 FEET
0 10 20 30 40 50 60 70 80 90

Plate 20: 'The New Market Hall, Huddesfield' This market embodies many of the characteristics of the nineteenth-century building type, the 'market hall:' a grand entrance front with plenty of architectural embellishment (in the 'Domestic Gothic' style of the day), a clock tower to announce the market's presence to its users and to advertise the good taste and economic progress of the town, its modern glass-plate shop fronts, and the rows of butchers' shops along the sides tell a story of a town government which is looking after its citizens' food needs.

was not able to wrest manorial ownership and control of the market from the local manorial owner, Lord Rawson, until 1867. At this point, after already handing over £200,000 to the Rawson family, two large market halls (1872, 1875), described as 'handsome buildings and a credit to the town,' replaced the street markets and what was regarded as a worthless market house. As in Birmingham, Bradford market officials made a conscious decision to use the new market hall to introduce cheap but nutritious fresh fish into the diet of Bradford citizens. The first of the halls, the Kirkgate market, (see Plate 21),[17] was a large brick/cast-iron/glass structure, the principal feature being two grand domed pavilions which opened to six avenues of shops and stalls and with considerable interior architectural embellishment of ornamental ironwork in green and bronze color. The shops were lined with white glazed brick to allow for cleansing. Within ten years of its opening, the town government established a tramway from the market to Bradford's new suburbs—and in doing so reversed a trend toward both suburban shopping and social distancing by bringing suburban people to the town center where food was cheaper, the choices more plentiful, and the mixing of classes encouraged.[18]

Typical of nineteenth-century market halls, and with equally typical Victorian interest in classification of nearly everything, Bradford's market authorities and their architects used the new market as a way of classifying food according to a hierarchy of ventilation and sanitation needs: one octagonal pavilion organized for the sale of fruits and vegetables, the other for fish, the shops with both internal and external access for butchers' meat sales, and the central avenues for ordinary stalls selling everything from dry goods to groceries. One obvious result of this classification was the preservation of market cleanliness and the segregation of foods such as meat and fish which required considerable water and ventilation; another benefit of such segregation of market foods by type was to give the buyer the advantage of competitive shopping and to provide an education on the importance of storage and sanitation for the both buyer and seller.[19]

Manchester's markets, notorious for the filth, noise, and congestion they spread throughout the town center, were owned by the local lord of the manor and managed by his manorial court until the town managed to purchase the markets in 1846 by way of an act of parliament. The town then set out to increase the town's food supply and reverse the market's reputation for chaos, which included a history of food riots. What transpired was a new centralized market hall, built in stages beginning in 1854—eventually becoming, at over 100,000 square feet, one of the largest indoor markets in Europe. The new market, it was claimed, brought to the town a larger and cheaper supply of food.

Plate 21: 'The Bradford New Covered Market' View of one of the two domed pavilions (the second part was not completed until 1878) which allowed for not only a revolutionary reinvention of the open-air street markets of old, but also for the classification and segregation of food and other consumer products. Like many market halls, the dazzle of the market was a way of encouraging shopping as a form of leisure. Spatially, the market acted as an avenue, which connected two of the town's principal streets. It was demolished in 1973.

The Transformation of Function

What do these fleeting excursions into the history of municipal space tell us about Victorian life? The answer, it appears, is that inside the hundreds of market halls that came to dot the Victorian townscape, a silent push into modernity was taking place. First, 'architecture' in a nineteenth-century sense was being translated as both a functional truism and an absolute necessity for the Victorian market. Through embellishment and the standard Victorian references to history, the public market was given an aesthetic quality which conveyed what many Victorians regarded as necessary links to a kind of collective historical memory for the promotion of beauty, truth, and civic virtue, be it Greek or Roman, Gothic, Renaissance, or some eclectic combination of architectural styles. It was understood and carried out with Victorian vigor that the new market buildings should be designed to direct its users' attention away from the low thoughts of the streets and the uninspired and often ugly uniformity of the town. The messages were specific: respectability, economic progress, personal morality, and, perhaps most of all, civic virtue. As the locus for physical nourishment, social exchange, and moral and civic instruction, the market hall, more than any other building of the Victorian age, was akin to the cathedral in past times in that it sought the integration of urban life by way of brick and stone.

From the design side, the market hall assumed a near universal formula. By the 1870s any urban dweller could easily describe a public market: a large structure, usually of brick, glass and iron, dominating the center of town, with multiple entrances (but one of them a grand central entrance), with considerable architectural appeal ('an ornament to the town') and most often with a clock tower which announced the market's presence to citizen and visitor for many miles around. Unfortunately all of this architectural context would be eventually forgotten, so that by the 1950s the brutal architectural utilitarianism of a new age would sweep the Victorian past away without a second thought.

Second, just as the ancient fairs had been largely shut down because they were regarded as centers of social chaos and crime, the market hall refashioned the social and economic behavior of the public in a manner compatible with the 'enlightened' bourgeois sensibilities with regard to work, gender, public behavior, entertainment, health and diet, and so forth. Consequently, the street became less multifunctional, and the days of the traditional market place being the turf of lower class street roughs and disreputable market sellers were over. The new market hall saved public market space for the 'respectable' classes, and in doing so served as an acceptable and 'elevating' gathering place for the middle and working classes, particularly women. Indeed, a reading of market hall regulations suggests that market hall policing was directed as much to market sellers as to market buyers. Whatever we wish to call it, 'social control' or 'social consensus,' the result was that the acts of buying and selling became segregated from the activities of the street and were redefined in what we would regard today as 'modern' sensibilities about behavior in public spaces.

Third, the market hall was the agency by which the people of the nineteenth century witnessed a real but now forgotten and little studied food revolution. The foremost function of the market was to promote the economic well-being of the town. From the day Liverpool opened its 74,000 square foot market hall in 1822, it became clear that market suppliers had a choice as to where to sell their goods: a clean, dry, and artificially lighted market hall or the traditional street market, where they were subject to cold, rain, riot, noise, and congestion. By the 1820s it had become municipal doctrine that the better the size, location, and layout of the public market the larger, more diverse, and more nutritious the town's food supply. Consequently, some towns were reborn as food-rich towns and others fell to the station of food-poor, a circumstance that was linked to how well market facilities attracted food retailers, be they big-city wholesalers or country butchers and farm people.

Equally important, the market hall acquired a new function: to encourage modern consumerism by providing expanded choice, by teaching about food preservation and food sanitation, and by cultivating and ritualizing the modern acts of 'shopping.' The selecting and planning of purchases were endorsed as leisure as well as necessity for people of the middle and lower classes. Although some market halls became known for catering to specific classes of consumers, in most towns the market hall was used to encourage social mixing. Some towns, such as Bradford and Accrington, even went a step further and linked the market hall to the local tramway system, thereby bringing the people of the suburbs back to the town center to mingle with the working classes in the public market.

Finally, a view from the market place suggests that early Victorian municipal leadership was perhaps less one of lethargy and more one of action. Population pressure certainly had much to do with a reinvention of market place function as did so-called bourgeois sensibilities regarding space and place, but as much as anything else, the timing of market reform from town to town was linked to who owned the market: the town itself or private interests. Until the town gained full powers over its market place, market reform was usually delayed. While this apparent link between municipal power and the local food supply needs further examination, we may say with assurance that there is much to be learned about nineteenth-century life by a foray into the Victorian market place.

NOTES

1   This essay is partly based on data included in the 'Gazetteer' portion of my recent study (with Kenneth Carls), *The British Market Hall* [and Gazetteer](New Haven, Yale University Press1999). I am grateful to Yale University Press for permission to draw upon this work.

2   The list is long and familiar to most students of the nineteenth century: the sanitary reformer, Edwin Chadwick, social commentators such as Charles Dickens, Mrs Gaskell, and Benjamin Disraeli, Henry Mayhew, and Friedrich Engels, and then, later, John and Barbara Hammond present unfavorable views of the new towns, while others, such as John Aikin, James Kay-Shuttleworth, and Andrew Ure find the new towns as places of opportunity and progressive change.

3   For a summary of the paucity of municipal services see E. C. Midwinter, *Victorian Social Reform* (London, 1968). It is the housing problem that gives the nineteenth-century town much of its unfavorable press. See John Burnett, *A Social History of Housing, 1815–1970* (Newton Abbott: David and Chandos, 1978); for a discussion of the impact of urbanization on working class life, see Rule, *The Labouring Classes in Early Industrial England, 1750–1850* (London: Longman, 1986). Rule stresses the working-class adjustments to deterioration in conditions and a loss of space. A new and generally optimistic view of the nineteenth-century spatial revolution is Thomas Markus, *Buildings and Power: Freedom and Control in the Origin of Modern Building Types* (London: Routledge, 1993); The Dickens quote is from Briggs, *Victorian Cities* (1963) p. 80. Social distancing as a way of classes to separate themselves from other classes is described in F. M. L. Thompson, *The Rise of Respectable Society* (Cambridge Mass: Harvard University Press, 1988), ch. 5.

4   Although there are as many histories of the market place as there are histories of the town, it is ironic that only recently has a general history of the market place come forth (see note 1) and there is still no comprehensive history of the street. For market riots see Rule, *The Labouring Classes,* pp. 348–53; and Roger Wells, 'Counting Riots in the Eighteenth Century,' *Bulletin for the Society for the Study of Labour History* 37 (1987). A discussion of the public market can be found in Thomas Markus, *Buildings and Power. Freedom and Control in the Origin of Modern Building Types* (1993).

5   Friederich Engels, *The Condition of the English Working Class* (1844, reprinted with an introduction by W.O. Henderson and W.H. Cahaloner, 1958), pp. 50–51, 80–81, 86.

6   The three regions which make up the so-called 'industrial north' (the Midlands, the northwest, and the north) account for about half of all market-building activity from about 1750 to about 1950. Very little market building took place in the southeast and east (including London). In terms of timing, the two major 'bursts' in market building were from about 1820 to 1840 and then from about 1870 through most of the 1880s. See Schmiechen and Carls, *The British Market Hall* (1999), ch. 8 and 'Gazetteer.'

7   In addition to Manchester and Liverpool, he lists eleven towns: Ashton, Bolton, Bury, Heywood, Middleton, Oldham, Preston, Rochdale, Stalybridge, Stockport, and Wigan.

8   Markets Comm. Rpt. V.9 1891.

9   *Liverpool Echo,* 7.14.1950 (Leeds Central Library Clippings File).

10 City of Liverpool, *Report of the Manager of the City Markets, Liverpool,*

1920, 1921, 1930; For Liverpool market regulations see, for example, the market by-laws set out in City of Liverpool, *Council Proceedings,* 13 December 1893, p. 66.

11 See plate 18.
12 Leeds Market Committee, 'Minutes,' vol. 5 (30 June 1878), p. 19, and British Parliamentary Papers, *Royal Commission on Market Rights and Tolls,* vol. IV, 1888: 'Leeds.' A good short history of the Leeds Kirkgate Market Hall is Steven Burt and Kevin Grady, *Kirkgate Market: An Illustrated History* (1992).
13 The *Bolton Chronicle,* 22 December 1855; the *Bolton Journal,* 3 November 1849; County Borough of Bolton, *Centenary Celebrations, the Market Hall, 1855–1955* (1955).
14 Plate 19. The exterior walls are fixed with shops. The center (C–C) holds a large fountain. The four entrances are marked KKKK. The upper gallery stairs are indicated as DDDDD. The market was (and still is) noted for its gigantic roof-transept of cast iron, creating a grand nave which reaches a height of 76 feet from the market floor. The floor arrangement was changed over time and today the market is a part of a larger shopping center. (Source: *The Builder,* January 8, 1853, p. 24.)
15 *Huddersfield Weekly News,* 3 April 1880. The purchase price of the market was £38,000 plus interest.
16 See plate 20.
17 See plate 21.
18 British Parliamentary Papers, *Royal Commission on Market Rights and Tolls,* vol. II, 1888: 'Bradford.'
19 *The Architect,* 19 October 1872, p. 218.

CHAPTER 12

Cinemas and their Managers in Depression England: a Social Function

Stephen Shafer

The 1930s in Great Britain were years of devastating economic problems. With the jobless rate rising from about 10.5 per cent in 1929 to over 22 per cent by 1932, and with the number of unemployed shifting between two and three million for much of the decade, those without positions faced grim prospects. Those fortunate enough to be employed could feel little security in the permanence of their jobs, and many workers derived little comfort from solutions proposed by politicians. After the National Government was formed in 1931, the decision to reduce unemployment benefits disappointed many among the working classes; critics complained that the government had little or no policy direction and was confused, unresponsive, and uncertain in its approach to the crisis. While the British economy began to recover by about 1933, which ultimately led to a material improvement for the working classes later in the decade, the continuing unemployment problem provided a gloomy perception of British conditions. As Walter Arnstein has written, 'prolonged and unrelenting unemployment put a lasting mark upon those British workingmen who experienced it,' leaving them with a 'sense of frustration and futility.'[1] Yet surprisingly little domestic unrest was observed among the working classes. A partial solution to this paradox may be found in the institution of the neighborhood cinemas and in the comforting social services provided by their managers.

   In Britain's gloomy economic, social, and political climate, people turned in increasing numbers to forms of escape, and films rapidly became recognized as 'easily the most important agency of popular entertainment.'[2] More specifically, movies had become by the 1930s '*par excellence* the "poor man's theatre" with minimum prices of admission averaging four pence to sixpence, and in many cases less for day performances'; thus the cinema was cheaper than the music hall, the chief amusement of the previous generations' working classes.[3] Yet, comparisons to other forms of amusement were seen at the time as inappropriate; movies were unique, said a contemporary sociological study, and the 'picture palace [could] be more fairly judged as a new agency, filling a place in the people's life which was previously void, than by comparison with the theater or other more elaborate forms of entertainment which have throughout been beyond the means of the average wage earner, as a very occasional luxury.'[4]

By 1937, an estimated 20 million of the country's 47.5 million people were attending movies weekly, and the cinemas were taking in £40 million annually.[5] In Liverpool, for example, at least 40 percent of the entire population was said to go to the movies at least once a week, and 25 percent went at least twice weekly.[6] As Branson and Heinemann observe, 'never had it been made so easy for the factory or office worker to live a complete fantasy life in substitution or compensation for the hardships of the real world'; thus, the writers conclude, 'the cinema, rather than religion, was "the heart of a heartless world, the opium of the world."'[7]

In fact, with film attendance so frequent, the relative success of the cinemas offered a dynamic and refreshing contrast to the depressed industries. The number of motion picture houses had expanded from about 3000 in 1926 to 4305 in 1933; by the end of the decade, this figure had risen to almost 5000.[8] Even during the gloomiest years, trade publications commented enthusiastically about the boom in cinema construction. Ernest Fredman, the editor of the *London Daily Film Renter*, who contributed an annual review of the industry in the United Kingdom to the *Film Daily Yearbook*, found himself repeatedly using adjectives like 'amazing' and 'tremendous' when referring to the expanded construction, though midway through the decade he began to have fears that too many theaters were being built.[9] Industry spokesmen were quick to emphasize the increased prosperity new cinemas brought to neighborhoods; as one trade paper commented, 'No sooner has a new cinema been planned than shops and houses quickly follow—an interesting exemplification of the fact that social life, as well as trade, follows the film.'[10] While the film industry and motion picture exhibitors were not immune from financial difficulties and seasonal slumps, picture houses served as beacons of recovery and prosperity. A studio executive noted that 'the public is impressed by our prosperity ... [and], perceives that we are happy in our work,' while another industry analyst concurred that, 'bad as is the industrial outlook, particularly in Lancashire, the cinema trade—always enterprising and progressing and never more so than now—resolutely refuses to be submerged in the stagnant waters of even cheerful complacency.'[11] The cinema outlook was upward and positive, and the managers did their best to share the point of view with their customers.

The architecture of the new cinemas, which were being built everywhere, including some working-class districts, reflected this optimism.[12] Larger, more luxurious, with plush seating, specially styled interiors, and almost 'palace-like' qualities, new movie houses were designed to take audiences away from reality and to give patrons the notion that the cinemas would cater to their needs. Filmgoers experienced amusements in extravagant surroundings and were treated with a respect they might not receive elsewhere. Although many of these 'super-cinemas' were constructed in the suburbs, far from the surroundings of a working-class clientele, improvements in transportation meant that working people in one district were not 'limited to places of entertainment within their immediate neighborhood;' thus, even in attending cinemas, laboring people sometimes could escape their everyday experiences.[13] Gradually, large cinema chains began to eliminate the small, independent exhibitor, often buying out smaller houses and replacing them with new cinema palaces. Yet, at least throughout the 1930s, small, independent houses survived, and in London, as of 1935, only about a third of the picture houses were part of a chain.[14] A 1936 film industry report observed that about 70 per cent of existing cinemas in the country still seated fewer than a thousand customers, and two in ten seated fewer than 500.[15]

But, as luxurious as the super cinemas were, the smaller, older, local picture houses often had the advantage of being cherished community fixtures. Managers were able to recognize regular customers, not only because they frequently would greet them at the door, but also because managers generally lived with their families in the district, often in modest accommodations adjacent to or above the cinema itself. As respected community members often serving on civic boards or participating in local charitable activities, they added a 'personal' quality. Chain cinemas, because they were under the authority of some distant, indistinct management, usually were regarded as being more remote and impersonal. Generally speaking, the working classes were more inclined to attend small, neighborhood cinemas.[16] Whether they went to the palatial 'Luxury Houses,' which contained shops and dining rooms, the middle-sized 'dumps', or the small 'bug-hutches' and 'fleapits' in the factory neighborhoods (as exhibitors themselves classified their establishments), the working classes patronized cinemas regularly throughout the decade.[17]

This fact troubled some individuals. Politicians predictably expressed irritation that those receiving unemployment benefits nevertheless could find enough money to attend movies. Neville Chamberlain, in a 1930 debate on the entertainments' tax, denied that the 'cinema pictures were a necessity in the household budget ... like food and clothes' and criticized those using unemployment benefits for such purposes.[18] But another MP, H.T. Muggeridge, disagreed, taking

> ... Chamberlain severely to task for his references to the
> unemployed attending cinemas. The cinema was catering for
> the common man ... The film industry, far from aggravating the

evils of unemployment, was making work for the unemployed and was proving an impetus to the industry of the country. Films had brought a world of make-believe in order to establish the well-being of the world of realities.[19]

Though the expenditure of unemployment benefits at picture houses may have been galling to some, such cinema-going helped keep what little money there was in circulation.[20]

While some politicians may have seemed unfeeling and indifferent to the plight of the working classes during the Slump, local businessmen running the cinemas, by contrast, were able repeatedly to demonstrate their attentiveness to working people by ministering to their needs and desires. Years earlier, a supplement to the *Kine Weekly*, in describing 'how to run a cinema,' had observed that 'a manager must show his primary concern for the welfare of the "labouring classes."'[21] Whether consciously or not, managers pursued this goal in a variety of ways.

First, the films themselves often boosted morale and gave people an opportunity to forget their anxieties, an opportunity they welcomed. Managers were aware of the 'escapist' quality of most features, accenting it in their publicity; one picture house even proclaimed in handbills, 'Free insurance–for two hours–against worries and troubles. Qualifies patrons for benefits from one thousand to ten thousand laughs.'[22] Lighter productions from America such as Frank Capra's upbeat social comedies were usually box office successes in Britain, and England's own motion picture releases often centered on positive themes emphasizing national unity and the indomitability of the British personality.[23]

But whatever the showings, by the 1930s movie houses had become a happy refuge for the working classes. One film industry observer described in glowing terms a cinema he had attended a few years earlier.

> I shall not forget the sight ... [of] ... [h]undreds ... of the toiling population of Salford ... gathered together for the purpose of enjoyment and recreation. Man and wife, sons and daughters, thronged the auditorium. The men fresh from work, and the women from the loom, sat together free from care for a couple of hours, so that the toil of the morrow could be faced with renewed courage and hope.[24]

Such authorities as Lord Beaverbrook agreed that 'motion picture entertainment does much to keep [public opinion] healthy.'[25]

Yet other reasons encouraged the working classes to frequent cinemas. During an earlier inquiry on public morale, a probation officer, discussing the housing problem in urban, working class areas, suggested that young people went to the movies to escape overcrowded conditions at home.

> Just imagine what the cinemas meant to tens of thousands of
> poor children herded in one room ... six or eight families under
> the same roof. For a few hours at the picture house at the corner
> they can find a breathing space, warmth, music ... and the
> pictures, where they can have a real laugh, a cheer and sometimes
> a shout ... . Those who have the least knowledge of the habits,
> the difficulties and the squalid lives of these one and two-roomed
> tenants talk the most foolish things against the cinema.[26]

Relief from other irritations also could be obtained at local cinemas. A
1930 issue of the *Bioscope* reported how a man 'summoned at North London
for assaulting his wife' pleaded that she was always nagging him; he claimed
that because 'she disturbs my rest at night, ... to keep the peace, I have to
go to the pictures to sleep.'[27]

But the appeal of the picture-house in the Depression years may have
been even more basic. Audrey Field observes in her informal reminiscence
of cinemas that,

> With high unemployment, what most cinema patrons wanted
> most of all was the fulfillment of their basic material needs ...
> cheap warmth in a chill northern winter is a useful adjunct [to
> the movie] ... [P]atrons in ... less wealthy parts of our towns
> and cities ... were getting for their money not just a film, but
> warmth, colour, comfort, opulent-looking surroundings
> [inexpensive refreshments], and a royal welcome from the
> manager, resplendent in white tie and tails. They were somebody,
> their approval was of supreme importance.[28]

She concludes that in the Depression the cinema served as 'an emblem, a
flag kept flying in token of no surrender and an unconquerable hope of
better things to come.'[29]

The cinema experience itself then may have been an attraction, but
picture-houses also helped interpersonal relations in giving individuals a
common experience and something to discuss. English sociologist J.P. Mayer
has observed that 'it is well known ... that in factories, shops, and offices–
during work and leisure hours–talk about films is probably the most frequent
type of conversation.'[30] One filmgoer interviewed in 1938 explained that
she attended movies because she 'like[d] sitting in a packed crowd in the
dark, among hundreds riveted on the same thing;' the pleasure of
experiencing something in common, she felt sure, was shared by factory
workers and professionals.[31] Before showings began, audience members
took advantage of opportunities to visit and meet with neighbors and friends
under relaxed conditions; older people sometimes came early just so they
could chat with others.[32] Like pubs, movie houses thus served as something
of a community center, a place where all could go for amusement, and one

of the few opportunities working class families had for recreation together.[33] Many smaller neighborhood cinemas, in fact, came to be called 'family halls,' and patrons often had substantial affection for these homey establishments; some were operated by the same family for years, and patrons became quite loyal to those who ran them.

Movie houses also helped commemorate various stages in the lives of the working classes. A child's imagination might be sparked for the first time by the exciting stories on the screen. Adolescents often had their first romantic encounters at cinemas, and poorer unmarried couples usually recognized cinemas as the most convenient place to do their courting. For the elderly, the cinema could be a haven where they could spend idle time that otherwise might leave them very lonely.[34] Young girls, away from rural homes for the first time to work in factories, sometimes found cinemas to be the place they felt most at home. Field tells of a teenage girl, who had come from the West Country to an industrial town to earn a living, who sent home a picture postcard of 'the picture house where I always go' which became 'a cherished momento of old times' in later years.[35]

Cinema managers encouraged this response with individual care and imaginative service. One enterprising exhibitor kept track of births, engagements, marriages, deaths, and 'other trivial occurrences in town and on every occasion [sent] messages of congratulations or sympathy–and two passes.'[36] For pensioners, special activities were undertaken. Some picture houses sponsored Sunday charity performances to benefit the Aged and Poor Fund of their respective communities.[37] Occasionally, a manager would see to it that the institutionalized old and infirm, or even those in correctional institutions, would be presented with free special programmes for which he often received the thanks of local government bodies; at the Olympia in Newcastle-upon-Tyne, such an event for pensioners was held annually with gifts distributed after the performance, and a programme for inmates at Barrow earned the manager the 'gratitude of that city's Town Council.'[38] To increase goodwill, many cinemas in larger cities, particularly those in the poorer districts, would allow free admission to matinees patrons who showed their old-age Pension Books.[39] Sometimes local politicians or an MP sponsored extra entertainments for the elderly; in one community, the Mayor (a film exhibitor himself) annually entertained 500 old folks from the town.[40]

Gestures of kindness to senior citizens often were the best services a manager could perform. Field relates that 'patrons, especially older, lonely ones, would come to the office' on a variety of pretexts but, more typically, 'for the pleasure of pouring their troubles into the manager's friendly ear;' while not all managers were equally patient, some allowed such customers to use the telephone on request, which sometimes itself was an excuse for a 'friendly get-together.'[41] Lasting friendships often developed from such relationships. Managers would be sought for advice, help, and understanding, and regular customers would reciprocate. As one manager's daughter reported, the 'patrons were so kind'; while they 'hadn't much money, ... they would bring me ... a small bar of chocolate or a bunch of flowers from their gardens, and when tomatoes were in season, one elderly couple used to bring me a bag of tomatoes every week. And the worse the times became, the more people loved the cinema.'[42]

Like pensioners, veterans often were accorded special performances and privileges. In Redditch, for example, a showing of the historical film *Disraeli* was sponsored by the exhibitor for the local veterans, and a cinema in Birmingham permitted reduced prices for ex-servicemen who wore their uniforms or carried their discharge papers.[43]

The cinema was often the site of fund-raisers, whether the cause was disabled children, a local boys' band, the British Legion, or the victims of a mining disaster.[44] The charities benefitting from these activities varied, but hospitals, the poor, and children were the most frequent beneficiaries. Before Sunday openings were legalized, cinemas sometimes were loaned to charities on Sundays for special performances; this involved considerable effort by the manager who had to provide custodial care and had to obtain a special permit from the London County Council Theatres' Committee or a comparable body elsewhere.[45] At Salford, Sunday evening choir concerts were scheduled periodically to raise money for the Salford Royal Hospital.[46] 'Hospital Sunday,' with all cinemas participating, was an annual event in Birmingham, Sheffield, Weston, and Manchester. Even in bad times, the amounts raised often were considerable. For example, in Sheffield in 1930, £945 was raised, a £94 increase over the previous year, with half the money going to the Sheffield Joint Hospitals' Council, £250 being sent to recondition an ambulance, and the remainder going to the general fund; in Birmingham, an even more impressive total of over £3500 was raised the same year.[47] Some cinemas reduced their prices at matinees for the unemployed, and in Scotland, special afternoon presentations for the jobless began in Glasgow and 'spread all over the country.'[48] Even those with jobs received special consideration. The Regent Cinema in East Kirkby, for example, ran morning performances each Thursday to enable miners working late shifts to see the latest features at a uniform reduced price.[49]

Probably the most widespread examples of charity were the annual Christmas shows. The pages of trade newspapers were filled with accounts of these events. Funds for the showings were raised by contributions from movie-house patrons, the management, local merchants, politicians, newspapers, and the local well-to-do. Such performances usually were held at larger picture palaces, though the format of each show and its funding varied. Sometimes youngsters would be admitted with cards the ticket-taker marked whenever they had attended the cinema; with fifty-two marks, signifying fifty-two visits to the movies, they could attend the free Christmas event. In Sunderland, the Havelock Cinema would hang hundreds of dolls on entrance walls for customers to take, dress, and return for distribution at their annual Poor Children's Treat.[50] In Sheffield, at two cinemas, the Regent and the Albert Hall, 4500 youngsters, described as 'Sheffield's poorest', were treated to a Christmas morning show and given toys as they left. At Leeds, toys, gifts, and dolls contributed by businesses and cinema patrons were mounted on a large Christmas tree and then distributed to 2500 youngsters on the Saturday night before Christmas. Newcastle's Grey Street Picture House was decorated to look like Toyland, and on Christmas Eve, the children of the unemployed were entertained and given gifts and goodies. Several Northern Ireland cinemas made their premises available for a Christmas Eve treat for workhouse children; six new pennies were distributed by local politicians to each child at the event. In Luton, teachers selected 1250 of the most needy children for a special Saturday morning program; gifts were provided by patrons, and the staff and orchestra volunteered their services, distributing toys to all.[51] In Salford, fatherless schoolchildren were recommended by patrons, clergy, magistrates and doctors for the Christmas show. Sometimes, the King and Queen would be sent a telegram of regards from the children at the outset of the performance; by the program's end, the royal couple would send greetings in return. Usually, in the live portion of the program, Father Christmas would be depicted, and at least one manager always reserved that part for himself. At another cinema, after the performance, the tree in the lobby was taken to a local hospital where still another performance was offered.

Even public health services were distributed through cinemas. Sometimes, with doctors and nurses stationed at the Christmas show, youngsters would be given a free clinical check-up as they waited in line, whereupon those particularly in need would be invited back for an additional New Year's show at which articles of clothing, clean underwear, shoes, and other necessities would be provided.[52] At one such medical clinic event, the theater manager reported that £200 had been raised by patrons to distribute to poor children at a 21 December Christmas party; at the free matinee, which included community singing, conjuring, and dancing acts, 2500 youngsters received toys, fruits, and sweets, while being examined by four local welfare nurses. The 500 neediest were given new boots or underfittings and were instructed to return on New Year's Eve when they were presented with additional gifts. Denying that it was 'a stunt to exploit' children, the manager concluded that the success of the idea and the money that was raised had demonstrated that he was 'expressing the wishes of his patrons in giving the kiddies a real happy surprise.'[53] Of course, the publicity the scheme received from the local press in the district was regarded as being 'well worth the hard work and time involved.'[54] These Christmas parties continued throughout the 1930s and helped improve both the physical and spiritual health of working class children by making what otherwise might have been some rather bleak holidays somewhat merrier.[55]

Charities for children were not confined to Christmas, however. Some picture houses provided contributions to a summer outing fund, while others arranged free special educational film showings.[56] In fact, local cinemas often were placed at the disposal of schools that did not have projectors for morning educational films.[57] Thus, movie houses participated in the formal educational process. Such 'civic-mindedness' not only helped youngsters develop the cinema-going habit at an early age, but also helped mute a potentially dangerous critic of youthful film-going: the school authority.

The most familiar association between British children and the cinema was the Saturday morning matinee. Managers sometimes lent or rented cinemas at nominal cost on Saturday mornings to a special Children's Cinema Council associated with the Education Authority to project selected educational and cultural features.[58] More common were Children's Matinees, commercial presentations provided in densely populated areas and attended by the children of the working classes. At such matinees, cartoons, short comedies, and interest films or serials, newsreels, and feature-length comedies, animal pictures, adventures, or westerns were shown along with health and safety films.[59] Initially, such presentations were viewed with suspicion if not outright disdain by educators and government authorities, many of whom continued to view cinemas as breeding-places of crime and vice. But, by the end of the decade, men like Sir Stafford Cripps recognized that it was not the cinema, but rather 'the circumstances of slumdom and dead-end employment' that were responsible for juvenile delinquency.[60] Others called attention to cases 'where the opening of ... cinema[s] ... [had] reduced hooliganism among boys, withdrawn young men from the public house, and supplied girls with a safer substitute for lounging with their friends in the alleys and the parks.'[61]

In fact, by the end of the decade, a Northern Ireland Government Report on the Protection and Welfare of the Young concluded that there was 'insufficient evidence' that juvenile delinquency could be attributed to the cinema's influence, and suggested that 'more attention' should be centered on providing special showings for children; 'these should not necessarily be of an educational nature, for children go to the cinema to seek recreation and they are apt to resent seeing anything reminiscent of the class-room during their leisure hours. The object should be to provide healthy films of a kind which children appreciate.'[62] What commercial cinemas showed to working-class children was apparently what at least one government report thought should be shown.

Children's matinees, however, meant considerable additional effort for managers. On Saturdays, managers' workdays began early and lasted until late at night with a variety of regular end-of-the-week activities in accounting, stock-taking, and staff payments. They had to book films appropriate for children, a problem 'not easily solved', and they had to learn to manage crowds of high-spirited youngsters with patience and skill. Although most managers were 'thoroughly frightened before taking their first children's matinee, ... nearly all of them ... quickly lost their fear and found a new and unexpected thrill in being with a mass of children'; managers became 'honestly enthusiastic' over children's matinees 'not only because it is an advertising medium, but also because it provides them with a stimulating experience and demands a technique which brings quick and lively response when it is used with success.'[63]

Since many picture house managers were family men themselves, they may have enjoyed in a 'paternalistic' way the contact with 'the many thousands of children who in post-war years had no fathers.'[64] Field cites one exhibitor in a working-class district who 'loved children' and had pioneered children's matinees before they became common; she observes that he 'always took special care with children's programmes ... . [Though] ... the cost of admission was a penny, each child was given a farthing bar of Fry's chocolate, which the proprietor insisted must be wrapped in silver paper.'[65] Another instance of fatherly concern occurred at another cinema when one working-class youngster, after an evening performance, was found asleep in a seat after everyone else had filed out. After the doorman sent the child home, the youngster returned saying that neither of his parents were home. The manager, who apparently lived in adjoining quarters, then made the boy comfortable in one of the roomier seats in the stalls, and allowed him to spend the night until one of his parents came to claim him the next day; Field concludes, 'With service like this ... the neighborhood hardly needed a children's club.'[66]

Obviously, not all managers were as humane as the one cited in Field's paean to the family picture house, and they were motivated by business as well as charitable considerations. Certainly, they benefitted from such favorable stories, and the fact that such 'publicity' and 'public service' ideas were shared in columns about attendance-boosting schemes in trade papers underscores this point; but to attribute such progressive-minded social benevolence entirely to profit motives would be a disservice to those who did perform extraordinary activities in a business they apparently enjoyed and from which they presumably derived satisfaction as well as a living. The fact remains that their services were often a relief and a help to the struggling working classes. A contemporary account concludes, 'there is no doubt that to many an anxious mother the cinema appears rather as a refuge where the children will be safe from the danger of the street, than as a means of entertainment or instruction.'[67] At least one police official in Wakefield maintained that 'the drinking of intoxicating liquor was on the

decline, especially among ... younger members of the community'
principally because 'entertainments, particularly the cinemas, had taken the
place of the public house.'[68] Even if the cinema's positive societal by-
products were unintended or motivated by profit, they were being
recognized.

Another trade gimmick with positive social benefits was the cinema club
movement, a development which transformed picture houses into social
and recreational youth organizations. In these clubs, Saturday morning
matinees became institutionalized into weekly gatherings of youngsters who
could identify with one another by their association with the cinema; in this
way, argued Richard Ford, children could enjoy

> ... belonging to an exclusive society—something which stands
> for their interests, ... [giving] them an impression of adult status
> ... and [a] feeling of superiority and importance, combined with
> a purpose and a job to be done. ... [A] well-run Children's
> Cinema Club ... helps considerably to maintain an even
> attendance at the cinema, and to provide a framework inside
> which charitable, competitive, and sporting activities can be
> organized.[69]

Clubs had individual names, depending on the cinema circuit or the
manager's imagination. The Odeon Circuit (the largest group of clubs) had
'Mickey Mouse Clubs' with each establishment having its own distinctive
cards and badges; the Bernstein Circuit (the Granada Cinemas) called its
organization the 'Grenadier Clubs.' The Union Circuit had 'Chums' Clubs,'
the Gaumont Circuit had 'Shirley Temple Clubs,' and various independent
cinemas had 'Popeye Clubs.' Each club had its own signs, greetings, badges,
emblems, and codes, and managers would contribute a 'Children's Club
Corner' column to the local newspaper with bits of information just for
youngsters. Members received cards with free passes on their birthdays
and get-well cards when they were ill; managers also solicited notes and
greetings from fellow club members for bed-ridden youngsters. By these
methods, clubs were giving children not only a feeling of belonging, but
also a realization that someone cared about them. Like scout leaders,
managers met with parents and served as counselors for problem youths;
they also arranged sports competitions with other clubs, amateur talent
events, and charity drives. Educational films and speakers on topics of
interest to children like animal care also were included at showings.
Managers often appointed a children's committee to oversee activities, to
make programming decisions, and to give children the experience of
responsibility and planning.[70]

Generally, clubs emphasized values with which most of society and most
children's authorities would have agreed. Membership cards might include

spaces to be marked verifying Saturday attendance so that the manager could recognize dependability and reward regular participants; sometimes youngsters even wrote notes explaining lack of attendance at film showings as if they were school absences.[71] Club rules often highlighted such virtues as 'order, cleanliness, and safety' or upheld desirable values like kindness, honesty, and respect for authority.[72] Rules encouraged youngsters to be 'truthful,' 'honourable,' and to 'always try to make [themselves].. good and useful young citizens'; members promised to 'obey ... elders and help the aged, the helpless and children smaller than myself', 'always [to] be kind to animals', and to 'learn and obey the simple rules of road safety ... [so that] when entering or leaving ... any public building, I will do so Quietly, Slowly, Without Pushing.'[73] Such values appealed to parents and public authorities. Patriotism also was encouraged; said one manager, 'children now stand and sing the National Anthem which is something of an achievement in a working class district.'[74] Public response thus was usually favorable; parents, citizens, government officials, and even headmasters expressed satisfaction with the matinees.[75] For children with little parental guidance, the manager might be one of the few disciplinary forces in their lives; not only for safety purposes, but also to maintain his reputation and prevent criticism, managers obviously had to patrol these organizations with a stern and watchful eye for the rowdy and for troublemakers.

Children's clubs drew a greater proportion of their membership from the working classes and industrial areas. As Field observes, while children of the affluent rarely if ever were allowed to go to cinemas, in poorer districts, virtually all youths went to the movies.[76] Therefore, the role of these cinema clubs is all the more remarkable. Youngsters might be asked to assist in charity drives by donating articles of produce, old toys, comic books, safety pins, bouillon cubes, or scrap material with prizes going to the contributor of the largest item; sometimes a manager would conduct a contest, and, as a prize, donate an item to a charitable organization on their behalf.[77] In general, then, the manager's duties with children could be likened to those of scoutmasters, schoolmasters, probation officers, welfare officers, and babysitters.[78] The cinema thus performed a remarkable variety of functions for working-class children whose opportunities for social and cultural activities would have been limited otherwise.

For adults, cinemas served an equally unusual mixture of functions. *Sight and Sound* diligently reports significant experimentation in the 1930s using film in education, including efforts to use movies in adult education; occasionally, cinema halls might be offered for these purposes.[79] Similarly, those churches which did not denounce film as a medium sometimes showed movies to raise money. Some churchmen organized film societies, using local cinemas to show films with religious content, such as *King of Kings*; occasionally, managers would lend the hall to a congregation to enable it to hold activities too large for the church or to conduct services when a disaster prevented utilization of church buildings.[80] Even town meetings occasionally were held in cinema halls, if no other facilities were available.

Cinemas also served as an information source for many individuals, with newsreels common in movie programs and the emergence of cinemas that were devoted entirely to news films.[81] The government position toward domestic and foreign policy generally was supported in these films.[82] Field concludes that cinemas helped prepare Britain for the ordeal of the coming war, noting that the film industry seemed to recognize 'what would shortly be demanded of it, which was nothing less than helping to weld into one classless, devoted, well-informed body of people, the whole British nation, at home and on the fighting fronts.'[83] Consequently, public-spirited managers showed short documentaries designed to encourage an appreciation for the working man, to develop an understanding of the nation's social problems, and to learn about people in the Empire and Commonwealth. During the foreign crises of the late 1930's, government films designed to disseminate safety instructions and air raid information or to encourage army recruitment routinely were accompanied in movie houses by demonstrations on how to use a gas mask and how to survive air attacks.[84] Additionally, free 'house magazines' like the *Rivoli News* themselves became sources of information for the community, with articles on general interest topics aside from promotional information; as many as 20,000 copies might be circulated weekly in the larger circuits. In smaller areas, 'the manager, with his little house magazine, acted as a local purveyor of news, for there was no local newspaper.'[85]

Managers clearly were aware of the cinema's importance for the working classes. As a Lancashire exhibitor noted in 1932, 'the men were nearly all out of work ... [b]ut somehow, the families still managed to come to the cinema.'[86] At a time when money was scarce, cinemas eased the guilt of those who thought it sinful to attend the movies in order to escape everyday frustrations by offering a chance to win a door prize that usually consisted of tea, sugar, bacon, and other groceries. Thus, concludes Field, cinemas provided 'a spice of gambling, ... glamour, fan worship, music, ... bright lights and the friendly dark–not to mention the more practical advantages of more warmth and comfort than the patron can afford in his own house'; they 'deserve[d]' to be regarded as 'Public Benefactor Number One.'[87] Trade publication advertisements argued that those who toiled needed the recreation and amusement movies provided so they could work properly, adding that better productivity could be achieved with proper relaxation. In fact, some industrial and mining employers, such as the Ashington Coal Company, ran a cinema expressly for their workers.[88]

In discussions within the Cinematograph Exhibitors' Association an awareness of the working class was continually evident. During the transition to sound, managers of small cinemas urged producers and distributors to keep silent films available, arguing that expenses of converting to sound would necessitate a ticket cost increase that would price them beyond what the working classes could afford.[89] While the fear that small exhibitors would be unable to survive proved unfounded, it is significant that managers would concentrate on this argument that working-class patrons would be unable to receive the services they now were providing.

Managers also argued for productions that would appeal to the working classes. One trade publication observed that, 'What the West End of London happens to like ... is no criterion for the provinces, ... for the masses of poor people who in the matter of paying for entertainment have to study every penny'; that is, movies popular in the West End 'cannot be considered the class of entertainment necessary for the industrial areas in the provinces.'[90] The writer concluded that 'the suburban cinema in the working-class districts has firmly established itself as practically the only entertainment caterer for the poorest of the poor bringing that little bit of brightness and good, clean and healthy entertainment to millions of workers.'[91]

When exhibitors lobbied for permission to open on Sundays, the argument again centered on the need to provide the working classes with amusement. A 1930 *Bioscope* editorial, for instance, noted that the 'large community of ... labourers forming the bulk' of Birmingham's population recently had demanded Sunday entertainment through their 'Labour organization'; it observed that many 'industrial centres' were overthrowing the 'forces of reaction' to obtain Sunday cinema openings, thereby finding a way to obtain 'reasonable recreation ... [on] a day [of] unutterable boredom.'[92] Likewise, Sir Hugo Rutherford, speaking at an exhibitors' banquet in Liverpool late in 1930, argued for Sunday openings. Suggesting that cinema's greatest 'responsibilities' involved 'entertainment', he implied that Sunday openings would provide a more beneficial alternative to pubs; 'why should we not have one competitor at least with the licensed houses? There are many people on Sunday nights who are at their wits' end for something to do, and I do not see any reason why it would not be a big benefit to the public if ... cinemas were allowed to put reasonable entertainment before them.'[93] Even the upper social classes thus had to consider whether cinema, for all its evils, was not a preferable vice when contrasted to other potential interests of the laboring classes. Though profits were undeniably significant in motivating their efforts, these arguments put forth by the industry, while self-serving, demonstrated clearly how aware exhibitors were of their patrons and of their connection to these laborers.

To the question of why cinema managers bothered to perform so many extra functions for the working classes, several answers might be postulated. Many of the most responsive exhibitors may have been products of the

working classes themselves and, therefore, may have felt a sense of
responsibility. Biographical sketches of various managers in the Gaumont–
British chain stressing their humble origins are suggestive of this
conclusion.[94] More intriguing is the thought that the service may have been
related to a professional empathy. While the working classes were, in an
economic and social sense, victims of a class structure, so too, in a cultural
sense, were those working in the film industry the victims of an artistic and
intellectual snobbery. L.C.B. Seaman has described how cultural leaders
denounced the cinema in the 1920s, calling the criticism part of 'the long
struggle to perpetuate the class war by the use of cultural weapons.'[95] Seaman
comments that 'culture had been for so long the preserve of the well-to-do
that it became an axiom that culture that was disseminated *ipso facto* ceased
to be culture,' and he notes that 'by the 1930s this was beginning to produce
an equally reactionary counter-attack on behalf of ... working-class
culture.'[96] He concludes that this 'hostility to mass culture so frequently
expressed from the 1920's onwards was often the result of a narrow
educational system, a too early hardening of the spiritual arteries and, above
all, ... an ingrained distaste for the masses as such.'[97] Field concurs, noting
that with 'intellectual snobbery ... [b]ecoming increasingly fashionable,
[and] ... social snobbery ... not yet gone out, ... the working man, and even
more, the working woman, were vulnerable to attack on both counts.'[98] As
purveyors of mass entertainment, itself the object of scorn, those in the
film industry were also vulnerable to this attack. Consequently, exhibitors,
unable to earn the respect of their middle-class social equals in business
because of the disreputable nature of the 'product' they 'sold', may have
felt akin to the working man and therefore may have embraced him more
closely than otherwise might have been expected, while simultaneously
trying to prove they were responsible, progressive members of both the
business community and the city at large. Certainly illustrations of this
sympathy for the working man were common. For instance, in a column in
a studio publication, written primarily for exhibitors, the author condemned
aesthetic, cultural and social snobbery to which both cinema managers and
working-class people were subject, concluding that exhibitors generally are
'thankful that the majority with whom [they work] are just plain ordinary
people,' because 'there is no room for the highbrow among practical, matter-
of-fact, work-a-day folk.'[99]

Obviously, to attribute too altruistic a motivation or too complex a reason
for this social service phenomenon would be dangerous. Basically, after
all, cinema managers were businessmen, and, in a climate of economic
failure and doubt, the argument can be made that they merely were
developing a spirited program to keep customers happy. But the exhibitor
was far more than just a businessman; he was a significant part of the
community. As Field has observed, 'He acted as banker to the patrons when

the bank was closed; he helped put out fires before the fire brigade arrived; when the last bus left before the end of the show he took stranded customers home in his own van. And besides being the manager, he was bill-poster, relief operator, and extra attendant ... .'[100] For these managers, the idea of 'service', not only for the individual but also for the community, constituted often-expressed values and goals that appeared repeatedly in trade publications.[101]

Cinema managers thus may have been a calming social influence during a difficult decade. Their efforts should not be overlooked, since they seem to have been not simply isolated occurrences but widespread throughout the country; as Field notes, 'there were a good many proprietors and managers up and down the country who carried on this same tradition of imaginative service to the people among whom they lived' for many years, and these 'dedicated managers who set out to perform a social service, besides showing films, did feel that they were not alone.'[102] Their customers, who probably would have sensed any phoniness in the sincerity of their motivation or services for them, remained loyal. The trust and security experienced in the cinema was illustrated by the fact that when movie houses were closed for the public's safety at the outset of the Second World War, the people demanded in spite of the risks that they be opened; as the *Kine Weekly* commented, such a response was 'a measure of the confidence with which patrons look to the cinema for so many pence worth of entertainment.'[103] The cinemas had earned that respect among their clientele especially during the economic crisis of the 1930s; thus, historians pondering the question of why there was not more domestic turmoil during this period may find a partial answer in the role these cinema managers played in maintaining social stability in their communities.

NOTES

1   Walter L. Arnstein, *Britain: Yesterday and Today*, 3rd edn. (Lexington: D.C. Heath, 1976), p. 287.
2   *New Survey of London Life and Labour*, London School of Economics and Political Science, IX (London: P.S. King and Son, 1930–35), p. 43.
3   Ibid., I, p. 100.
4   Ibid., p. 295.
5   N. Branson and M. Heinemann, *Britain in the 1930s* (New York: Praeger, 1971), p. 251; see also C. L. Mowat, *Britain Between the Wars: 1918–1940* (Boston: Beacon Press, 1955), p. 501.
6   John Stevenson, *Social Conditions in Britain Between the Wars* (Harmondsworth: Penguin Books, 1977), p. 43.
7   Branson and Heinemann, *Britain in the 1930s*, pp. 246–8.
8   See sections on the 1930s (particularly pp. 37 and 56) in the Political and Economic Planning Report in *The British Film Industry: A Report on its History* (London: P.E.P.), 1952.

9   See yearly review sections in *The Film Daily Yearbook* (New York: Film Daily, 1930–39). See also *International Motion Picture Almanac* (New York: Quigley Publishing, 1934–35, 1936–37, 1939–40).
10 *Bioscope*, (19 February 1930), p. 2.
11 Ibid., (10 September 1930), p. vii, and (31 December 1930), p. 43.
12 See P. Morton Shand, *Modern Theatres and Cinemas* (B.T. Batsford, 1930) for early consideration of cinema architecture. Recently, various publications, some inspired by nostalgic memories, have appeared, preserving pictures and descriptions of movie houses that have long since been demolished. See Dennis Sharp, *The Picture Palace and other Buildings for the Movies* (Hugh Evelyn, 1969); David Atwell, *Cathedrals of the Movies* (Architectural Press, 1980); Richard Gray, *Cinemas in Britain* (Lund Humphries, 1996); and Allen Eyles's three books: *ABC – The First Name in Entertainment* (London: Cinema Theatre Association/British Film Institute, 1993); *Gaumont British Cinemas* (London: Cinema Theatre Association/British Film Institute, 1996); and (with Keith Skone), *London's West End Cinemas* (Keytone, 1991). An excellent internet site on England's Picture Palaces can be found at <http://easyweb.easynet.co.uk/ ~lfbarfe/>.
13 *New Survey of London Life and Labour*, I, p. 295. For a detailed overview of cinema circuits, see *The British Film Industry*, cited in note 8.
14 *New Survey of London Life and Labour*, IX, p. 11.
15 S. Rowson, 'A Statistical Survey of the Cinema Industry in Great Britain in 1934,' *Proceedings of the Royal Statistical Society* (1935), pp. 77–8.
16 Audrey Field, *Picture Palaces: A Social History of the Cinema* (London: Gentry Books, 1974), p. 128.
17 Ibid.
18 *Bioscope* (20 December 1930), p. 20.
19 Ibid.
20 Field, *Picture Palaces*, p. 67.
21 Cited in Ibid., p. 39.
22 *Bioscope: Modern Cinema Technique Supplement* (3 September 1930), pp. xii–xiii.
23 See R. Graves and A. Hodges, *The Long Weekend* (New York: Norton, 1940), pp. 297, 344–6. See also F.H. Vaughn and T. Ormiston, 'Does the Public Get the Films it Wants,' in *The Listener* (15 April 1936), pp. 711–13, and S. Shafer, *British Popular Films, 1929–39: The Cinema of Reassurance* (London: Routledge, 1997).
24 Quoted in Field, op.cit., p. 49.
25 Ibid., p. 67.
26 Ibid., p. 61.
27 *Bioscope* (19 March 1930), p. 27.
28 Field, *Picture Palaces*, pp. 94–5.
29 Ibid. p. 70.
30 J.P. Mayer, *Sociology of Film* (London: Faber, 1946), p. 274.
31 Elizabeth Bowen, 'Why I Go to the Cinema,' in Charles Davey ed., *Footnotes to the Film* (London: Readers' Union, 1938). Also see J. P. Mayer's *British Cinemas and Their Audiences* (London: Dennis Dobson, 1946) and B. Seebohm Rowntree and G.R. Lavers, *English Life and Leisure* (London: Longman's, 1951).
32 Field, *Picture Palaces*, p. 96.
33 Report of the Commission on Educational and Cultural Films, *The Film in National Life* (London: Allen and Unwin, 1932), p. 246.

34 Field, *Picture Palaces*, pp. 74–76.
35 Ibid., p. 77.
36 *Bioscope: Modern Cinema Techniques Supplement* (3 September 1930), p. xiii.
37 *Bioscope* (24 December 1930), p. 16; (19 November 1930), p. 41.
38 Ibid., (6 August 1930), p. 35; (8 October 1930), p. 52.
39 Ibid., (21 May 1930), p. 28; Field, *Picture Palaces*, p. 96.
40 *Bioscope*, (January 7, 1931), p.41.
41 Field, *Picture Palaces*, p. 97.
42 Ibid., p. 125.
43 *Bioscope* (November 19, 1930), p. 41; (24 September 1930), p. 53.
44 Ibid., (19 November 1930), p. 41; (3 December 1930), p. 43.
45 Ibid., (24 June 1930), p. 34 for an outline of permit requirements for a charity Sunday showing.
46 Ibid., (26 November 1930), p. 37.
47 Ibid., (28 May 1930), p. 51; (20 August 1930), p. 40; (19 November 1930), p. 41, and (24 December 1930), p. 5.
48 Ibid., (3 December 1930), p. 43; Field, *Picture Palaces*, p. 96.
49 *Bioscope*, (16 December 1930), p. 44.
50 Ibid., p. 41.
51 Ibid., (1 January 1930), p. 95.
52 Ibid., (31 December 1931), p. 40.
53 'Exploitation Matter Reviewed', Ibid., (8 January 1930), p. x.
54 Ibid.
55 Field, *Picture Palaces*, p. 138. See Richard Ford, *Children in the Cinema* (London: Allen and Unwin, 1939), p. 175 for an example of a parent's gratitude.
56 *Bioscope*, (10 December 1930), p. 43.
57 *Film in National Life*, p. 71; *Bioscope*, (8 October 1930), p. 52. See also Ford, *Children in the Cinema*.
58 Ford, *Children in the Cinema*, pp. 18–24.
59 Ibid., pp. 198, 205.
60 Ibid., p. 80.
61 Ibid., p. 82.
62 Cited in Ibid., p. 102.
63 Ibid., p. 156.
64 Field, *Picture Palaces*, p. 74.
65 Ibid.
66 Ibid., p. 97.
67 *New Survey of London Life and Labour*, IX, p. 74.
68 *Bioscope* (12 February 1930), p. 37.
69 Ford, *Children in the Cinema*, pp. 154–5.
70 Ibid., pp. 70, 162–185. Ford includes minutes of a 'typical' cinema club committee meeting from an industrial area.
71 Ibid., pp. 173–74.
72 Field, *Picture Palaces*, p. 123.
73 Ford, *Children in the Cinema*, p. 161.
74 Ibid., p. 166.
75 Ibid., p. 178.
76 Field, *Picture Palaces.*, pp. 37–8.
77 Ford, *Children in the Cinema*, pp. 179–85.
78 Field, *Picture Palaces*, p. 99.

79   See F.G. Thomas, 'With the Cinema in Devon,' *Sight and Sound*, I, 2 (Summer 1932), pp. 38–40.

80   See 'A Religious Film Society,' *Sight and Sound*, I, 3 (Autumn, 1932), p. 67; also 'The Film in Religion', p. 75 (same issue).

81   For movie patrons' regard for newsreels, see interviews in Mayer's *British Cinemas and Their Audiences* (op.cit.) and Norman Hulbert, 'News Films and Their Public,' *Sight and Sound*, II, 8 (Winter, 1934). For children and newsfilms, see Ford, *Children in the Cinema*, pp. 135–38.

82   On censorship regarding the Spanish Civil War, see A. Aldgate, '1930's Newsreels: Censorship and Controversy,' *Sight and Sound*, XLVI, 3, (Summer, 1977), pp. 154–57. Jonathon Lewis, 'Before Hindsight,' *Sight and Sound*, XLVI, 2, (Spring, 1977), pp. 60–73 explores non-fiction film attitudes toward pre war events. For issues neglected in newsreels see Bert Hogenkemp, 'Films and the Workers' Movement in Britain, 1929–39,' XLV, 2 (Spring, 1976): pp. 69–76, and Aldgate, *Cinema and Society: British Newsreels and the Spanish Civil War*, (London: Scolar Press, 1979).

83   Field, *Picture Palaces*, p. 107.

84   Ford, *Children in the Cinema*, pp. 198, 205.

85   Field, *Picture Palaces*, pp. 98, 124.

86   Ibid., p. 102.

87   Ibid.

88   *Bioscope* (7 January 1931), p.41.

89   Harry Hopkins, 'Are Silent Houses Doomed to Die the Death of a Dog,' *Bioscope* (1 January 1930), p. 62.

90   Ibid.

91   Ibid.

92   'Birmingham's Bunce,' *Bioscope* (12 February 1930), p. 15.

93   *Bioscope* (10 December 1930), p. 41.

94   See career sketches and biographies in the *Gaumont-British News* published from 1930 to 1936.

95   L.C.B. Seaman, *Post-Victorian Britain* (London: Methuen, 1966), p. 161

96   Ibid.

97   Ibid.

98   Field, *Picture Palaces*, p. 85.

99   *Gaumont-British News*, I, 1 (January, 1930), p. 10.

100 Field, *Picture Palaces*, p. 124.

101 See E.H. Lundy, '"Gaumont-British Service". To Theatre Staffs Everywhere,' *Gaumont-British News*, VII, 1, (January 1936), p. 74; also R. Bennell's, 'Service,' ibid., II, 1 (January 1931); pp. 10–11.

102 Field, *Picture Palaces*, pp. 75, 98.

103 Quoted in Ibid., p. 135.

CHAPTER 13

'I used to take her to the doctor and get the *proper* thing:' Twentieth-Century Health Care Choices in Lancashire Working-Class Communities

Lucinda McCray Beier

The history of health policy tends to be studied either within the broader context of social and welfare policy or as one possible focus for study of the relationship between scientific research and government priorities. According to a leading authority, Daniel Fox,

> Health policy, like policy for retirement income, job security and unemployment, social services and housing, has been profoundly influenced by the politics of economic productivity, social justice, and demographic change in each country. However, health policy has also been guided by perceptions of the nature and course of disease and opinions about the probability that particular medical interventions, organized and distributed in particular ways, would ameliorate its effects.[1]

In a recent article, Virginia Berridge identifies a need for research situating post-Second-World-War developments in medical science and disease in their policy context, pointing out that 'The translation of scientific "truth" into policy "fact" is a vital and under-researched conjuncture.'[2]

These and other scholars correctly perceive the interplay between medical science, scientific researchers, health care professionals, policy-makers, and administrators as being crucial; however, their analysis leaves out other important stakeholders in policy history – the individuals and groups composing the public for whom policies are designed and upon whom they are imposed. Indeed, members of the general population tend implicitly to be viewed as either passive recipients or uncritical consumers of needed, valued, and utilized services.[3] Furthermore, health policy historians have devoted little attention to social, economic, class, gender, and other differences among health care consumers that potentially affect popular perception and use of services. In a preliminary step toward filling this gap in health policy history, this paper will consider the response of working-class residents of three Lancashire communities to the introduction of the British National Health Service (NHS) in 1948.

The paper focuses not on the healthy/hungry thirties debate, nor on the political wrangling and financial horse trading leading up to the extension of National Insurance, nor on the evolution and restructuring of the British health care delivery system.[4] Instead it uses oral history evidence to explore mid-twentieth-century changes in working-class management of health incidents, including birth, ill-health, and death. It argues that working-class health culture remained traditional – even old-fashioned – until after 1948 due to factors including economic realities, relatively low expectations of professional medicine, and the often-ignored issue of class disparity between official health care providers and patients. It concludes that improvement in access to health and medical services, divorce of health care provision from means-tested charity, and the coincidental introduction of effective new therapies transformed working-class health culture and behavior in the years immediately following the Second World War.

Oral History Methods and the Experience of Ill-Health and Health Care

There is little doubt of the close relationship between poverty and ill-health. Despite declining death rates in Britain during the first half of the twentieth century, both contemporary observers and historians recognize the disproportionate burden of both morbidity and mortality upon the poor, particularly upon poor women and children.[5] Although official statistics illustrate the damage inflicted by bad nutrition, poor housing, high unemployment, and infectious disease, they do not tell us how people dealt with these challenges. Oral history is a powerful tool for examining attitudes toward health, illness, and healers; approaches used to manage health incidents; and health care choices of people whose experiences are otherwise not articulated.

There is a growing body of oral history evidence about popular experience of ill health and medical care in Britain.[6] None the less, there is little published work on the huge changes in that experience that have occurred in living memory. Jocelyn Cornwell's *Hard-Earned Lives: Accounts of Health and Illness from East London* uses a case study approach to explore the 'commonsense' health concepts and behavior of twenty-four adults interviewed in the early 1980s.[7] The resulting information provides an in-depth snapshot of working-class London health culture; it does not offer an historical perspective on either that culture or changing experience and expectations regarding health, ill-health, or health care providers.

Elizabeth Roberts has published widely on working-class Lancashire social and family life. Her paper, 'Oral history investigations of disease and its management by the Lancashire working class, 1890-1939,'[8] offers invaluable insight into early twentieth-century working-class health culture and behavior. Her books, *A Woman's Place: An Oral History of Working-Class Women 1890-1940* and *Women and Families: An Oral History, 1940-1970*, although not primarily focused on health issues, provide useful information about working-class approaches to birth control, child-bearing, and neighborhood support in times of illness and death.[9]

This paper is largely based on information resulting from life history interviews of ninety-eight working-class residents of three northern English towns – Lancaster, Barrow, and Preston – conducted between 1987 and 1989 by Elizabeth Roberts and myself for a project entitled 'Familiar and Social Change and Continuity in Working-Class Families, 1940-1970.'[10] As Table 13.1 indicates, every attempt was made to ensure a balance regarding the age, sex, and residence of interviewees:

Table 13.1 Life history interviews

Date of Birth	Town		
	Barrow	**Lancaster**	**Preston**
1910-1919	2 men	1 man	–
	2 women	1 woman	1 woman
1920-1929	5 men	6 men	4 men
	4 women	5 women	4 women
1930-1939	6 men	5 men	4 men
	6 women	6 women	6 women
1940-1949	4 men	4 men	6 men
	4 women	7 women	4 women
1950-1959	–	–	1 woman
Totals	17 men	16 men	14 men
	16 women	19 women	16 women

Overall Total: 47 men + 51 women = 98 respondents

Interview respondents were recruited through social and family networks, community organizations, and casual contacts. Respondents identified themselves as working class; most (79 per cent) reported that their fathers had been either unskilled or skilled wage earners.[11] All of the interviewees had spent most of their lives in Lancaster, Barrow, or Preston – communities whose economies and cultures have been largely dependent upon manufacturing industries.[12] Semi-structured interviews were conducted using a questionnaire that contained a substantial number of questions concerning the experience and management of health, illness, childbearing, and medical care.

Traditional Working-Class Management of Health, Ill-Health, and Death

Medical anthropologists, sociologists, and historians have distinguished between dominant, officially sanctioned Western medical theories and practices, currently summarized by the term 'biomedicine', and other approaches to dealing with ill-health that are variously designated as, among other terms, 'popular,' 'traditional,' 'lay,' 'folk,' and 'alternative.' As one recent study points out, 'Several scholars have created typologies that attempt to describe the range and use of various therapeutic systems or modalities and to highlight related cultural issues. Despite the best of intentions, most typologies are founded on ethnocentric assumptions, such as the primacy or superiority of one system over another.'[13] Contrary to the conventional polarization of biomedicine and other ways of dealing with health and illness, the oral evidence suggests that older theories about disease causation comfortably co-exist with newer theories; for example, the same person can believe that a cold is caused by sitting in a draught (a humoral explanation) or by contracting a virus (a biomedical explanation).[14] In addition, oral history evidence indicates that people are willing to use healers and therapies ranging from home remedies or amateur neighborhood authorities to the latest biomedical treatment and specialist physician, depending upon factors including perception of danger, interpretation of symptoms, authoritative advice, and access to resources and services. Finally, it suggests that working-class health beliefs and practices followed a generation or two behind middle-class health culture in terms of accepting the 'cultural authority' of official health care providers – hardly surprising, since the providers themselves tended to be middle-class.[15]

Despite the explosion of discoveries in medical science during the late nineteenth and early twentieth centuries and the related development of a burgeoning number of health care professions, working-class Lancashire health culture remained quite traditional before the Second World War. Lay people – mainly women – managed most health incidents. Although a range of formal health services were available, mothers, grandmothers, and neighborhood health authorities provided advice, prescribed and administered medicine, attended births and deaths, and nursed the sick.[16]

Health maintenance and care were part of women's nurturing role: 'From a young age girls were expected to help with domestic work, such as cooking, cleaning and sewing, and to help look after sick relatives and neighbors.'[17] Families also took advice from chemists (i.e. druggists), who served as a kind of cultural bridge between working-class sufferers and middle-class physicians – an informal conduit of official medical information on the one hand, and validators of popular medical ideas on the other.

Generally speaking, injuries and illnesses perceived to be minor were first treated within the household. Respondents born before 1940 remembered a host of remedies (some prepared at home, some purchased ready-made over the counter) used before outside help was sought. Children inhaled tar fumes for whooping cough, had warm olive oil applied to their ears for earache, and took syrups internally and hot compresses externally for sore throats. Many of these compresses were very imaginative: one respondent's family used hot mashed potatoes in a sock; another reported application of boiled onions. Until at least 1950, the dominant remedy for a bad chest was goose grease, often plastered on with brown paper. Every family had its own favorite cough mixture recipe. Sore eyes were treated with Golden Eye Ointment (purchased from the chemist) or, in one case, by being rubbed with a gold ring. Boils were 'drawn' with a variety of preparations, among which bread poultices or a mixture of soap and sugar were the most common. And before 1941, opium was widely purchased in a variety of preparations to quiet fussy babies and sooth tooth- and stomach-aches, coughs, sleeplessness, and other discomforts.[18] For example, Mrs Fleming, born in 1921, remembered paregoric, an alcohol-based preparation of opium and camphor, being used by her family when she was small. Of her mother, she said,

> She used to make some cough medicine, and it were gorgeous, but you can't do it now. It was butter, sugar, vinegar, black treacle and, I don't know whether you have heard? We used to call it paregoric ... And old-fashioned fireplaces had a shelf, you know, above, and it used to be in a basin covered up until it had all melted down. And that cured your cold ... I went for it once when our Pat [her daughter, born in 1942] had a right bad cough and I thought, 'I'll try this.' And the chemist nearly booted me out of the shop.[19]

As far as both family and community were concerned, an ounce of prevention was worth a pound of cure. In the period before the Second World War, before antibiotics or commercially prepared vitamins were generally available, many people took tonics and laxatives to stave off illness. Virtually all respondents remember being given 'emulsion,' either at home or at school. Mr Newberry, born in 1931, said

Well, we were given emulsion at school and we were given cod-liver oil capsules at school, but again this was during the war where ... vitamins were in short supply anyway. And we didn't decide to have these things, it was decided for us ... . And we were all told we had got to bring our own spoon to school ... . And in order to identify a particular spoon it was suggested that we wrap a piece of colored wool round it or rafia, so that you knew whose spoon was whose.[20]

Many respondents were given cod liver oil – either on its own, or combined with malt. In addition, many families took weekly 'physics' to maintain health. Mrs Howard, born in 1931, said:

I'll tell you what my mother swore by. Phennings Cooling Powders, and that was it, oh we used to love that. Friday night was bath night, we'd all have baths, put clean nighties on, we all had clean sheets on. And then we used to get our hair dried. Sometimes my dad used to dry our hair for us; it was marvelous, my dad giving us a towel rub. And then out would come the Phennings Cooling Powders. Now, they went in ages. It was, if you was between two and three year old, it was half a powder, and three and five, it was one powder, or one and a half powders, or two. And she used to put a spoonful of milk and then shake this powder on, and it was the most gorgeous tasting stuff I've ever tasted ... . And we were dying to get that age, oh, where we could have three powders.[21]

Respondents were not certain what long-term effects were expected from these treatments, but at least one respondent, harking back to humoral theory, speculated that the Friday night dose of Syrup of Figs was administered 'So that we were cleaned out for the rest of the week to go to school.'[22] In his *The Classic Slum: Salford Life in the First Quarter of the Century*, Robert Roberts recalled similar behavior among an earlier generation of working-class northerners: 'At weekends people purged themselves with great doses of black draught, senna pods, cascara sagrada, and their young with Gregory powder, licorice powder, and California syrup of figs.'[23]

Despite such preventative measures, people became ill. If home treatment failed, external help was sought. Many respondents remembered neighborhood authorities who were consulted in time of illness, helped with home confinements, and laid out the dead. Mr Newberry said that his mother had performed these services for neighbors on a Lancaster council housing estate during the 1930s, '40s, and '50s. He reported that people would consult her for 'Any kind of illness, particularly as far as youngsters were concerned. She diagnosed after looking at the kids and I don't remember her being wrong, she probably was, but I don't remember her being wrong.

And if she felt the doctor was needed, then the doctor was sent for.'[24] His mother also 'helped with deliveries and she helped with ... laying people out, people who had died' in an area of 'maybe two or three streets, that's all ... There was probably somebody equally as competent in the next road.'[25]

Mrs Burton, born in 1931, made a similar statement, 'There always seemed to be one woman in the street that would help. She wouldn't be a qualified midwife, but she used to go when there was any babies born. And she used to do the same thing if anybody died.'[26] Mr Morton, born in 1948, recalled:

> R. Every street had its 'lady' who was ... experienced in these matters. Ours was actually the lady across the road that I was telling you has just died [1988], Mrs Riley. Who had actually had some nursing experience.
> I. Was she a kind of unofficial midwife to the neighborhood then?
> R. She was unofficial everything, father confessor, helper, supporter, advisor, nurse, everything, was Nana Riley ... There was another lady around the corner who has been long since dead. We used to call her Aunty Viv, although of course she was actually no aunty at all. She was just a very close family friend ... . Even Mum and Dad called her Aunty Viv, and she died when she was about ninety-three and always looked very much the way that old ladies did in the pictures that I have got upstairs. Very leathery wrinkled skin, old-fashioned shawls and clogs, and they [such ladies] were still quite common when I was a child.[27]

Mrs Turner, born in 1932, recalled that her great aunt had been one of the unofficial healers on a Lancaster council housing estate who 'used to go and help people, delivering and laying out and everything.' She had had no formal training, but people trusted her abilities: 'She always looked old to us ... but she just did it, and I suppose they would take it for granted.'[28] This woman continued providing services until she was quite elderly.

Mrs Howard, born in 1931, described another neighborhood healer:

> I think she had been a nurse in her time, and she must have left to have a family ... . But she was the nurse on our street, whether she had ever been a proper nurse, I don't know. But everybody ran for Mrs Myrtle when anybody was ill. Because I remember two brothers being badly scalded, and she came both times. One had pulled a kettle off the fire onto his legs and I seem to remember her dipping his leg in a bag of flour ... . I know my sister jumped on a rusty tin once and gashed her leg. 'Go for

Mrs Myrtle!' you know, and she used to come back, she used to bring a box with her, and it was full of iodine, cotton wool, and ointments and things. And she used to really make you better, and she used to come and dress it for you and stuff like that.[29]

During the inter-war years, management of childbirth was in transition among working-class families. While many respondents had been born or had their babies at home, an increasing number were born or gave birth in maternity homes or hospitals. Furthermore, women whose mothers had been delivered by unlicensed midwives consulted licensed midwives or general Practitioners for their own deliveries. Dr Ackerman, who began working as a general practitioner in 1948, recalled that in the early years of his practice he delivered many babies at home, but as time went on, hospital births became common:

Facilities became more available. It isn't terribly long since we had a maternity hospital here, and for awhile we hadn't very much in the way of beds available to us as General Practitioners. But then of course you see the advice of the consultant obstetricians was, 'All right, don't have a first birth at home; once you get to four, come and tell us. So deal with your ... second and third children if there is no hint of trouble.'

Mr Newberry, who in many ways exemplified the transition from traditional to 'modern' management of ill-health, said that all of his children were born at home in the 1950s. When asked why, he said:

I don't know, possibly the freedom of access for visitors and that sort of thing. She [his wife] felt more comfortable, I think. I don't think any of our generation, I think even now, don't enjoy hospitals. Because, I think, of the regimentation and ... restriction and that sort of thing. I suppose it's part of our in-built way of life, that we don't like regimentation ... . And the children have been born at home, well since dot, so why on earth change it? Thank goodness, we were very lucky, there were no complications ... . We did visit the doctor. She did have visits from the midwife prior to the birth and we were told that everything was going to be natural, sort of thing. As indeed it was.[30]

Mrs Turner's experience summarizes both the options available to women and changes in working-class approaches to childbearing that took place between her own birth in 1932 and the births of her children in the 1950s and 1971:

I. Were you born at home as well?
R. We were born at home, yes. Born in my granny's parlor.

I. So there was no talk, even though it was twins, of having you in hospital?
R. No. But, like I said, my mother didn't know she was having twins until we were born ... Got the shock of her life, my granny. I couldn't tell you what she said. No, shock of her life, you know, being left with two of us, just little things. They couldn't put real clothes on us, so they had to wrap us up in olive oil and cotton wool ... My grandma, when we was born, they used to keep us warm in the side oven. Because they had no incubators then, you see.

This woman's mother also had a later child, born in 1946, who was delivered at home by an unlicensed midwife. However, when Mrs Turner herself had children, two out of three births were in hospital. When asked why she made this decision, she replied, 'Well, it was just the sensible thing to do, you know.'[31]

Barriers to Working-Class Use of Official Medicine

The main reasons respondents chose to depend on unofficial, neighborhood medical authorities were cost and social class issues. Cost was a particularly important factor in the decision to consult a physician before 1948. Mrs Allen, born in 1932, described the way illnesses were managed in her home when she was a child: 'Well, all depending what it was, really. If she [mother] thought I was really ill, she would send for the doctor. She would try and probably cure me first herself, because then they'd to pay. And then, if it didn't work, she would send for the doctor then. But I know I used to take fever cure and all sorts of stuff.'[32] Another interviewee, Mr Kendall who was born in 1931, remembered, 'I should have had glasses when I were a little lad because I had a lazy eye ... and my Mum couldn't afford them, so I never got them. So consequently I'm still bothered with this one lazy eye.'[33]

Interviewees were affected by national trends regarding health care expenses. Most wage earners received treatment free at the point of use under the 'Lloyd George' National Insurance program, implemented in 1911 and extended until by 1939 approximately half the population was covered.[34] Unfortunately, most women and children were not insured. Thus, respondents born before 1940 remember their families paying the doctor's 'man' (collector) a small amount – often a penny – every Friday in order to defray medical expenses. Mr Fleming, born in 1917, said, 'Oh well, they used to send a collector round, if you didn't go to pay or you couldn't afford to pay. They would send a man round to collect a penny or tuppence a week off you.'[35]

Some interviewees also remembered their families belonging to Friendly Societies that helped cover medical costs. Mrs Barber, born in 1929, said, 'We were also in a Friendly Society, the National Deposit it was called, and we went once a month in a school at the back of Abbey Road and paid. I don't know how much we paid, so much for Mother and so much for me.'[36] However, many Friendly Societies did not cover women and children.[37]

Those unable to pay for medical attention were forced to seek help from welfare authorities – a last resort because of the shame and discomfort of taking charity. Mr Billings offered one explanation for why means-tested welfare was universally loathed:

> The government of the day decided that they wouldn't give you any help financial-wise, but until they got right down unto the fundamentals. That was, if you'd got a piano you sold it. Anything that was valuable you had to sell it, so all you were left with were just the essentials in the house. That was the means test ... If you had a son working whatever menial job it was, maybe five bob a week as a newspaper boy, they would knock that off your money. So the result was that boys went out and they used to camp on the beach.[38]

None the less, health services offered by the Poor Law doctor and the workhouse were sometimes the only alternative.[39] Mrs Norton, born in 1919, became pregnant out of wedlock in 1940 and, at first, kept her condition secret from her parents. However, when she became ill, she talked to her father:

> He said, 'Are you all right?' I said, 'Well, I don't know.' Because I was losing blood ... Anyway, they brought the doctor and I had this toxemia, I had kidney trouble and that. Eventually she was born seven months ... Three pound, two ounces.
> I. Did you have her at home?
> R. No. I'll tell you where. I was put where they were put in them days. My mother put me in the workhouse.
> I. Did she? ... Why did she do that?
> R. Because she thought it was wrong what I had done ... Yes, that was the place you [had to] go to. Well, when you were put in there while the time come that you had to have your baby, you had to work. But I couldn't work because I was ill, I was so ill. And then I was taken – I was really ill this particular night and I remember saying to the lady in the next bed, 'I've got a pain.' And this nurse come and they brought the doctor. I remember the doctor, Dr. Mathers, that was the Poor Law doctor that run that home. He came and I had her, I had Maureen ... I stayed there [in the workhouse] and had her, and then I had to

stay in until she got up to the weight of five pounds, and then
they told me I could go home. Now, I didn't have a taxi, I didn't
have nothing ... I came home on the bus.[40]

When Mrs Norton chose, after her marriage, to have her second child in the
workhouse, her husband was enraged. He said:

The workhouse in those days, you had to be really hard up. If
you got into the workhouse, you had to be really rock bottom.
... This time when she had her baby, I didn't think that as being
rock bottom, because we weren't rock bottom. No, I was
working. No, we weren't rock bottom. She had no cause. I never
drove her into that position ... No.[41]

Along with means-tested financial assistance, medical care provided by Poor
Law doctors was avoided if at all possible.

Oral history evidence suggests that members of the working class may
have avoided or resented the services of many types of official health care
providers because of social class issues. Mr Boyle, born in 1937, was shamed
by his experience with health clinic services as a child:

Now, on Harrison Hill, they classed theirselves as different
families than what we were. We were scum to them. I'll give
you an instance. Me, my brothers and sisters all got what they
called at the time, impetigo, which is scabies. So you had to go
to this place which is called Atkinson Street and it must have
been a public house at one time and they had changed it, the
Health must have changed it ... And you went there and there
were big tin baths and you got in them baths of hot water, and
this bloke used to come ... and scrub these scabs ... until he
made them bleed. Then you got out of the bath and he filled you
with this ointment. He had a name for it, it were thick yellow
ointment. And then you could put your clothes back on, which
you had a woolen vest and one thing and another, and then my
Mam would walk us back down the street, and then you would
see on the other side were these kids ... 'Don't go up near
[Boyles's], they've all got scabies, keep away from them, they've
impetigo.' And it went on from that, you see. And that was just
around the corner from me.[42]

Class preference may also partially account for women's continued use of
unqualified midwives long after the passage of the 1902 Midwives Act. In
A Woman's Place, Elizabeth Roberts writes, 'Unqualified midwives were
cheaper; they were generally thought to be friendlier, and less "starchy";
and they were certainly less likely to tell the woman what to do, being more
likely to cooperate both with her and her female relatives.'[43] There was

also some working-class resistance to services provided by health visitors, who were often middle class in origin. In *Women and Families*, Roberts quotes Mrs Jenkins, who reported, 'My mother-in-law wouldn't let her [health visitor] in the house. She said that she was an interfering busybody.'[44]

Some interviewees indicated that their families avoided physicians for class reasons. According to Mr Newberry, the doctor 'Was a distant character that was held in some reverence and we didn't particularly want to see him .... That was no disrespect to him as an individual, but the best relationship in our family – as in most working families – was distant.'[45]

Many respondents consulted chemists before going to the doctor. Chemists' advice was cheaper than that available from GPs. Mrs Burrell, born in 1931, reported:

> R. If you had falls in the street or something like that, you always went to the chemist. Mr Last, he was called, he was a lovely old man, and it was like a doctor, because at that time you used to have to pay ... your doctor for a consultation, but if you went to the chemist, I mean you would get six penny-worth of liquorice and chlorodine for your cough, that was the bottle then.
> I. Do you have a feeling that you were getting different kinds of medicine from the chemist than you would have gotten from a GP?
> R. No, I think it would be all the same ... but you would pay a lot more for the doctor.[46]

Furthermore, because chemists were tradespeople, serving and living among their working-class customers, they presented less of a class barrier than did the physicians.[47] Cuthbert's on the corner of Cable Street and North Road in Lancaster, was particularly popular. Mr Newberry said that his family preferred Mr Cuthbert to the doctor because there was 'No waiting room, no long-winded detail and explanations. We could mention to Cuthbert, and I don't think he was ever confronted as a chemist by an original illness, everything he treated, somebody had had before. And he produced these bottles you would describe as snake oil, and it worked.'[48]

Respondents described a less pleasant relationship with dentists, whom they consulted mainly for extractions. Their unpleasant memories were due less to class issues than to discomfort caused by the treatment they received. Many reported having gone to school dentists, whose services were offered by local education authorities as part of the School Medical Service initiated in 1907.[49] There was no charge for school dental services, but respondents remember school dentists as harsh and unsympathetic. The 'ordinary' dentist charged a fee. According to Mr Logan, born in 1919, 'A normal dentist, if you went to him, it was a shilling for a straight pull out. If you wanted anaesthetic, it was five shillings, so you didn't have it [the anaesthetic] ... .'[50]

Change in Working-Class Health Culture

The introduction of the National Health Service (NHS) in 1948 promised a brave new world where medical care would be a right, not a privilege. Heralded by war-time Coalition Government promises, the NHS was part of a larger Welfare State of which much was expected – particularly for the working class. For example, Barrow's Medical Officer of Health, A.R. Forrest, wrote in his 1945 Report,

> There is no doubt ... that such factors as economic distress, due to unemployment or low wages, bad and over-crowded houses, the employment of married women in industry, and the social class of the parents, namely unskilled or semi-skilled workers, has the effect of raising the infantile mortality rate. One hopes that in the future post-war world that we shall see freedom from want, economic security for the family by full employment and adequate wages which will not require the mothers to work in industry, and better housing so that each family can have a decent home of their own in order to bring up their children.[51]

Free at the point of use, health care services based on the latest biomedical science was expected to improve overall quality of life and eliminate differences in health between social classes.

Experts agree that inequalities in health and access to health services persisted after the introduction of the NHS.[52] While life expectancy improved and death rates declined in the generation after 1948, these advances were slower than in the years before the Second World War and slower than in many other European countries.[53] None the less, from its introduction, the National Health Service was popular with users, regardless of social class. Historians and oral history respondents agree that the flood of early and continued demand for service indicated health care needs that had previously gone unmet. According to Helen Jones,

> It would seem that women, who had not normally been covered by National Health Insurance, and who had probably been hardest hit by poverty, gained most from the NHS. The full extent of women's ill health had never before been revealed. One woman doctor who qualified on the day the NHS came into operation recalled women queuing with thyroid deficiency, gynecological problems, painful varicose veins, or with menopausal difficulties. The biggest increase in visits to the GP came from the elderly and from women aged up to thirty-five.[54]

Mr Boswell, born in 1920, remembered:

> People wanted their teeth out ... and wanted a set of dentures,

they just could not afford to buy them, so they had aching teeth
... Or somebody was ill, send for the doctor, you would get a
bill. So they would go down to the chemist and make a bottle up
or something like that, you know, and of course the result was
that people snuffed it. They had diseases that could have been
cured, but they went on too far, so the population was beset
with illnesses... And they could not afford to get them treated,
so it was the best thing since wearing boots when that [the NHS]
came on.[55]

In addition, respondents remember that the advent of the NHS did away
with class and economic disparities in the ways doctors treated patients.
Mrs Horwick, born in 1945, remembered her mother's account of the doctor
before the NHS:

R. Dr. Simpson. He didn't like the National Health Service when
it came on. He was a mean Scotsman. He used to make you
wash your bandages and those sorts of things then ... .
I. Did your mother ever talk to you about the pre-Health Service
days? I mean, she was presumably very keen on the Health
Service, was she?
R. Yes, she was. I mean, Bevan was her hero, certainly. Yes,
she thought it was wonderful, you know, after experiencing the
meanness of doctors like Simpson and others, the discretionary
treatment.[56]

Arguably, partly as a result of reduction of economic and class barriers
between patients and health care providers, working-class health culture
changed rapidly. People who had experienced traditional domestic and
community management of illness and children made different choices within
their adult households. When asked where he and his wife obtained medical
advice for their own children, Mr Newberry, whose mother had served as a
neighborhood healer, said:

R. Well, the doctor. If Mum had called, we would ask, but
basically, no, we talked to the doctor.
I. Why was there this change?
R. Because, I think, the world had changed, the responsibility
levels had changed, knowledge had changed. The doctors had
got a lot more knowledge and were a lot more available ... .
I. Was this because of the National Health Service, do you think,
in part?
R. Well, again, basically there were more doctors. Obviously
during the war there was a shortage, but, yes, there were certainly
more doctors. They were certainly more mobile in that they had

got motor cars then so that they could travel about.[57]

Other respondents reported this change – higher levels of consultation of doctors combined with reduced confidence in amateur medical authorities. Mrs Owen's only daughter was born in 1940. While continuing her close relationship with her mother, who lived nearby, she transferred her reliance in medical matters to her G.P. She said, 'If something happened to her, I used to take her to the doctor's and get the *proper* thing.' She tolerated her mother's home remedies, allowing

> Mum to goose grease her if she had a bad chest. I used to say, 'That child's got a bad chest,' and out would come the jar of goose grease. An earthenware jar with a piece of brown paper with a rubber ring round, and she would come down and rub her back and front. In the end, I took her [daughter] to the doctor, and he gave me some antibiotics, and it cleared up in no time.[58]

Doctor Ackerman, who began practicing in Lancaster in 1948, said that when he first arrived, infant management depended on the traditional authority: Granny.[58] His explanation for the trend away from dependency on grandmothers for information and advice was that, as more housing became available after the Second World War, fewer grandparents lived with their children's families. However, taking Mrs Owen's cue, I believe that there were more important factors, including reduction in economic and class barriers, together with official medicine's new success in dealing with old problems, that contributed to this trend.

Like changes in the health care delivery itself, the development of working-class acceptance of the cultural authority of health care professionals was evolutionary rather than revolutionary. Certainly, a range of health care providers had regarded themselves as medical authorities for centuries. It is equally true that medical education, professional licensing, medical institutions, and public health services and regulations had been the object of government policy since the early modern period. Nevertheless, although working-class English people had accepted advice and treatment from representatives of official medicine before 1948, as we have seen, these representatives were peripheral to traditional working-class health culture. Paul Starr, who coined the phrase, describes the relationship as being dominated by the *cultural authority* of the physician:

> Patients consult physicians not just for advice, but first of all to find out whether they are 'really' sick and what their symptoms mean. 'What have I got, doc?' they ask. 'Is it serious?' Cultural authority, in this context, is antecedent to action. The authority to interpret signs and symptoms, to diagnose health or illness, to name diseases, and to offer prognoses is the foundation of

any social authority the physician can assume. By shaping the patients' understanding of their own experience, physicians create the conditions under which their advice seems appropriate.[59]

Only after the introduction of the National Health Service did General Practitioners, Consultants, and other health care professionals gain this authority among working-class residents of Lancaster, Barrow, and Preston.

This cultural shift was aided by the introduction, after the Second World War, of penicillin and other powerful antibiotics to the civilian population – a development that heralded a revolution in medicine and surgery. No longer were traditional killers such as pneumonia, tuberculosis, puerperal fever, and post-operative infection accepted with fatalism. These new weapons against disease were controlled by doctors who possessed the exclusive right to prescribe them.[60] Before twentieth-century legislation, the doctor's ability to prescribe had depended on his or her expertise in medical theory; after this legislation, license to prescribe became both a significant badge of the doctor's professional status and an important reason people consulted doctors.

Together with increased dissemination of a growing range of vaccines and a flood of new medical technology, introduction of antibiotics changed people's fears and expectations regarding disease and its management. Very soon after the Second World War, policies and institutions organized to control infection – quarantining, stoving, and isolation hospitals – became virtually obsolete.[61] At the same time, the power of medical intervention and the demand for medical services grew dramatically. People who had depended on family and neighborhood authorities to raise children, deal with illness and disability, and manage death relied increasingly on the advice and services of experts. According to Elizabeth Roberts, after the Second World War 'There was a strong feeling that professional services were better than those provided by well-meaning amateurs. Professional help was particularly sought by mothers of babies and small children. Increasingly, the advice of doctors and health visitors was preferred to that of older women in the family or neighborhood.'[62]

The flip side of this development was that ordinary people lost confidence in their own ability to handle health incidents. The younger the respondent, the more dependent on the advice of both doctors and infant and child welfare clinics which for an earlier generation had mainly been a source of cheap or free supplies.[63] As the elderly neighborhood authorities on ill health, childbearing, and death retired or died in the post-War period, no one took their place. Although patent medicine sales continued and remain healthy, remedies truly concocted at home went so completely out of fashion that they only barely remain in living memory. Increasingly, official medical theories were accepted by the lay community, for whom germs and viruses began to occupy the danger zones vacated by bad air, cold, and draughts.[64]

Perhaps it is not a coincidence that rising expectations regarding medical services and results came at the same time as post-war prosperity improved both living standards and expectations of members of the working class. Full employment, rising wages, aggressive public housing policies, and the proliferation of consumer goods revolutionized people's ideas about the necessities of life. Along with the indoor flush toilet, three-piece living room suite, and Hoover vacuum cleaner, working-class people increasingly viewed access to official professional medical services as a necessary component of a decent life.

Despite the inevitable criticisms and complaints, the oral evidence indicates that the National Health Service lived up to expectations. In contrast to their otherwise conservative views, many respondents praised the service the NHS provided (particularly up to 1970, when our study ended) and looked back without nostalgia to the bad old days of amateur management of birth, illness, injury, and death.

Conclusions and Implications for Further Study

This study clearly indicates that policy does not necessarily dictate behavior. Some government-provided pre-Second World War health services, including clinics and Poor Law health care facilities, were under-used or used only as a last resort. Other officially-endorsed services, such as those provided by General Practitioners, were used sparingly, depending on the circumstances. In contrast, the policy creating the National Health Service affected working-class behavior and, eventually, health culture because the way it was implemented reduced barriers to the utilization of official health services. Furthermore, the continued popularity and use of NHS services have embedded them deeply in working-class health culture.

Historians study change and continuity. Perhaps no endeavor has altered as dramatically in the twentieth century as health care. Although public statistics, published literature, institutional documents, and records kept by health care providers are useful sources for information about developments in this area, they can only imply information about the experience of the people who lived through these developments. Furthermore, these sources generally reflect the viewpoint of some professional or political elite. As Paul Thompson, among other practitioners, tells us, oral history gives voice to the inarticulate – ordinary people whose experiences would not otherwise be documented.[65] Oral history generations are short; most of the people Elizabeth Roberts interviewed in the 1970s for A Woman's Place are now dead. Their memories died with them. It is important that we collect the remaining memories of health, ill-health, and medical care in order to provide a complete and balanced history of health care and policy in the twentieth century.

NOTES

1   Daniel Fox, 'Health Policy and the History of Welfare States: A Reinterpretation,' *Journal of Policy History*, Vol. 10, No. 2 (1998), p. 239.
2   Virginia Berridge, 'Health and Medicine in the Twentieth Century: Contemporary History and Health Policy,' *Social History of Medicine*, Vol. 5, No. 2 (1992), p. 307.
3   This is not to say that consumers have not contributed to policy debate. Ivan Illich's *Medical Nemesis* (New York: Pantheon Books, 1976), arguably launched the first post-Second World War critique of the dominance of professional allopathic medicine. This critique has had enormous influence on consumer-led health care reform movements. Similarly, women's questioning of the way professional medicine has managed childbearing has led to widespread change in this area. See, e.g., Ann Oakley, *The Captured Womb: A History of the Medical Care of Pregnant Women* (Oxford: Blackwell, 1984). Also influential was the anti-psychiatry movement of the 1970s, spearheaded by critics including R.D. Laing, Thomas Szasz, and David Cooper, which has had an enormous impact on mental health policy. None the less, critiques of health care have generally focused on medical practitioners and institutions as if they operated entirely independently of policy. Furthermore, the perspectives and experiences of consumers, either as individuals or as organized groups, has not attracted much attention from health policy historians.
4   See, e.g., Charles Webster, 'Healthy or Hungry Thirties?' *History Workshop*, no. 13 (1982), pp. 110–29; Virginia Berridge, Mark Harrison, and Paul Weindling, 'The Impact of War and Depression, 1918 to 1948' in Charles Webster, ed., *Caring for Health: History and Diversity* (Open University Press, 1993); Charles Webster, *The Health Services Since the War: Problems of Health Care, The National Health Service Before 1957* (Her Majesty's Stationery Office, 1988); Brian Watkin, *The National Health Service: The First Phase 1948-1974 and After* (London: George Allen & Unwin, 1978); Audrey Leathard, *Health Care Provision Past, Present, and Future* (London and New York: Chapman and Hall, 1990).
5   See, e.g., Helen Jones, *Health and Society in Twentieth-Century Britain*, (London and New York: Longman, 1994), pp. 58–87; Margery Spring Rice, *Working-Class Wives* (London: Penguin, 1939); Webster, 'Healthy or Hungry Thirties?.'
6   For a discussion of sources see Paul Thompson, 'Oral History and the History of Medicine: A Review,' *Social History of Medicine*, Vol. 4, No. 2 (1991), pp. 371–83. See also Rachel Adam and Rachel Van Riel, *In Sickness and in Health* (1987) and *Can We Afford the Doctor?* (Age Exchange, 1985).
7   Jocelyn Cornwell, *Hard-Earned Lives: Accounts of Health and Illness from East London* (London: Tavistock, 1984).
8   Published in John Pickstone, ed., *Health, Disease and Medicine in Lancashire, 1750–1950* (Manchester: UMIST Occasional Publications, No. 2, 1980).
9   Elizabeth Roberts, *A Woman's Place: An Oral History of Working-Class Women 1890–1940* (Oxford: Blackwell, 1984) and *Women and Families: An*

Oral History, 1940–1970 (Oxford: Blackwell, 1995). Among other things, this paper owes to Dr. Roberts its recognition of the mid-twentieth century shift among working-class women from reliance on lay authorities to dependence on professional carers in matters related to health. See Elizabeth Roberts, *Women and Families,* pp. 145–54.

10 This project was funded by the Economic and Social Research Council (ESRC). Interviews conducted for this project also served as the basis for Roberts, *Women and Families.*

11 See Roberts, *Women and Families*, pp. 1–7 for a discussion of the communities and the respondents.

12 Preston, largest of the three communities with a population ranging from 119,001 in 1930 to 100,140 in 1970, had a large but declining cotton industry and port during the period under consideration. Lancaster, with a population ranging from 43,383 in 1930 to 48,500 in 1970, had a mixed economy composed of manufacturing, service (health care and education), and retail sectors. The economy of Barrow, with a population ranging from 66,202 in 1930 to 63,460 in 1970, was dependent on heavy engineering and dominated by its shipyards.

13 Martha O. Loustanau and Elisa J. Sobo, *The Cultural Context of Health, Illness, and Medicine* (Westport, CT. and London: Bergin and Garvey, 1997), p. 74. This chaper (pp. 73–105) contains a useful critique of several influential anthropological classifications of therapeutic systems. A recent critique of sociological scholarship on lay and professional medical perspectives and behavior appears in Michael Bury, *Health and Illness in a Changing Society* (London and New York: Routledge, 1997), pp. 1–46.

14 See, e.g., Cecil G. Helman, '"Feed a Cold, Starve a Fever": Folk Models of Infection in an English Suburban Community, and Their Relation to Medical Treatment,' in Caroline Currer and Meg Stacey, *Concepts of Health, Illness and Disease: A Comparative Perspective* (Leamington Spa, Hamburg, and New York: Berg, 1986), pp. 211–232.

15 For discussion of the cultural authority of allopathic physicians, see Paul Starr, *The Social Transformation of American Medicine* (Basic Books, 1982), pp. 9–21.

16 My earlier research, resulting in *Sufferers and Healers: The Experience of Illness in Seventeenth-Century England* (Routledge and Kegan Paul, 1987), found that early modern English women of all social classes served as medical authorities in their families and communities. Thus, I feel confident about describing twentieth-century Lancashire working-class health culture as 'traditional.'

17 Jones, *Health and Society in Twentieth-Century Britain*, p. 59.

18 Sale of opiates was increasingly regulated after passage of the Dangerous Drugs Act in 1921. The Pharmacy and Medicines Act of 1941, among other things, restricted the retail sale of medicines and poisons to authorized classes of persons including physicians, dentists, 'authorized sellers of poisons, and persons who have served a regular apprenticeship and who come within specified conditions.' Leslie G. Matthews, *History of Pharmacy in Britain* (Edinburgh and London: E. & S. Livingstone, Ltd, 1962) pp. 367–8, 377–8.

19 Fleming is not this respondent's real name. All identifying information about interviewees is confidential. Thus, names used in this paper are fictitious. References to interview transcripts, housed by the Center for North West Regional Studies, Lancaster University, Lancaster, Great Britain, are given by the respondent's code name and transcript page number: Mrs F1L, p. 49.

20 Mr N2L, pp. 52–3. See, also, e.g., Mrs A4L, p. 74 and Mr N3L, pp. 128, 133–4.
21 Mrs H5L, p. 58.
22 Mrs T2L, p. 77.
23 Robert Roberts, *The Classic Slum: Salford Life in the First Quarter of the Century* (New York: Penguin, 1971), p. 124.
24 Mr N2L, p. 50.
25 Ibid., p. 55.
26 Mrs B2B, p. 31.
27 Mr M10L, pp. 19–20. In quotations from interview transcripts, I=interviewer and R=respondent.
28 Mrs T2L, p. 79.
29 Mrs H5L, pp. 56–7.
30 Mr N2L, p. 60.
31 Mrs T2L, pp. 27, 34, 54–6, 66–7. See Roberts, *A Woman's Place*, pp. 104–10, for discussion of childbirth in the early years of the twentieth century.
32 Mrs A4L, p. 75.
33 Mr K2P, p. 83.
34 Jones, *Health and Society in Twentieth-Century Britain*, pp. 26–27.
35 Mr F1L, p. 29.
36 Mrs B3B, p. 62.
37 Jones, *Health and Society in Twentieth-Century Britain*, p. 20.
38 Mr B4B, p. 43.
39 Jones, *Health and Society in Twentieth-Century Britain*, p. 21.
40 Mrs N3L, p. 66.
41 Mr N3L, p. 137.
42 Mrs B11P, p. 17.
43 Roberts, *A Woman's Place*, p. 107.
44 Roberts, *Women and Families*, p. 148.
45 Mr N2L, p. 53.
46 Mrs B2B, p. 40.
47 See Stuart Anderson, "I Remember it Well': Oral History in the History of Pharmacy,' *Social History of Medicine*, Vol. 10, No. 2 (1997), p. 338.
48 Mr N2L, p. 53. See also, Mr I2L, p. 41.
49 Watkin, *The National Health Service*, pp. 31–2.
50 Mr L3P, p. 120.
51 A. R. Forrest, *Report of the Medical Officer of Health, Barrow*, 1945, p. 12.
52 See, e.g., *The Black Report: The Health Divide* (New York: Penguin, 1988); John Whitelegg, *Inequalities in Health Care: Problems of Access and Provision* (Staw Barnes, 1982); Jones, *Health and Society in Twentieth-Century Britain*, pp. 125–7.
53 David Widgery, *Health in Danger* (London: Macmillan, 1979), pp. 33–5.
54 Jones, *Health and Society in Twentieth-Century Britain*, pp. 123–4
55 Mr B4B, p. 30.
56 Mrs H9P, pp. 38–9.
57 Mr N2L, p. 58.
58 Mrs O1B, p. 58.
59 Dr. A5L, p. 17.
60 Starr, *The Social Transformation of American Medicine*, p. 14.
61 The Penicillin Act of 1947 provided for the control of manufacture and sale of penicillin. 'Similar control was applied to streptomycin when it made its appearance a little later.' Matthews, *History of Pharmacy in Britain*, p. 381.

62 'Stoving' involved a form of fumigation of houses where infectious disease had occurred.

63 Roberts, *Women and Families*, p. 12.

64 Ibid., p. 148. See also, Roberts, *A Woman's Place*, p. 177.

65 It is ironic that, according to some authorities, in order to accommodate prevailing popular beliefs, representatives of official medicine routinely adopt traditional explanatory models to discuss diagnoses, therapies, and prognoses with patients. Examples, discussed by Arthur Kleinman and Cecil G. Helman in *Concepts of Health, Illness and Disease*, pp. 27–50 and 211–32, are 'nervous breakdown,' 'cold and chill,' and fever.

66 Paul Thompson, *The Voice of the Past: Oral History* (Oxford: Oxford University Press, 1978).

Walter L. Arnstein: a Bibliography

Books

The Bradlaugh Case: a Study in Late Victorian Opinion and Politics (Oxford: Oxford University Press, 1965). A paperback and hardback reprint with a new postscript chapter was published as *The Bradlaugh Case: Atheism, Sex, and Politics Among the Late Victorians* (Columbia, MO: University of Missouri Press, 1984).
Britain Yesterday and Today: 1830 to the Present (Lexington, MA: D.C. Heath & Co., 1966; 2nd edn, 1971; 3rd edn 1976; 4th edn, 1983; 5th edn, 1988; 6th edn, 1992; 7th edn, 1996; 8th edn, Boston: Houghton Mifflin Co. 2001).
Compiler and Editor, *The Past Speaks: Sources and Problems in British History Since 1688* (Lexington, MA: D.C. Heath & Co., 1981; 2nd edn, 1993).
With William B. Willcox, *The Age of Aristocracy: 1688–1830* (Lexington, MA: D.C. Heath & Co., 3rd edn 1976; 4th edn, 1983; 5th edn, 1988; 6th edn, 1992; 7th edn, 1996; 8th edn, Boston: Houghton Mifflin Co. 2001).
Protestant Versus Catholic in Mid-Victorian England: Mr. Newdegate and the Nuns (Columbia, MO: University of Missouri Press, 1982).
Editor and Contributor, *Recent Historians of Great Britain: Essays on the Post-1945 Generation* (Ames, IA: Iowa State University Press, 1990).

Articles and Essays

'The Bradlaugh Case: a Reappraisal,' *Journal of the History of Ideas* 18 (April, 1957): pp. 254–69.
'The Industrial Revolution Reconsidered,' *Business and Society* 2 (Spring, 1962): pp. 26–30.
'Gladstone and the Bradlaugh Case,' *Victorian Studies* 5 (June, 1962): pp. 303–30.
'Britain's Common Market Crisis,' *Business and Society* 2 (Autumn, 1962): pp. 14–17.
'Parnell and the Bradlaugh Case,' *Irish Historical Studies* 13 (March, 1963): pp. 212–35.

'Votes for Women: Myths and Reality,' *History Today* 18 (August, 1968): pp. 531–39.

'Charles Bradlaugh: The Freethinker as Statesman,' *Question* 2 (January, 1969): pp. 86–98.

'Victorian Prejudice Reexamined,' *Victorian Studies* 12 (4): pp. 452–57.

Editor and Translator, 'A German View of English Society: 1851,' *Victorian Studies* 16 (December, 1972): pp. 134–43.

'The Religious Issue in Mid-Victorian Politics: a Note on a Neglected Source,' *Albion* 4 (Summer, 1974): pp. 183–204.

'The Survival of the Victorian Aristocracy,' in Frederick Jaher, ed., *The Rich, the Well-Born, and the Powerful* (Urbana: University of Illinois Press, 1973), pp. 203–57. Reprinted in paperback by Citadel Press, 1975.

'The Myth of the Triumphant Victorian Middle Class,' *The Historian* 37 (February, 1975): pp. 205–21.

'The Liberals and the General Election of 1945: a Skeptical Note,' *Journal of British Studies* 14 (May, 1975): pp. 120–26.

'The Murphy Riots: a Victorian Dilemma,' *Victorian Studies* 19 (September, 1975): pp. 51–71.

'George Macaulay Trevelyan and the Art of History: a Centenary Reappraisal,' *The Midwest Quarterly* (18 (Autumn, 1976): pp. 78–97.

'In Queen Victoria's Golden Days,' *Reviews in European History* 3 (June, 1977): pp. 226–33.

'Edwardian Politics: Turbulent Spring or Indian Summer?' In *The Edwardian Age: Conflict and Stability 1900–14*, Alan O'Day, ed., (London: Macmillan, 1979; Hamden, CT: Archon, 1981), pp. 60–78, 183–5.

With Randall E. McGowan, 'The Mid-Victorians and the Two-Party System,' *Albion* 11 (Fall, 1979): pp. 242–58.

'The Great Victorian Convent Case,' *History Today* (February, 1980): pp. 46–50.

'Victorian Politics: The Age of Peel and Palmerston,' (Fifty-minute lecture on cassette tape), (Wilmington, DE: Michael Glazier, Inc., 1980).

'Victorian Politics: Gladstone and Disraeli,' (Fifty-minute lecture on cassette tape), (Wilmington, DE: Michael Glazier, Inc., 1980).

'Reflections on the Histories of Childhood,' in *Research About Nineteenth-Century Children and Books*, Selma K. Richardson, ed., (Urbana: University of Illinois Graduate School of Library Science, 1980), pp. 41–60.

'Great Britain Since 1707,' *Funk & Wagnalls New Encyclopedia* (1983), Vol. 12, pp. 139–53; 2nd edn, 1991.

Review Essay, involving surveys of British History by Eric Evans, Keith Robbins, and Brian Harrison, *Albion* 17 (Summer, 1985): pp. 187–93.

'Queen Victoria and Religion,' in *Religion in the Lives of English Women, 1760–1930*, Gail Malmgreen, ed., (London: Croom Helm; Bloomington: Indiana University Press, 1986), pp. 88–128.

'Queen Victoria,' in *Victorian Britain: an Encyclopedia,* Sally Mitchell, ed., (New York: Garland Press, 1988), pp. 835–37.

'Recent Studies in Victorian Religion: History,' *Victorian Studies* 33 (Autumn, 1989), pp. 149–63.

'Queen Victorian Opens Parliament: the Disinvention of Tradition,' *Historical Research* 63 (June 1990): pp. 178–94.

'Religious Victorians,' *Journal of British Studies* 31 (July 1992): pp. 300–306 (a review essay based primarily on Ian Kerr, *John Henry Newman: a Biography* (1989), David Brown, ed., *Newman: a Man for Our Time* (1990), and David Forrester, *Young Doctor Pusey: a Study in Development* (1989)).

'Queen Victoria,' *Victorian Studies* 36 (Spring, 1993): pp. 377–80 (a review essay based primarily on Giles St. Aubyn, *Queen Victoria: a Portrait* (1992), Theo Aronson, *Heart of a Queen: Queen Victoria's Romantic Attachments* (1991), and Agatha Ramm, ed., *Beloved and Darling Child: Last Letters Between Queen Victoria and Her Eldest Daughter, 1886–1901* (1990).

'My Interview with Bertrand Russell,' *The American Scholar,* Vol. 63, 1(Winter, 1994), pp. 123–29

'Queen Victoria's Speeches from the Throne: a New Look,' in *Government and Institutions in the Post-1832 United Kingdom,* Alan O'Day, ed., (Lewiston, NY: The Edwin Mellen Press, 1995), pp. 127–53.

'Queen Victoria and the Challenge of Roman Catholicism,' *The Historian* 58 (Winter, 1996): 295–314.

'Queen Victoria's Diamond Jubilee,' *The American Scholar* 66 (Autumn, 1997): pp. 591–7.

'The Merry-Go-Round,' 'World's Fair,' and 'Redrawing the Globe,' in *Imagining the Twentieth Century,* Charles C. Stewart and Peter Fritzsche, eds., (Urbana and Chicago: University of Illinois Press, 1997).

'Queen Victoria' in ENCARTA (Microsoft Encyclopedia on the World Wide Web), 1998.

'The Warrior Queen: Reflections on Victoria and Her World,' *Albion* 30 (Spring, 1998): pp. 1–28.

'Queen Victoria's Other Island,' in *More Adventures with Britannia: Personalities, Politics and Culture in Britain,* William Roger Louis, ed., (Austin: University of Texas Press, 1998), pp. 45–65.

'Queen Victoria and the United States,' in *Anglo-American Attitudes: From Revolution to Partnership.* Fred M. Leventhal and Roland Quinault, eds. (London: Ashgate, 2000), pp. 91–106.

Book Reviews

As of December 2000, not counting the review essays listed above, reviews of 133 books had been published in the following scholarly journals: *Journal of Modern History* (23); *Victorian Studies* (22); *American Historical Review* (15); *Journal of Social History* (13): *Albion* (12); *The Historian* (11); *History: a Review of New Books* (9); *Religious Studies Review* (4); *Victorian Periodicals Review* (3); *Labor History* (2); *Catholic Historical Review* (2); *Anglican & Episcopal History* (2); other journals (15).

Conference Papers and Invited Guest Lectures

More than fifty papers presented at conferences ranging from the Anglo-American Conference of Historians to the American Historical Association and the North American Conference on British Studies. Lectures at more than forty institutions ranging from the University of Chicago, Yale University, the University of Kentucky, and Miami University in the United States to the Universities of London, Cambridge, Edinburgh, Durham, York, and Southampton in Britain and the University of Mannheim in Germany.

Index